COLIN A. ROSS, M.D.

The Osiris Complex:
Case-Studies in Multiple
Personality Disorder

UNIVERSITY OF TORONTO PRESS
Toronto   Buffalo   London

© University of Toronto Press Incorporated 1994
Toronto Buffalo London
Printed in Canada

ISBN 0-8020-2858-6 (cloth)
ISBN 0-8020-7358-1 (paper)

Printed on acid-free paper

Canadian Cataloguing in Publication Data

Ross, Colin, 1950–
  The Osiris complex : case studies in multiple
  personality disorder

  ISBN 0-8020-2858-6 (bound)   ISBN 0-8020-7358-1 (pbk.)

  1. Multiple personality. 2. Multiple personality –
  Case studies. I. Title.

  RC569.5.M8R6 1994   616.85′236   C93-095100-X

THE OSIRIS COMPLEX: CASE-STUDIES IN MULTIPLE PERSONALITY DISORDER

Contents

Part Two
Case-Studies Related to Multiple Personality Disorder 217

Introduction

I diagnosed my first case of multiple personality disorder (MPD) as a third-year medical student in 1979. Over the fourteen years since then, my patients have been my greatest teachers: they have been creative, open, and honest, and their conversation has been real and intelligent. Day in and day out in my professional life since 1985, the year I started working intensively with MPD as a psychiatrist, I have had the privilege of participating in serious conversations about identity and the nature of the human mind. Many of the people I have conversed with have not been well educated, but they have had much to teach me, because they have a deep experience and understanding of life.

What is multiple personality disorder? As I say in my book *Multiple Personality Disorder: Diagnosis, Clinical Features, and Treatment* (Ross 1989), multiple personality disorder is a little girl imagining that the abuse is happening to someone else. The imaging is so intense and subjectively compelling, and is reinforced so many times by the ongoing trauma, that the created identities seem to take on a life of their own, though they are all parts of one person.

Two basic psychological manoueuvres form the foundation of multiple personality disorder. First, the little girl who is being repeatedly sexually abused has an out-of-body experience: detached from her body and what is going on, she may float up to the ceiling and imagine that she is watching another little girl being abused. Since that unfortunate little girl on the bed below may have a different name and a different physical appearance, the abuse is not so terrifying and overwhelming because it is happening to someone else, and the child is buffered from the direct impact of the trauma. Second, an amnesia barrier is erected between the original child and the newly created identity. Now not only is the abuse not happening to the original little girl, she doesn't even remember it: this process is reinforced over and over as the abuse continues. Various identities may be created to deal with different aspects of the trauma, resulting in an eventual total of ten, twenty, or more alter personalities. Once the mind is in the habit of creating new identities in this way, alter personalities may be generated to cope with many non-trauma events, tasks, or functions in life, including going to school and dealing with peers.

Adult patients with MPD experience a number of core symptoms that should be enquired about in psychiatric assessments. These include voices in the head and ongoing blank spells or periods of missing time. The voices are the different personalities talking to each other, and to the main, presenting part of the person who first comes for treatment. The periods of missing time occur when different personalities take turns being in control of the body, and are attributable to the memory barriers between the personalities.

MPD patients also experience numerous other symptoms such as those associated with depression, anxiety, eating disorders, substance abuse, sleep disorders, sexual dysfunctions, and psychosomatic disorders, and symptoms that mimic those of schizophrenia. The assessment and treatment of multiple personality disorder must take this large array of trauma-related symptoms and problems into account. The complexity of the patients' symptoms often results in misdiagnosis and the institution of treatments that are not effective. In fact, in two different published research studies, MPD patients were found to spend an average of just under seven years in the mental health system before being correctly diagnosed (Putnam 1989; Ross 1989). During this time, they received many different diagnoses and treatments, none of which took the trauma into account.

Although MPD patients are, by definition, diagnosed as having more than one personality, they in fact don't. The different 'personalities' are fragmented components of a single personality that are abnormally personified, dissociated from each other, and amnesic for each other. We call these fragmented components 'personalities' by historical convention: much of the scepticism about MPD is based on the erroneous assumption that such patients have more than one personality, which is, in fact, impossible.

In order to correct misconceptions arising from use of the term 'personality' in this context, the official name of the disorder has been changed to Dissociative Identity Disorder in the fourth edition of the *Diagnostic and Statistical Manual of Mental Disorders* (*DSM-IV*) of the American Psychiatric Association (1993), which is the official diagnostic manual of psychiatry in North America. The term 'Multiple Personality Disorder' will be retained, in brackets, in *DSM-IV*, and thus may still be used diagnostically.

I decided not to cite references within the case-studies in this book in order not to detract from their immediacy, but will give a brief description of the literature on dissociation here. The literature on dissociative disorders is still relatively small and can be entered quite easily; however, it is growing at a rate that now makes it impossible for any one clinician to read everything that is being published. That was not so five years ago, when it was still possible to read pretty well everything published about MPD in the mental-health literature.

Carole Goettman, George Greaves, and Philip Coons have produced a comprehensive bibliography of the MPD literature, entitled *Multiple Personality and Dissociation, 1791–1990. A Complete Bibliography*. It is available for purchase in updated versions from George Greaves, PHD, at 529 Pharr Road, Atlanta, Georgia, 30305. Two other entries into the literature are Frank Putnam's *Diagnosis and Treatment of Multiple Personality Disorder* (1989), and my *Multiple Personality Disorder: Diagnosis, Clinical Features, and Treatment* (1989). Both include extensive bibliographies and literature reviews, indentifying the key references in the field up until the late 1980s.

The journal *Dissociation*, published quarterly since its founding in 1988, is edited by Richard Kluft, and is available from the Ridgeview Institute, 3995 South Cobb Drive, Smyrna, Georgia, 30080. The articles and references in this journal will keep the reader current with the dissociative-disorders literature. Other essential reading is the September 1991 special issue of *Psychiatric Clinics of North America* on MPD, edited by Richard Loewenstein and published by W.B. Saunders Company, The Curtis Center, Independence Square West, Philadelphia, Pennsylvania, 19106.

I highly recommend *Multiple Personality Disorder From the Inside Out*, edited by Barry Cohen, Esther Miller, and Lynne W. This collection of anonymous poems and writings by people with MPD is published by the Sidran Press, 211 Southway, Baltimore, Maryland, 21218. Besides the wonderful material from the contributors, it contains lists of resources, support networks, newsletters, and suggested readings.

The professional society for study of MPD, of which I am the 1993–4 president, is the International Society for the Study of Multiple Personality and Dissociation, which is based at 5700 Old Orchard Road, First Floor, Skokie, Illinois, 60077. Besides conducting an annual meeting, the society publishes a newsletter and a membership directory, and has component societies and study groups throughout North America.

These sources of information are sufficient to lead the interested reader into both the professional and lay literatures on MPD. Research papers of mine published since 1989 can be found in the May 1990, November 1990, and December 1991 issues of *The American Journal of Psychiatry*. Other psychiatric journals to which I have contributed and which could be scanned for recent MPD publications include *Hospital and Community Psychiatry, General Hospital Psychiatry, The Journal of Nervous and Mental Disease, The American Journal of Clinical Hypnosis, The International Journal of Clinical and Experimental Hypnosis, Comprehensive Psychiatry, The American Journal of Psychotherapy,* and *Psychiatry*.

Over the last ten years, the MPD literature has evolved from prescientific to scientific status, although this transition isn't yet fully appreciated by the majority of mental health professionals. The quality of the data supporting the reliability and validity of the diagnosis is as good as for any other psychiatric disorder, though the quantity of literature is still relatively small.

Most of the quantitative research on MPD has been conducted using the Dissociative Experiences Scale (DES), the Dissociative Disorders Interview Schedule (DDIS), and the Structured Clinical Interview for *DSM-III-R* Dissociative Disorders (SCID-D). Data on and discussion of these three measures can be found in several 1991 issues and the January 1992 issue of the *American Journal of Psychiatry*; the relevant references are cited in those papers.

The DES is a self-report measure of dissociation developed as a screening tool for dissociative disorders. It consists of 28 items, can be completed and scored in 15 minutes, and yields an overall score ranging from 0 to 100. The factor structure of the DES has been replicated in a number of studies, large-N general population norms are available, and the ability of group median scores on the DES to differentiate MPD from other diagnostic groups has been replicated. Using a computer algorithm based on weighted item scores, the DES can predict with a high rate of sensitivity and specificity who in a large pool of clinically heterogeneous psychiatric patients has a clinical diagnosis of MPD. The performance of the DES in this regard is as good as that of any other self-report measure used to screen for any other disorder, and it has been translated into many different languages.

Among the several other self-report measures of dissociation, particularly promising is a scale developed in Europe by Vanderlinden. This scale has been translated into English, and studies using it in North America are underway. State-of-the-art discussion of the self-report measurement of dissociation now deals with subtle questions about variations in the factor structure of the DES in different populations, correlations of DES factors with other measures, and similar concerns. Whether the DES is reliable and valid as a screening tool for MPD is no longer a research question, but an established fact.

The DDIS and SCID-D are structured interviews developed for making dissociative-disorder diagnoses in both research and clinical settings. Both have established validity and reliability, but further studies with larger numbers of subjects are required in order to irrefutably establish their diagnostic validity in terms of MPD. Research projects are underway in which the interrater agreement of these two methods of diagnosing MPD is being determined, and I expect that the level of agreement between the two interviews will be as good as the structured-interview reliability for any other psychiatric disorder. Both the DDIS and the SCID-D have been translated into a number of different languages.

MPD is the most important and interesting disorder in psychiatry, which is why I study it. I believe it to be the key diagnosis in an impending paradigm shift in psychiatry, because MPD best illustrates the characteristic response of the human organism to severe psychosocial trauma, and because trauma is a major cause of mental illness, from a public health point of view. Trauma, I believe, is a major underlying theme in much mental illness, including depression, eating disorders, personality disorders, substance abuse, psychosomatic illness, and all forms of self-abuse and violence. Biological psychiatry might obtain more clinically meaningful results if it focused on the psychobiology of trauma and abandoned the search for causality in genes and endogenous chemical derangements. Since MPD patients have experienced the most extreme childhood trauma of any diagnostic group, they exhibit the psychobiology and psychopathology of trauma to an extreme degree.

I believe that the traumatized subgroup of any given diagnostic category has a distinct phenomenology, response to psychotherapy and psychopharmacology, set of biological markers, pattern of family transmission, course, and prognosis. Until the confounding effects of trauma are taken into account and properly controlled for, it may not be possible to detect a gene for depression because the etiological influence of trauma is likely to swamp out any genetic effect, or any pedigrees in which a genetic cause is predominant.

MPD patients have taught me that virtually all symptoms in

psychiatry are potentially trauma-driven and dissociative in nature. The purpose of this book, then, is not simply to present interesting stories or provide a window into current goings-on in the dissociative-disorders field. It is to help foster an understanding of the relationship between childhood trauma and serious mental illness. The MPD literature is heading inevitably in the direction of a general trauma model of psychopathology. The model will produce a paradigm shift out of the two dominant schools of thought of twentieth-century psychiatry, the psychoanalytical and the biomedical-reductionist: the case-studies in *The Osiris Complex* illustrate the clinical roots of this paradigm transformation.

In the pages of this book, I can portray only a shadow of the intense reality of MPD therapy. I have disguised the identities of all the patients except Anne Sexton: all the information about her is a matter of public record, and is contained in the biography by Diane Wood Middlebrook (1991). Some of the patients are Canadian, and some are people I have met since moving to Texas.

Each chapter has a specific purpose. Each case of MPD illustrates a different facet of the dissociative response to trauma; together they depict the range and variability of the disorder. The cases of psychogenic fugue and dissociative disorder not otherwise specified in Part II were also included because they illustrate the full range of dissociative disorders, of which MPD is the extreme, and because each case raises a problem about the nature of identity and memory, or defines an aspect of my work with the dissociative disorders. I have written this book primarily for a mental health audience, but it should be of interest to the general educated reader as well. At times I have explained certain details about medications or symptoms on the assumption that the reader is not a psychiatrist, and I have deliberately avoided professional jargon as much as possible.

Why have I chosen *The Osiris Complex* as the title of this book? I coined the term in my previous book, *Multiple Personality Disorder: Diagnosis, Clinical Features, and Treatment*. The Osiris complex designates what I believe is the most important motif in psychopathology: the fragmentation of the self in response to external trauma. In the Isis–Osiris myth from ancient Egypt, Osiris is murdered by his jealous brother Set, who cuts him into pieces and scatters them far and wide. Isis then gathers her brother Osiris's fragments together, reintegrates them, and resurrects Osiris in a new form: this healing of the traumatized self is my task as a therapist. Fathered by Ra, Isis and Osiris were siblings who married and begot a son Horus, who in turn defeated his uncle Set in battle. The idea communicated by the phrase 'the Osiris complex' is that incest and other psychosocial trauma are at the root of much psychopathology, and can be a direct and overwhelming cause of serious mental illness.

Institutional, social, and economic barriers stand in the way of traumatized children and their recovery, in our society and throughout the world. Like many forms of inflammation, MPD is a normal human response to trauma that has become self-destructive. MPD is an autoimmune disorder in which the psyche has become confused about the distinction between self and non-self, and has learned to turn its destructive mechanisms on the self, mistaking it for a foreign invader. Fortunately, over the last thirty years, a specific and effective method for treating this condition has been created through the joint effort of many clinicians.

To the people with dissociative disorders who have taught me, I dedicate this book.

REFERENCES

American Psychiatric Association. 1993. DSM-IV Draft Criteria. Washington, DC
Middlebrook, D. Wood. 1991. Anne Sexton: A Biography. Boston: Houghton Mifflin
Putnam, F.W. 1989. Diagnosis and Treatment of Multiple Personality Disorder. New York: Guilford Publications
Ross, C.A. 1989. Multiple Personality Disorder: Diagnosis, Clinical Features, and Treatment. New York: John Wiley & Sons

Part One

Case-Studies of Multiple Personality Disorder

1

The Case of Jenny Z

During the first year I was on staff as a psychiatrist at St Boniface Hospital, a therapist working outside the hospital asked me to see a woman in consultation. The therapist knew I was interested in dissociative disorders and wanted to watch me do the assessment because she had no prior experience with such disorders. That is how I met Jenny Z.

At the time I met her, in August 1985, Jenny was a thirty-two-year-old married woman with two children, a girl age seven and a boy age five. The children were at home with their father in Vancouver, and Jenny had been living in Winnipeg for about two years. She had come to therapy, she said, because of blank spells, and said on questioning, 'I'm mixed up; I need help.' The previous day she had returned from a three-day visit to Vancouver by plane. She couldn't remember anything about how she got to Vancouver or back to Winnipeg, or anything she did during the three days.

A week before that, Jenny had 'come to' at the Winnipeg airport, having just got off the plane from Vancouver. She had no memory of a period of a month prior to that moment: the last thing she remembered was a day in June in Winnipeg.

As I assessed her memory, concentration, general knowledge, and ability to think clearly, Jenny appeared to be normal, except for the period of missing time. Her thought processes were rational, she did not appear strange or in a trance state, the was no sign of any medical illness, and she did not seem to be under the influence of drugs or alcohol. However, she was very vague about her childhood, which she described as generally happy. Her memory of life before age five was 'zero'; from age five to ten, 'I made it – it wasn't too bad'; and from age ten to fifteen, 'I don't know ... I know ... I just don't want to remember.'

At age twelve, Jenny was raped and beaten by her father while her mother was in hospital. The beating produced a 'concussion,' for which she spent a 'long' but unknown period in hospital. She has had painful breasts since the time of the rape, and said she has always been 'frigid' – 'cold, afraid, it's dirty to me.' At age fifteen, she was forced to quit school to go to work, and for the next three years, she worked forty hours per week at a manufacturing plant, plus twenty-two hours per week at a retail store: 'Dad didn't believe in working,' she said.

When Jenny's father threatened her with rape again three months after the initial attack, she stabbed him three times in the leg: 'he should have got treatment, but didn't.' She said her father was a 'creep,' and her mother a 'liar' and 'hypochondriac.' Her father, she said, weighs 280 pounds, and her mother 410 pounds, and she has a sister who weighs 350 pounds, while Jenny herself is of normal weight.

Jenny started dating in high school and married her husband in her early twenties. She said they had intercourse twenty times a month, but that she had orgasm only once a month. Even with orgasm, though, sex was a chore she performed to please her husband, and afterwards she always felt 'dirty.' The marital relationship was quite good most of the time, Jenny said, so it wasn't really clear why they had split up or why she had moved to Winnipeg on her own. She said she missed her kids a lot.

When I asked Jenny her age, she told me she was thirty-two, but when I asked her birthdate, she said 12 May 1952, which would have made her thirty-three. I didn't pursue this discrepancy in the initial consultation, but took note of it. She had trouble remembering my name, although I had told her it several times, which seemed odd because otherwise she had no trouble with her concentration or short-term memory. Physical tests done subsequently, including blood work and a computerized tomography (CT) scan of her head, were normal, as was an electroencephalogram done later.

One thing Jenny did mention during the initial interview was that she often heard voices calling her name when no one was there. She said that her first memory blank had occurred in 1976, but that spells of memory loss began to increase in frequency in 1984, and especially so in the previous few months. In the year prior to coming to see me in consultation, Jenny had cashed $5,000 worth of cheques on an account held jointly with her boyfriend. She did not know what had become of $4,000 worth of the money, but the rest had been spent on records, an expensive mirror, and other items in their home that she couldn't remember buying.

It wasn't very clear why Jenny had been referred at this particular time, rather than a week or a month earlier, and she couldn't explain it other than by saying she needed help. Because of the large amount of money that was being spent during the blank spells, I decided to see her for further assessment on a daily basis.

Within the first couple of days, I learned that Jenny was in trouble with the law. While in Vancouver for a month, she had cleared up some bad cheques she had cashed there, but she was held in jail overnight and made a court appearance concerning other bad cheques. These events she was able to reconstruct from documents she had and a very hazy recall of what had happened. She also told me that she had written bad cheques in Winnipeg in May and June, and that she had made appointments to see her bank manager and a detective about them during the three-day blank spell immediately prior to hospitalization. She had missed these appointments because she was in Vancouver. I was not sure, at this point, how much of the amnesia was real and how much was malingering.

Jenny also explained another conflict that likely contributed to her amnesia and her hospitalization. She didn't want to leave her boyfriend, but she wanted to have her children back:

her boyfriend refused to live with the children, and her husband didn't want them either; in fact, they were living with Jenny's mother. Jenny just couldn't make a decision about what to do.

Jenny had felt suicidal in the past, and had similar feelings now. She said she had been depressed much of the time since 1976, and that she had taken an overdose of phenobarbital in 1973 because of 'trouble with my husband, not getting my own way.' She had overdosed with her father's 'nerve pills' in 1975 because of jealousy and an argument with her husband, but she wasn't sure what she had been jealous about, or exactly what kind of pills she had taken.

Jenny had worked throughout most of the previous two years and had taken a number of evening courses in bookkeeping. In 1984, she said, her drinking had 'gotten out of hand,' by which she meant that she had been consuming two twenty-six-ounce bottles of whiskey per week. Her relationship with her boyfriend, Ted, was quite good, and her sex life with him was more pleasurable than that with her husband; however, she used alcohol to relax prior to intercourse.

When I interviewed Jenny's boyfriend, he described two 'fits' he had witnessed. The first occurred in December 1984. Jenny, Ted, and some friends were sitting at a table in Jenny's home when she excused herself and went to the bathroom. She had been gone about twenty minutes when Ted went to check on her and found her lying in a foetal position on the bathroom floor, clutching her stomach, moaning, groaning, and rolling around. There were no tonic or clonic contractions, as would occur in a seizure. Ted held her down, and an ambulance was called to take her to the hospital. 'The doctor kicked me out for making too much noise – figured I was on dope,' she said. From that emergency department, she went to another hospital, was given a shot, settled down, and went home. The 'fit' lasted for one hour: Jenny could remember having abdominal pain and getting up to go to the washroom, but nothing of the intervening time before she arrived at the first emergency department.

The second episode occurred in January or February 1985, while Ted, Jenny, and others were at a lounge. She went outside in Ted's absence, accompanied by a friend. When Ted went to look for her, he found her sitting on a bench, hunched over, shaking, but not screaming. She was taken by car to a hospital but appeared to stop breathing on the way, at which point Ted gave her mouth-to-mouth resuscitation. At the hospital, she was given a shot, kept overnight for observation, and released the next day. This second 'fit' lasted twenty minutes: Jenny could remember feeling faint at the lounge and getting up to go outside, but nothing more till the next day.

Ted had never observed any hints of neurological illness in Jenny – no sleepwalking, no strange behaviour while asleep, no trance states, and no severe disturbance of her thinking. He had never had reason to think she was hallucinating and had never seen her faint, bump into things, or behave strangely in any other way that suggested she was disoriented.

In light of this background information, it was virtually certain that Jenny's blank spells were psychological in nature, and that they were helping her cope with difficult decisions, plus perhaps allowing her to do things she would feel bad about if she remembered them, such as cashing numerous cheques on her joint account. Most of the money in the account was actually earned by Ted.

I decided to try using hypnosis to recover the memories of the missing periods of time that occurred just prior to my first seeing her. Jenny easily entered a deep trance and immediately provided the details of her trips to Vancouver and activities while there. She remembered the location of $6,100 she had placed in two bank accounts in Winnipeg: the money came from cheques she had cashed on her joint account. Both new accounts were under the name of Jenny Z. I gave her suggestions for recall of the hypnotic session, good mood upon awakening, and easy induction of hypnosis the next day. Jenny responded to all three suggestions and telephoned Ted immediately after the session, telling him about the money.

The next day, Jenny again entered a deep trance, and I

explored the period during July when she was in Vancouver. No other secret bank accounts in Winnipeg or Vancouver were discovered. I regressed Jenny to ages three, eight, ten, eleven, and twelve: she described the weather, what she had for breakfast, and details of the scenery at these ages. Then I asked Jenny to imagine that it was 'the morning of the day your dad did something bad to you when you were twelve.'

Step by step, Jenny relived the events of the day until she got to night-time. At night her father came into her bedroom and raped her orally and vaginally, coming to orgasm in her mouth. Her reliving of the rape was very dramatic: Jenny screamed, cried, writhed, and called out for her brother. As she relived the period after her father left the room, Jenny called out to her two sisters, who were in a second bed in the room. She comforted them, tears on her cheeks, telling them, 'It'll be okay, don't worry, it'll be okay. We'll go and stay with Aunt Carol. Don't cry now. Don't cry.'

Since I thought Jenny should work through the trauma in a controlled trance before fully confronting the memory in a waking state, I suggested to her that she not remember the session upon awakening. The next couple of sessions were devoted to further reliving of childhood sexual abuse at the hands of her father, and filling in her more recent periods of missing time. I learned that the sexual abuse had been extensive and that all the girls in the family had been used sexually by their father and his alcoholic friends.

I also discovered that the $6,100 had been spent. Most of it went to Vancouver to buy things for Jenny's children. The existence of the two bank accounts in Winnipeg and the amounts deposited and withdrawn were later confirmed by bank records. One interesting bit of information came to light incidentally: I learned that Jenny was actually born in 1953 and that she had changed her birthdate to 1952 in order to get a job when she was fifteen. She had never corrected the birthdate on her identification, but had corrected her age later on, so that Ted, for instance, knew she was thirty-two but didn't know that her identification showed her to be thirty-three. I discussed this point with Jenny after one of the hypnotic sessions, and she said she had already told Ted that her psychiatrist was suspicious about her age, and had explained to him the reason for the discrepancy. I therefore knew that, at times, she consciously withheld information and distorted the truth. It was during the first hypnotic sessions that I made the diagnosis of multiple personality disorder. Jenny had mentioned, but only once, that she and her boyfriend sometimes joked about a second Jenny. Sometimes Jenny would kiss Ted then say, 'It was Sally who did it, not me. You were kissing Sally.' Both of them treated this as a joke and nothing more.

My usual procedure after induction of a hypnotic trance was to say, 'How are you feeling today, Jenny?' During one session I decided to say instead, 'How are you feeling today, Sally?' Not really expecting much to happen, I was surprised to find myself in conversation not with Jenny but with Sally. As I hadn't had much experience with multiple personality disorder at this point, I was not accustomed to it and didn't expect to encounter it very often.

I spent the next few sessions getting acquainted with Sally. Jenny was confused and didn't know what she thought about things, except that she felt lost and hopeless, had little self-confidence, didn't know what to do next, and was anxious and depressed. Jenny was soft-spoken, quiet in manner, compliant, somewhat dependent, and very nice. She never spoke critically of her husband, boyfriend, doctors, or children. However, I soon discovered that Sally was sarcastic, aggressive, opinionated, and impulsive. She was a practical joker; spoke in a firm, confident manner; and described Jenny's husband as 'an idiot.' Sally was the dominant character of the two, but Jenny had no idea that she existed as more than a harmless joke.

It was Sally, at least so Sally claimed, who directed Jenny to cash $6,100 worth of cheques drawn on Ted's account, and it was Sally who decided to return to Vancouver twice to see Jenny's children. Sally was the decision maker, and she spoke scornfully of Jenny's inability to cope with life. During the amnesic periods, Sally was conscious while Jenny was blanked out. My therapeutic strategy was to get to know Sally better and then to establish a three-way conversation between myself, Sally, and Jenny under hypnosis. I proposed to suggest to Jenny that she be amnesic, at least initially, about my contact with Sally.

During this period, legal complications arose. Jenny was facing charges for fraud in reference to the cheques Sally had cashed in Vancouver. I spoke with three bank managers, a lawyer in Vancouver, and a city detective in Winnipeg; as well as planning psychiatric strategy, I became embroiled, temporarily, in an intricate web of legal considerations.

After a week of talking with Sally for an hour a day under hypnosis, I had established a three-way conversation. One morning, having done my now brief hypnotic induction, I age-regressed Jenny back to age ten. I then said, 'How are you today, Jenny?' There was no answer. I said the same thing again. Still no answer. I was wondering what to do next when Jenny suddenly said, in a ten-year-old girl's voice, 'My name is Barbara Anne.' My immediate thought was that I had contacted another personality, so I decided to find out more about Barbara Anne.

I asked Barbara Anne where she lived. She gave me the same Vancouver address Jenny had. On questioning, she gave me the same list of brothers and sisters. Then, I'm not sure why, I decided to ask Barbara Anne her mother's maiden name. She gave me the surname Jenny had used on being registered in the Out-patient Department for the initial consultation when she identified herself as Jenny Z. I was puzzled. I then returned Jenny to age thirty-two, still in trance, and asked her what her maiden name was. She gave me a second surname, X! I then asked her what her married name was, and she gave a third surname, Y. With questioning, I discovered a reason for this proliferation of names.

Jenny's maiden name was Barbara Anne X. Her married name was Barbara Anne Y. But she had always been called Jenny as a nickname. All these names referred to the same person, not to alter personalities. Her mother's maiden name was Z. It turned out that, when Jenny left Vancouver for Winnipeg to evade fraud charges, she deliberately adopted an alias, using her mother's maiden name as her surname. Thus I knew her as Jenny Z.

I suggested to Jenny that she not remember this session upon awakening, which she didn't, and we talked for quite a while afterwards. We were discussing my phoning her lawyer in Vancouver, since she was due to appear in court there in a few weeks. I was writing down some information I might need for the phone call, when I decided to try playing a bit of a game with Jenny.

As I wrote down her children's Christian names and ages, I casually asked, 'And what's their last name? Y?' I was not supposed to have heard of this name.

A look of panic registered on Jenny's face, her eyes opened wide, and she gasped, 'How did you know that? Where'd you get that name from?' Then an expression of realization flashed across her face, and she buried her face in her hands and began to cry. We talked for a long time, and I concluded that her amnesia was genuine. I explained how I had learned about her alias under hypnosis. She decided to phone Ted immediately and tell him about her alias, which she did. One can imagine what Jenny's treatment to that point had been like for Ted: in the space of a week, he had learned that his girlfriend had been repeatedly raped by her father; that she was living under an alias; that she had fraud charges pending against her in another city; that she had multiple personality disorder; and that $6,100 of his money had been deposited into two bank accounts he knew nothing about, then withdrawn and spent!

The legal considerations were complex. The Vancouver charges were against Barbara Anne Y, and the Winnipeg charges were against Jenny Z. The police in the two cities did not know that the two were the same person. There were arguments in favour of bringing the Vancouver charges to Winnipeg: all charges could then be read at once; there could be psychiatric testimony; plane fares would be saved; and we wouldn't have to risk a decision by Sally to run away to another city. There were also arguments in favour of having the charges heard in Vancouver: the Vancouver charges had already been gathered together from several different jurisdictions in British Columbia and had been read in court; and Jenny had a lawyer there who felt he had already successfully negotiated with the prosecution. If sentence was passed in Winnipeg before Jenny went to court in Vancouver, through, her Vancouver charges would be her second offence, and she would be subject to a more severe sentence in Vancouver.

The lawyer in Vancouver had based his negotiations with the prosecutor on the following premise. Barbara Anne, as his client was called, intended to return to Vancouver to live with her husband and children, having recovered from a period of emotional turmoil in her life, during which she passed bad cheques. Jenny told him on the phone, however, in my presence, that she intended to live in Winnipeg with Ted. Neither the lawyer nor Jenny's husband knew before this phone call that she had adopted an alias, and the lawyer did not know that she had charges pending in Winnipeg. Jenny's parents-in-law had agreed to appear in court in Vancouver as character witnesses, but when they learned about her plans to stay in Winnipeg with Ted they would refuse to do so. After I had made the initial contacts and arrangements, these matters were all dealt with by detectives, lawyers, and bank managers.

During this period, both Jenny and Sally threatened suicide. Jenny said she would kill herself if she went to jail. Sally said she would kill herself and take Jenny with her, even though Jenny didn't really want to die. At other times Sally confessed that she was scared to die and said she didn't know if she could stop Jenny from killing her. At still other times, Jenny said that she didn't want to die but thought Sally would take over and force her to commit suicide: this fear was voiced after Jenny and Sally had gotten to know each other. Since Jenny had become distraught and confused about spending time in hypnosis without remembering anything, I had given suggestions that eliminated the amnesia barrier between the two personalities.

As I got to know Sally better, I wanted to learn how and when she came into existence as a distinct personality. As part of finding this out, I asked Sally to relive an incident Jenny had relived earlier. On Christmas Eve 1963, Jenny was at a Christmas party when she developed a stomach ache. Her aunt Carol had made a doll for her and had arranged for the doll to be given to Jenny as a party prize. Jenny's brother called a taxi and they went home together, Jenny taking the doll with her. She named it Sally.

When they arrived home, the house was dark and locked, though their mother was supposed to be there. Jenny's brother kicked in a screen door at the back of the house, came through the house, let Jenny in, then turned on the lights. They then discovered their mother in bed with another man and, in anger, Jenny ripped Sally to pieces.

As Sally relived this incident, she reported observing it through the doll's eyes. When Jenny ripped up the doll, Sally floated up into the air – she was made out of 'floating stuff, like jelly' – then entered Jenny's body through her leg. When I asked what would happen if Jenny died, Sally told me that she would enter the body of another woman on the ward. I decided to learn more about how Sally was created.

Sally told me that she was made by her aunt Carol. I then asked her to describe the occasion when Aunt Carol brought her to the hall for the Christmas party, during the afternoon of 24 December, 1963. Barbara Anne obviously was not present at that time. Sally told me that her aunt Carol was wearing green slacks and a white top. When I asked Sally how she could see the room, she replied, 'I'm looking through my eyes.'

Then I asked her, 'But whose eyes are you looking through? If Barbara Anne isn't there, how can you see?'

At this point, Sally began to look confused, and said, 'What do you mean?' In a stern interrogator's manner I cross-examined Sally: she soon broke down and admitted that she had made it all up. She was never in the doll, she didn't know where she came from, and she had no idea how long she had been an autonomous character inside Jenny's body.

I asked Sally why she made up the story about the doll, and she replied, 'Because you're a psychiatrist.'

Her reply was disconcerting: it meant that I could never be sure what was truth, what fantasy, and what just lies. I now knew, though, how Sally experienced herself. She did not feel that Jenny's skin and flesh were her skin and flesh; rather, Sally was locked inside, out of contact with everything and everyone in the world except me. I was the only person who knew she existed (her therapist had withdrawn from the case by this time for reasons unrelated to Jenny) and she had never spoken to anyone else except when passing herself off as Jenny. Sally had never been sexually abused; the abuse had been of Jenny's body, not hers, and Jenny's father was not Sally's.

Many mental health professionals would have thought that Jenny was malingering, that there was no dissociative disorder, and that the diagnosis was antisocial personality disorder. I did not agree with this viewpoint for a number of reasons. First, Jenny did not fulfil all the diagnostic criteria for antisocial personality disorder, especially those concerning juvenile delinquency. Second, we discussed all potential legal gains to be derived from her diagnosis and treatment, and she freely admitted to all of them. Third, because she agreed to *every* change of legal strategy I recommended, including telling her lawyer in Vancouver, city detectives, and bank managers about her alias, which she had not wanted to do, she did not appear to be malingering.

At the time of discharge, Jenny had taken out a loan from her bank for $1,600 to repay what she had withdrawn by forging Ted's signature in June. This was to the bank's advantage, since she now owed them a properly documented $1,600 loan, whereas before she had simply defrauded them of $1,600. All in all, as she was deceiving Ted, the police, and her lawyer less at discharge than on admission, it would be difficult to believe she had outmanoeuvred me. Additionally, she was no longer claiming to be amnesic about her cheque fraud, and I never testified in court, nor did her lawyer introduce any psychiatric or psychological evidence.

Despite my believing that she had genuine multiple personality disorder, I listened with scepticism to everything both personalities told me.

As the therapy proceeded, I saw my role as analogous to that of a diplomat or labour–management mediator. I was an intermediary whose job was to get the two sides talking so that they could work out a mutually advantageous way of living together. Their current way of handling life was taking them in the direction of alcoholism and jail.

Sally had never been part of Jenny's surface being. The only method she had devised of signalling her existence to the outside world was 'playing tricks,' but no one besides Ted had deduced her existence as a result of observing that behaviour. Ted told me he had suspected all along that Sally was more than just a joke. Nevertheless, Sally was isolated and, as a consequence, bitter, angry, and frustrated. At first she did not even want to talk to Jenny; she preferred to stay inside, play tricks, and have fun. I easily convinced her, though, that it was very lonely being stuck inside Jenny's body and that the situation had gotten out of control. The tricks – cheque cashing, forgetting things, seeing things that weren't there, not seeing things that *were* there, physical symptoms, and trance states – had placed both Sally and Jenny in a bad position. There was a good chance they would go to jail.

Two examples of trick playing Sally engaged in during the hospitalization come to mind. One involved nightmares that Jenny had about Chinese men chasing her. Jenny didn't know why the men should be Chinese, but Sally explained that Jenny had watched a frightening movie on television with Chinese men in it. She had since forgotten about the movie but had been afflicted with nightmares. Sally exacerbated these nightmares by making them come more frequently and with greater intensity. One night Jenny woke up from a nightmare in a trance state, believing that Chinese people were in her apartment. She had to sedate herself with medication to get back to sleep.

On the second-last weekend of this phase of the therapy, Sally made her take $100 from Ted's wallet without being able to remember doing so. Jenny carried the money with her to an appointment with me. It became apparent that Sally had done this out of spite; she was angry with Ted because he was about to go way on a week's vacation. Also, they had had little time together on the weekend because of Ted's business commitments. Ted phoned me on Monday morning to tell me about the $100 and during the next session I investigated the matter. I suggested to Jenny that she remember everything about the $100 on waking up from hypnosis, which she did.

I was able to provided four reasons for Sally's pulling this 'trick': 1 / she was upset about Ted's vacation; 2 / she was upset about not getting enough attention on the weekend; 3 / she was still trying to get revenge on Jenny's father by taking her anger out on Ted; and 4 / it's hard to break a habit. One of the goals of therapy was to help Sally understand the destructiveness of this kind of behaviour.

During the early stages of therapy, Sally did not want to give up her independent being since, once she became fully integrated with Jenny, she could no longer play tricks. I pointed out to Sally numerous times that the tricks were backfiring: for example, during the night Jenny had to take a sedative, Jenny had become so frightened that Sally got frightened too. My general strategy was to convince both personalities that they needed each other. I also reinforced the idea that Sally could have real adult fun, rather than the kind she was accustomed to, if she could partake fully in Jenny's life. Sally could also help Jenny to be more assertive, more outgoing, more confident, and more decisive. Jenny could help Sally by letting her have a fair say, by controlling her impulsiveness for their mutual benefit, and by changing her behaviour in small ways that would better suit Sally's preferences.

We agreed between the three of us to set up a 'testing weekend.' During that weekend, Sally would try to play one or two small pranks, and Jenny would try to be alert so that she wouldn't get fooled. The purpose of this exercise was to provide them with some fun, to enable them to interact more, and to help Jenny realize that becoming integrated requires effort and vigilance.

On the Saturday afternoon, Jenny was cleaning up her apartment. She put a garbage can on the floor and emptied all the ashtrays and wastepaper baskets into it: some other odds and ends went into the same garbage can. Jenny was happily cleaning and was glad to have this domestic job completed. However, when she went to move the garbage can, she discovered there wasn't one! Jenny had emptied all the ashtrays onto the rug. She had to pick up the mess, clean the rug, and continue her work.

This trick typifies Sally's sense of humour, which resembles that of Sally Beauchamp, a mischievous personality in a case described by Morton Prince in his book *The Dissociation of a Personality* early in the twentieth century, and Eve Black, a similar alter personality in the heroine of *The Three Faces of Eve*. The trouble with Sally was that, on her own admission, she was too impulsive. She would force Jenny to do things that got both of them in trouble. Before very long, Sally was happily admitting that it would be to her advantage to be integrated with Jenny's more methodical character.

Sally did not, however, have control over all the symptoms she and Jenny experienced. Jenny was prone to nightmares and having vivid hallucinations as she was falling asleep, which were entirely out of Sally's control, and which frightened her. As I got to know Sally better, and as she and Jenny were now thought of by all three of us as being two sides of one person's character, I still did not understand the fundamental purpose of the dissociation. Why did Barbara Anne have to split into two? Since Jenny had relived different episodes of sexual abuse by her father, could now remember and talk about them, and was not so intensely disturbed by them, I decided to ask Sally to relive the rape at age twelve.

There was a great deal of resistance on Sally's part, and I had to talk with her at length in order to get her to agree to the abreaction (a therapeutic technique whereby the patient relives a past event so vividly that it seems to be happening over again in the present). This kind of intense reliving and remembering, combined with conscious processing and mastery of the experience, as all mental health professionals know, is an essential part of recovery from severe trauma.

As she relived the rape, Sally's face contorted in anger, fear, pain, and hatred. She was lying on her back in my office reclining chair, arms by her side, with a blanket over her. Suddenly, she leapt up, eyes closed; on her knees, she furiously pounded the chair, screaming, 'He's not my dad, he's not my dad! I don't want to remember, I don't want to remember!'

She was violently upset. After a few minutes I suggested that Sally lie down on her back and to to sleep, which she did. I had tapped a reservoir of psychic pain and anger of greater depth and intensity than I had imagined. The abreaction, done initially within the protection of hypnotic trance, acted as an exploratory drill, probing down through previously impenetrable strata of psychic rock, gaining access to the deep source of dissociation. Sally would not admit that the man who raped her was her father; he was Jenny's father, not hers. It was Jenny's body that was raped; that disgusting, dirty, evil thing had happened to Jenny, not Sally, because Sally was a dissociated and purely psychic being, separate from Jenny, with no physical body. It was Jenny, not Sally, who had felt her father's penis in her vagina and tasted his semen as he came to orgasm in her mouth.

I had understood this in a dim, theoretical way beforehand. Now I understood it vividly as a firsthand experience, almost as if I had been present at the original event. This is one of the sources of stress for the therapist working with victims of childhood sexual abuse: it is almost as if one has to watch children being raped, then talk to them afterwards. There is great emotional intensity for the therapist. However, what the therapist goes through is a minute fraction of what the patient has experienced, and must re-experience in the therapy in order to overcome the past.

It is said that those who do not remember the past are condemned to repeat it: Jenny's younger sister was still living at home with her parents and her baby; the father of this baby is probably Jenny's father. Jenny's sister had not yet begun the difficult work of remembering, recovering, and becoming free of the past.

As Jenny and Sally got to know each other, we had many touching conversations. Often, I felt I was in conversation with two innocent and naïve girls. Sally would pout and refuse to talk to Jenny over some trivial matter, so I would act the part of the kind father and patch things up. Then Jenny would not want to talk to Sally because Sally was angry with her, so I would have to convince Jenny to talk to Sally. Sally, I learned, was a part of Jenny with self-confidence, independence, and a will to live which allowed her to dissociate herself from the father she hated, and to maintain a core of pure, undefiled selfhood. The cost of this survival strategy was that Jenny was left on her own, uncentred, unable to manage life, lost and confused. My therapeutic intent was to bring the two personalities back together, blending the strengths of both.

Unfortunately, Jenny had to return to Vancouver after four weeks of assessment and therapy. She missed her children, there was a court appearance to be made, and it seemed inevitable that she and Ted were going to break up – all good reasons to leave Winnipeg. Sally was not integrated when she left, but the two personalities were able to converse with each other freely and had resolved to work together cooperatively. Jenny promised to stay in touch, but I lost track of her for three years.

Then, one day in 1988, I got a phone call and heard a familiar voice on the other end of the line. Jenny had moved back to Winnipeg, much had happened in her life, and she wanted to get back into treatment. The rest of her therapy also took place on an out-patient basis with no need for hospital admissions.

The amnesia barrier between Jenny and Sally was partially reconstituted, but there was considerable conversation between the two of them. Jenny had experienced many black spells over the three years and had difficulty putting her life during that period into a narrative sequence. She had been seeing a psychologist occasionally, but he hadn't done any work with her multiple personality disorder.

Jenny had spent two months in jail in British Columbia on fraud charges in 1986; as far as she was aware, no other bad cheques had been written. She had had only occasional contact with her children, who were in a foster home and were apparently doing fairly well, despite some behaviour problems. She had ended a common-law relationship she had been involved in for two years, and said she had forgotten most of the details of her prior treatment and had forgotten my name until she moved back to Winnipeg. That move appeared to have triggered memories of her previous treatment, but she couldn't recall much about the conversations with Sally in my office.

After reviewing the events of the three years, I asked if I could talk to Sally. During the intervening three years I had acquired a great deal more experience with multiple personality disorder and had greatly reduced my use of hypnosis. I had learned that it simply wasn't necessary to do a lengthy hypnotic induction to get the work done, and I suspected that Jenny's trouble recalling her previous treatment might, in part, be related to my overuse of hypnosis.

A simple request to speak to Sally sufficed. Jenny nodded her head, briefly closed her eyes, and in a couple of seconds Sally was there – bright, chipper, enthusiastic, bubbly, and flashing me a big grin. Sally's memory of the prior psychotherapy was clear and detailed. She had been carefully observing everything that Jenny did from 1985 to 1988, and had intervened in many small ways to help out. She sometimes would give Jenny extra strength; at other times, she would just whisper support and encouragement into her ear.

Sally was both critical of the recent common-law boyfriend, Bill, and fond of him. She said that Bill had found out about her from Jenny and had gotten to know her well. In fact, Sally called him 'Daddy.' Much of the time she referred to Jenny as 'Mummy.' Sally had adopted the role of Bill and Jenny's fun-loving adolescent child, and was involved in day-to-day life with them. For instance, Bill would call Sally out, the two of them would go shopping and buy Jenny a dress, which Sally tried on to make sure it fit. When they returned home, Sally would put the dress on, Bill would call Jenny back out, and Jenny would suddenly 'come to' wearing a new dress.

When Bill and Jenny wanted to have sex, they would ask Sally to go away and play with her friends and dolls somewhere, which she would do. Although this relationship was lots of 'fun,' it was a re-enactment of Jenny's incestuous relationship with her father. It was as if Jenny and Sally had created a happier, more playful version of the incest relationship in order to lessen the pain of the abuse by their father: sex with Bill was a pretend game which made incest seem acceptable.

The dissociation between Jenny and Sally had been reinforced by this relationship countless times, as had the illusion that Sally was actually a separate person inside. When I asked Sally about whether she was a separate person or part of Jenny, she acknowledged in theory that they were both aspects of one person, but said that wasn't really how she felt about it.

I had learned during the three years from 1985 to 1988 always to ask whether there were any other personalities inside. This question is posed in an indirect manner by asking the known personalities if any of them have had blank spells or heard voices other than the voices of the known personalities. I didn't have to be subtle in my enquiry because Sally readily provided names and descriptions of five other personalities. Three of them had been in existence for many years, and two were created in 1986 after Jenny got out of jail.

I had, in fact, met Margaret in 1985 but hadn't realized she was distinct from Sally. Margaret was fifteen years old and had been the victim of much of the incest. I should have realized in 1985 that, since Jenny was initially amnesic for the incest and Sally did not have a physical body, someone else must have taken control during the sexual abuse. It was technically straightforward to call Margaret out just by asking, after receiving confirmation from Sally that it would be all right to do so. I requested that Sally ask Margaret if it would be all right if I talked to her. Margaret said it would be, and Sally passed this message on to me. Margaret had a bit of a chip on her shoulder but was not hard to get along with. She knew who I was, and remembered talking with me. When I asked why she hadn't identified herself to me in 1985, she replied that I hadn't asked, so she hadn't come forward. Margaret hated her father intensely. There were two other adolescent personalities as well: one, Liz, was a victim of other sexual assaults by a boyfriend and her father's friends. The other, Sheila, was drunk all the time.

When Sheila was in control of the body, she acted drunk, presenting a very convincing picture of alcohol intoxication. She was giddy, slightly slurred in her speech, unsteady in her gait, and looked intoxicated. She had been in this state continuously since adolescence. It took only a few sessions to learn why Sheila was drunk: she had been sexually assaulted while on a date at age seventeen, and had been intoxicated at the time.

Many alter personalities become frozen in time, stuck in the trauma in a never-ending abreaction which brings no healing. Often child personalities expect to be sexually assaulted at any moment and do not realize that any time had passed since the abuse happened, say, twenty or thirty years earlier. Some alter personalities may mistake the doctor or therapist for an abuser from the past and cower in the corner, head buried between the knees.

Sheila was a variation on this theme: she was stuck in the intoxicated, traumatized state in which she had been created eighteen years earlier. During subsequent years, she took executive control of the body only a few times for brief durations, apparently on a spontaneous basis. She never developed relationships with outside people or participated directly in life.

The two other personalities, Roseanne and Samantha, were created in 1986. They were prostitutes. Bill had been working as their driver, and they had been running an escort service. According to Sally, Bill carried a gun and handled the money. The reason for entering prostitution that Sally gave was to earn money to move to California and start a new life, but in fact most of the money had been spent on cars, fur coats, and other material possessions.

Jenny was never a very sophisticated criminal. For instance, one of Samantha's customers was a married man who paid for her services by cheque. When the customer's wife found cancelled cheques made out to Samantha's escort service, she phoned Samantha and threatened to take her to court if she did not pay the money back, a sum of over $1,000. Rather than 'cause trouble,' Samantha paid the money back, without consulting a lawyer. I have had other patients who gave away most of their trick money because they didn't want it, the purpose of their prostitution being entirely psychological and self-punitive in nature.

Samantha had employed three other women at one point and had a number and agency name listed in the phone book. She had been in a number of potentially dangerous situations, had been beaten up several times, and had been threatened with a knife. Samantha and Roseanne told me that part of the reason for moving back to Winnipeg was to get out of prostitution. Surprisingly, and thankfully, neither of them had been involved with drugs, and Jenny hadn't been infected with the AIDS virus.

In her book *Voices*, Trula Michaels La Calle tells the story of a man with multiple personality disorder whose lover died of AIDS. In research studies I have published, I found that about 20 per cent of multiple personality patients have worked as prostitutes, and also that many prostitutes have dissociative disorders. These victims of childhood incest, like Jenny, are often amnesic for their prostitution, which is carried out by alter personalities. I suspect that the spread of the AIDS virus in both homosexuals and heterosexuals may be driven by dissociation and amnesia to a significant extent. For many sexually promiscuous individuals and infected prostitutes, their behaviour may be driven by unresolved child abuse and untreated dissociative disorders. If this is correct, it represents a major social cost of childhood trauma and its long-term consequences.

The re-creation of the original paternal incest with Bill, I now realized, was more complicated than I had at first understood. Bill, in the role of Sally's father, was also a variant on the original father who had lent his daughters out to his alcoholic friends for sexual use. With Bill, it was customers instead of friends, but the logic was the same. Like many abuse victims, Jenny was entrapped in the past in several ways, one of which was the repetition of abusive and exploitative relationships. Her moving back to Winnipeg was a major step in breaking this pattern.

The second phase of the therapy proceeded very quickly. I got to know the five other personalities, and with Sally's help the amnesia barriers between Jenny and her other 'people' were removed. Jenny had a great deal of work to do learning about her involvement in prostitution; recovering and processing the abuse memories held by Margaret, Liz, and Sheila; and coming to understand the destructive aspects of her relationship with Bill.

The relationship with Bill was not all negative or destructive, or course. Jenny acknowledged that entering into prostitution was her idea, not his, and that she had created alter personalities to do the work and to hold the memories of the prostitution. Jenny herself couldn't have turned the tricks, for emotional and moral reasons and because of fear. One component of the therapy involved helping Jenny take responsibility for all her behaviour and actually experience it, psychologically, as her own behaviour and past, rather than as something other people had done.

The relationship with Bill contained many positive moments. They really did have fun together, and were genuinely fond of each other, but the foundation of the relationship was not sound.

The integration of the seven different personalities was not achieved without some difficulties. Several times, Roseanne and Samantha appeared to be integrated but then came back again. There was no further involvement in prostitution, though, and Jenny never drank heavily again. She was able to work much of the time, though at one job she was a victim of sexual harassment and created a new personality state to deal with the situation: this transient personality state was integrated shortly afterwards.

The integration of all the personalities into a single unified self is the goal of the therapy. Through this process the person recovers all his or her memories and feelings, and comes to terms with them as much as possible. The integrated person feels that all her life experiences happened to her, just as anyone else would. Integration is a by-product of the hard work of therapy: once the memories, thoughts, and feelings are shared, and the conflicts and disagreements between personalities resolved, the blending together of the personalities happens quite readily. The final integration may occur spontaneously or may be assisted with a verbal ritual provided by the therapist.

When her integration appeared to be complete and stable, Jenny arranged for her children to move to Winnipeg but live with someone else, while she spent an increasing amount of time with them. She is not experiencing blank spells or hearing voices in her head, and she feels that Sally is with her in her heart, but not separate in the old way. The quality of her life is much improved, and she is not plagued by anxiety or depression. I last spoke to Jenny in the spring of 1993, at which time she was still integrated.

If Jenny had been able to get treatment for her multiple personality disorder earlier in life, she might not have had to give up her children, might have avoided involvement in prostitution and alcohol abuse, and might not have committed fraud or been sent to jail. This would have saved her much suffering, and the taxpayer a great deal of money. Despite her not getting treatment until she was in her thirties, though, her future is hopeful.

2

An Abused, Agoraphobic Housewife

When I first met Charlene on the ward in January 1986, she was a thin, pale, nervous thirty-three-year-old housewife. She had a strange way of hunching over and holding her shoulders into herself, and she appeared to be cringing all the time, like an abused animal. When she walked, her steps were short, hesitant, and inhibited. She was so frail and overwrought that it seemed a loud noise might shatter her into fragments. When I introduced myself, she spoke in a frightened, childish voice, saying, 'The doctor [her family physician] told me I have irrational fears.'

Charlene had short wavy brown hair, tense forehead muscles, and frightened-looking eyes, and she radiated an intense nervous energy. Her hands trembled as her thin, white fingers grasped a cup of coffee. I wasn't surprised to learn that she drank more than twenty cups of tea a day, and I felt she must be suffering from caffeine toxicity.

Why had she come to hospital? Charlene was to begin a trial of an antidepressant and was so worried about possible side-effects that her family doctor was unable to start the medication on an out-patient basis. When I enquired about her fear of medication, I learned that she was worried about nausea, skin reactions, fainting, changes in her perception, and a dozen other potential calamities. These were relatively minor concerns, however.

The main problem with starting medication, she said, was

that, if she suffered irreversible brain damage (an unheard-of complication with such medications), her husband, Mark, would leave her. Where did this idea of hers come from? I learned upon enquiry that Mark's father had emigrated from Yugoslavia with the children when Mark was very young, leaving Mark's mother behind in an institution. According to the family myth, Mark's father left his mother because her brain was irreversibly damaged by her anti-epileptic medication. The story was dubious, but Charlene was afraid that the pattern would be repeated in her marriage.

Why did Charlene need an antidepressant? For two reasons: since the death of her alcoholic father in September 1985, Charlene had developed a clinical depression, and severe panic disorder with agoraphobia. She had been almost completely housebound for four months, and had gone out only a couple of times since the funeral. She had been experiencing many severe panic attacks per day, with all the classical symptoms – intense fear, palpitations, a racing heart, sweatiness, feeling faint, shortness of breath, fearing she was going crazy or about to die, an upset stomach, weak legs, tingling in her hands and feet, a choking sensation, and feeling unreal or depersonalized. The attacks would come on very quickly and unpredictably, and last up to half an hour. She had never had panic attacks prior to her father's death.

Antidepressant medications are effective for depression, but they also often block the occurrence of panic attacks, thereby allowing a person to overcome his or her agoraphobia.

Charlene also told me that she was an abused wife, and that the beatings had started during her first pregnancy (she had children aged eight and six, a boy and a girl). Mark, she said, controlled her with the threat of beatings. He gave her $100 a month to spend, but she was not allowed to use a cheque-book or charge card. He worked long hours as a tradesman, and treated her as a domestic and sexual slave at home. If dinner was not ready when he arrived home, Mark flew into a rage. Most of his spare time was devoted to drinking and speaking in Yugoslavian with his father; he spent almost no time with the children and never took Charlene out. He had fractured two of her ribs on one occasion and at other times had inflicted innumerable bruises on her. If she took the medication and got irreversible side-effects, he would take the children and leave her: if the subject of her leaving him ever came up, Mark commented, 'If you move out, it'll be in an ambulance.'

After years of being controlled and abused, Charlene said, she had finally made a decision. She was going to take the medication no matter what Mark said: she was finally going to do what she wanted. She told me this on a Wednesday, the day of her admission, and we decided to start the medication on Friday.

After breakfast on Thursday, Charlene phoned Mark and told him to come and take her home. She was too worried about brain damage to stay in hospital longer or risk taking the medication. When Mark arrived at the hospital, however, she told him there was no way he could stop her from taking the antidepressant, and sent him home.

Before she took the first 25 milligrams of antidepressant on Friday morning, we had a long talk about anxiety and side-effects. I explained that people participating in drug studies who do not realize they are taking a placebo often get better, and also often develop side-effects. I drew a comparison with the panic attacks she had if she tried to drive her car: it is not the car itself that causes the symptoms, I explained; rather, they come from within the person. Similarly, she would almost certainly experience side-effects from the antidepressant but these would be produced by her own anxiety and not the medication.

Actually, the situation was somewhat more complicated than that, since the tricyclic antidepressants do have minor side-effects that can trigger panic attacks in people with panic disorder. I didn't mention this to Charlene, however.

Several times we went over the reasons for prescribing the medication, the small starting dose, the safety of the ward environment, and the plan to gradually increase the dose to 150 milligrams per day. Before the medication could possibly have been absorbed through the lining of her stomach, Charlene developed numerous 'side-effects.' She was nauseated and faint; felt funny all over; felt panicky, then drowsy, then hyper-aroused, with a sense that everything looked very clear and sharp. She was very bitter about the fact that there was not a nurse with her constantly the entire day. She thought it an injustice that the ward routine went on as usual while she endured this ordeal in solitude, although in fact the nurse checked on her regularly.

Charlene took another 50 milligrams that evening and never did have any serious side-effects.

The following week I heard more about Mark. I found myself feeling angry at the brutality of this man. How could he beat such a frail, small, and ill woman, one who weighed eighty-nine pounds at the time of her hospitalization? I arranged a family interview to be attended by both children and both parents.

Mark, I learned, is indeed big and strong. He is not psy-chologically minded and gets angry very easily. He disciplined the children harshly, worked constantly, could not relax, and had no hobbies or friends. However, he was a good provider, and did all the shopping and driving of the kids to lessons and activities while Charlene had been housebound with agora-phobia for four months.

By the time the family interview was over, my view of Mark had changed. I no longer saw him as the stereotypical chauvin-ist Charlene had described. He spoke kindly of his wife, and was frank about how frustrating she could be and how difficult she was for him to deal with. He was, to some extent, genuine-ly concerned about the harm the medication might cause, but his main worry was expressed in the question 'What good would she be to me?'.

Mark perceived Charlene as purely instrumental, as a domes-tic and sexual worker in the home. However, this was also how he perceived himself, except that his job was outside the home. If Charlene suffered irreversible brain damage, she would no longer be able to function, and the family unit would collapse economically. It was true that he beat her and that that behaviour was inexcusable, unjustifiable, and criminal, but everything wasn't as black and white as Charlene made it out to be.

The most interesting interaction during the family interview was between Charlene and her six-year-old son. Mark's father had been babysitting during the day while Mark was at work. When Mark came home, he found that a towel rack in the bathroom had been broken, but both children denied responsibility. Mark couldn't extract a confession out of either of them. When this incident was discussed in the session, both Charlene and Mark interrogated their son, but neither could get anything out of him. Charlene then called him over, sat him on her lap, and began cooing and baby-talking to him. She said repeatedly, 'You can tell Mommy. Don't be frightened. You can tell Mommy.'

With a repentant expression on his face, the boy hung his head down and the questioning continued: 'Did you do it? Did you break the towel rack? You can tell Mommy.' This was repeated many times while mother and son shared a cuddle.

Finally, the boy nodded his head, yes. Immediately, Charlene said, 'That's all I wanted to know.' She pushed her son off her lap, ignored him completely, and continued the conversation with me.

In this set of interactions, Mark took the role of a frightening ogre who disciplines harshly and tries to intimidate the children into confessing. Charlene's role, comparatively, was more subtle, devious, and effective. She needed Mark to behave as the monster in order for her son to feel safe and protected on her lap, so that she could extract the confession. The technique was a family adaptation of the good guy–bad guy strategy used in police interrogation around the world. In this family, though, Charlene saw herself as the good mother and victim, and Mark as the bad father and abuser: they were playing reciprocal, interdigitated roles in the family system.

Charlene had no empathy whatsoever for Mark as a man with his own pain. A story she told me of a family argument illustrated the pattern: one day their son was playing too roughly with his sister. Mark got mad at him, grabbed him and threw him on the couch; afterward, when the boy came crying to Charlene, she blew up at Mark. Mark's father was there, and Charlene launched into a bitter tirade about how Mark cared more for his father than his wife, how he treated the children badly in front of his father, and how she wasn't going to tolerate it anymore.

Mark's father then got up, said he wasn't going to come over for Christmas dinner, and left. The next day Mark bought Charlene a new television set and a VCR. Charlene told me this story with humour. Everyone reconciled in time for the father-in-law to come over for Christmas, of course, and a day of heavy drinking with Mark. Charlene regarded this incident as evidence of Mark's brutality, insensitivity, and constant efforts to bribe her with material things. When I pointed out that she didn't seem to have difficulty accepting the gifts, she replied, 'I'm not that stupid.' Charlene had her most satisfying sexual relations with Mark following a beating.

Charlene always referred to her mother as 'the witch.' Just as Mark was seen as a malevolent monster with no positive features, so too her mother was all bad. She absolutely refused to admit that she ever loved or needed her mother in any way. 'I don't need her. What do I need her for?' was a constant refrain.

Her mother had never been to her father's grave, which had no tombstone, and Charlene had been only once. Her mother suffered from a chronic illness which at times required that she be hospitalized, and on one occasion her mother was in hospital for three weeks and didn't notify her daughter, who did not learn about it until after her mother had been discharged. On other occasions she would blame Charlene for having made her sick again, induce massive guilt in her through manipulative statements, and insist she visit regularly. Charlene's sister lived at home with her mother, and was housebound by agoraphobia.

Dad, in contrast, was idealized to an amazing degree. According to Charlene's description, he was an ineffectual, lazy alcoholic who died of pancreatic cancer. When Charlene was an adult, the two of them were extremely uncomfortable with each other and, when left alone together, had no idea what to say or talk about. Yet father was all good and all wonderful: you couldn't say a word against him. Charlene's depression, panic attacks, and agoraphobia started immediately after he died.

I asked Charlene numerous times during her hospitalization whether anything bad had happened during her childhood, but she always replied that there was nothing. She responded very well to the antidepressants within three weeks, with full resolution of her clinical depression, and a dramatic reduction in her anxiety level and number of panic attacks. The discharge plan included marital therapy, attendance at an out-patient agoraphobia group, and monitoring of her medication. She was discharged on a Friday in good spirits.

On the following Monday, I received a phone call. Charlene had to talk to me. Over the weekend, horrible memories had come flooding back in an uncontrollable torrent, and she was terrified of what else she might remember. When she was a girl, men had done things to her, she said. She had to talk.

Before I saw her the next day, I discussed the situation with the social worker, and we agreed to postpone the marital therapy and to proceed with individual therapy for Charlene with me to find out what was going on and to help her piece together these memories. She would continue taking the antidepressant and would go to the agoraphobia group. This plan was accepted by Charlene, though she never did attend the agoraphobia group. During the first six months of out-patient therapy, I decreased and then discontinued Charlene's antidepressant, and also discontinued the sleeping pill she had been taking for years.

I told her that I thought her memories were flooding back at this time for several reasons: it might have something to do with the medication; with her feeling she had a supportive therapeutic environment, and thus the safety necessary for remembering; or with her needing to have a reason to continue seeing me as a therapist. It was clear very early in my sessions with her that, besides working hard in therapy and benefiting from it, Charlene would become dependent on me, and often be difficult and manipulative.

One problem I had to deal with was phone calls. Charlene would phone every day with a crisis or emergency which only I could resolve. These crises were always minor, never needed immediate attention, and could usually have been resolved quite easily by Charlene on her own. Some days she would phone ten to fifteen times, and would yell at the secretaries and accuse them of lying if they could not get me immediately. One day I arrived at work to find three emergency phone messages, and a fourth saying it was all right, I didn't have to respond to the previous messages. She phoned again shortly after leaving the fourth message.

Over the several years of Charlene's therapy, the were prolonged periods during which I refused to answer any phone calls or have any contact with her outside scheduled sessions. Then I would allow one phone call per week on a trial basis, and shortly she would be phoning every day again. Then I would completely cut out phone calls for several months, and the pattern would be repeated. Several times she came to the building, demanding to see me, and was sent home, and once she complained to the head of the department and threatened to contact the media. Although much of Charlene's behaviour was annoying and tiresome, I saw it as stemming from her childhood sexual, physical, and emotional abuse.

When she was five years old, the local minister had called Charlene into the church while she was at summer Bible school. There he exposed himself and attempted to penetrate her. The minister held her naked on his lap while he sat on a pew: she faced away from him as he tried to penetrate her from the rear. As she relived the experience in therapy, Charlene felt the pain in her genital area again, and re-experienced the panicky choking feeling as the minister held his hand over her mouth. It was exactly the same feeling that she had during panic attacks – that she wouldn't be able to get any air with her next breath – and the pelvic pain was exactly the same as that she had felt so often during intercourse. With therapy, both the panic attacks and the pain during intercourse were cured.

Charlene recovered her abuse memories in fragments at home, during sessions, and in dreams. Often she went into a trance in my office if the memories were coming back too quickly, at which times she spoke in a childish voice. Quite a few times, she simply put her head down on my desk and went to sleep if the memories became too painful. I had to shake her to wake her up, so that we could continue with other therapeutic work.

Another memory involved a molestation in some bushes, but this time she wasn't sure if it was the minister. He's chasing her. She's running. He's coming closer and closer. She's hiding in some bushes and he finds her. Now he's doing something. What's he doing? She's frightened. She wants him to go away. Why is he doing that? He's masturbating. Then Charlene would come out of trance, without resolving the question of the man's identity. Charlene would 'hypnotize' herself during sessions, and I never did perform a formal hypnotic induction myself.

There is another memory: she is washing blood and semen off her panties in a small pond, before going home. When she gets home, her mother becomes angry at her and gives her an aspirin. It tastes bitter. It's the same bitter taste she gets as an adult whenever she's anxious. And so it goes, in these early months: more memories are relived, and patchy fragments fit together into coherent stories, and Charlene's symptoms become less and less severe.

Another 'incident,' as she calls them, is relived in therapy: she walks into her parents' bedroom and finds her mother in bed with a man, but she isn't sure if it's her father or the minister. He gets out of bed and begins molesting her. That is all she remembers.

By the time this fragment was reconstructed into a complete memory, Charlene had had to deal with the fact that her mother had an affair with the minister who molested her while her father was away on business. Worse than that, her mother used to charge the minister five dollars to allow him to sexually abuse her daughter. At first Charlene felt she must be crazy to have such memories because such things could not possibly have happened. There was a great deal of confusion about what was real and what was not, which took a long time to resolve.

Charlene remembered thinking that, when her father came home, he wouldn't let her mother make 'wristwatches' on her anymore. Her mother used to bite her wrists so hard that distinct teeth marks remained for a while, which her mother called 'wristwatches.' There was a long list of different abuses perpetrated by her mother, including locking her in the basement for hours, child prostitution, emotional cruelty, and massive induction of guilt and self-blame in Charlene.

Once, in the second year of therapy, Charlene received a phone call from a collection agency. Her sister, unbeknownst to her, had cited her as a reference in subscribing to a magazine, but then had decided that she didn't want the magazine anymore. The woman from the collection agency, not realizing that the two women were sisters, wanted Charlene's sister's phone number. Charlene pretended she didn't know it. A few minutes later, the woman phoned back, having talked to Charlene's mother, and asked her, 'Is that woman insane?'.

Charlene's mother had told the woman from the collection agency that her sister had not paid for the subscription 'because she's on welfare and she's insane.' The woman thought that was a horrible way for any mother to talk about her daughter, but Charlene thought it was typical.

Right up to the time of her father's death, Charlene used to spend countless hours doing housework for her parents, in addition to her own domestic work. She ran errands, was constantly being called over to do something, and performed this slavery for years without complaint, and without rewards of any kind. Why? Charlene said it was because she felt 'an obligation.' Yet, while doing this extensive labour for her parents without resentment, she was very bitter that Mark consistently forced her into the servant role.

Whenever Charlene tried not to fulfil her exaggerated obligations to her parents, she was overcome with guilt. Why? The guilt made her feel sick and anxious and, over the years, had resulted in countless tests and prescriptions from doctors for physical symptoms they could never explain. She had filled literally dozens of prescriptions and never taken any of them. Why?

The only way Charlene could relieve her guilt was to function as a slave. She needed the guilt to motivate her to work, and she needed to work to prove over and over again to herself and her parents that she was not a bad girl. She was never successful. If only she could work a little harder, sacrifice herself a little more, be a little bit closer to perfect, maybe she wouldn't be bad anymore and the abuse would stop. This childish logic is almost universal in victims of severe childhood sexual abuse, but Charlene's behaviour was driven by it in an extreme fashion.

Charlene was also frightened of getting better. With every small step forward she was overcome with anxiety, and developed a rush of symptoms. Getting better might mean that she would have to risk real intimacy with someone. This was too dangerous to even consider, because of the cruel violations of intimacy perpetrated on her by her parents. Yes, she learned eventually that her father had sexually abused her too. It really wasn't safe when the knight in shining armour came back from his business trip, and he really didn't protect her from the witch.

To be a slave, Charlene required slave masters. This was Mark's role, which he was very willing to fill. Her perception of herself as purely a victim, and Mark as purely a perpetrator, actually helped to keep her locked into the abusive pattern, because it blinded her to her own contribution to the pattern, and the pattern's origin in her childhood. In all her relationships, including with me, Charlene exerted immense unconscious pressure to re-enact an abuse scenario. She told me directly that she wished I would beat her to prove that I really cared.

At times Charlene's behaviour was so annoying that I did feel like beating her up. She would whine, complain, manipulate, threaten, or refuse to leave at the end of a session. Several times

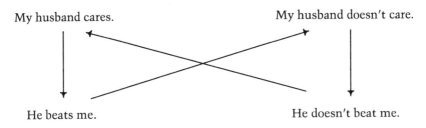

My husband cares.   My husband doesn't care.

He beats me.   He doesn't beat me.

Figure 1
Battered-Wife Loop

I left my office and went down to the ward at the end of a session, and she sat there for a while till she got bored and left. She would cling to me tenaciously and then abuse and reject me.

Charlene was caught in what I call a 'Battered-Wife Loop,' which is depicted in figure 1.

Based on the childish logic of the victim, abuse is transformed into evidence of caring: at least Mommy and Daddy care enough to beat me, the child reasons, which is better than abandoning me or ignoring me completely. I must mean something to them. Often abusive parents actually tell children that they are beating or raping them out of love.

Trapped in this logic, Charlene often felt that her husband cared about her: the proof of his love was that he beat her and used her as a sexual object. Yet, at the same time, she thought that Mark didn't care for her because he mistreated her. She also had a set of cognitions in which Mark didn't care about her because he didn't beat her. The beatings were not continuous, so Charlene kept moving round the loop. Additionally, of course, the fact that Mark didn't beat her functioned as evidence that he did care, when Charlene was using the logic of a non-traumatized adult. As soon as Charlene had come to the conclusion that Mark did, in fact, care about her, though, the childish logic was activated again, and she needed to be beaten to reinforce the feeling that he cared.

The Battered-Wife Loop is a very difficult trap from which to escape. Much of the therapy involved defining how Charlene was stuck in abusive patterns of relating to others, trying to help her see how she was contributing to the pattern, and supporting her efforts to change. She was also trapped in her marriage by lack of education and skills, economic dependency on Mark, and responsibility for the majority of the parenting, in addition to her symptoms and unresolved abuse history. She could not overcome these long-term consequences of child abuse until the trauma was accurately remembered.

I came to understand a reciprocal relationship between anger and anxiety which also helped to keep Charlene immobilized in her home. During the months following her father's death, she spent many hours per day sitting in exactly the same spot on the same couch, drinking tea, and feeling depressed, anxious, and frightened.

Charlene could not bear it when Mark left for work in the morning. It took him half an hour to get out of the house. As soon as he touched his jacket, she would burst into tears. Then Mark would comfort her until she settled down. This sequence would be repeated three or four times, then, after he left, it would take her an hour to settle down and be able to do her domestic chores.

Charlene was too anxious to leave Mark. I asked myself whether the main problem was anxiety, in which case treatment of the anxiety would help her to leave, or whether the anxiety was actually helpful and necessary, in that it protected her from ever having to seriously consider leaving. Charlene saw her 'anxiety' as similar to an infection, something from outside her that she was afflicted with, and which had no direct connection with her personal life or past. She said she would never put up with the beatings if it weren't for her anxiety.

When she was angry, though, the anxiety went away. To be sufficiently angry, Charlene needed Mark to be extremely abusive. When the anger came, her physical symptoms and 'irrational fears' evaporated: once she had left with the kids for two weeks, but her anxiety symptoms had gotten so bad that she moved back in, which resulted in a marked temporary relief of her symptoms.

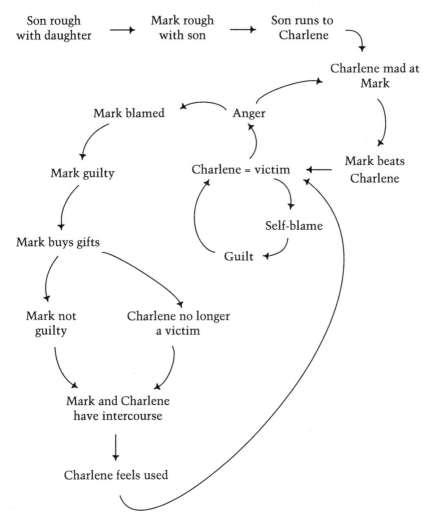

Figure 2
Ogre–Victim Transactional Pattern

Charlene was also trapped in another more complicated pattern I call the 'Ogre–Victim Transactional Pattern.' It is depicted in figure 2.

The therapy session in which Charlene extracted the confession about the broken towel rack illustrates a point of entry into the Ogre–Victim Transactional Pattern. A typical example, shown in the diagram, starts with the son being too rough with the daughter (son in ogre role, daughter in victim role). Mark responds with harsh discipline of the son (Mark in ogre role, son in victim role). The son runs to Charlene in the victim role and gets comfort from her, Charlene then gets angry at Mark and takes on the ogre role. In reaction, Mark activates his ogre role again, and switches Charlene into the victim role by beating her.

This makes Charlene angry and propels her back into the victim–spouse abuse loop. It also sends her into a loop of self-blame and guilt originally indoctrinated into her by her parents, and it makes her blame Mark for being abusive. Mark responds with guilt, and then he buys her things. The material bribes result in Mark no longer being guilty and Charlene no longer being a victim: instead, she is a loved and well-treated wife. In the next step, Mark and Charlene have intercourse, but this makes Charlene feel used, again because of her abuse history, and she is propelled back into the victim role, in preparation for yet another tour through the loops.

One can understand why Mark sought oblivion in alcohol and why Charlene was so symptomatic. The Ogre–Victim Transactional Pattern was driven by a complicated set of rules that Charlene lived by. These were:

1 / Victims are anxious.
2 / Ogres are angry.
3 / Anger and anxiety are inversely related.
4 / Bad girls deserve to be beaten.
5 / Men are ogres.
6 / Bad girls must be beaten to prove their mothers were right.
7 / Good fathers protect girls from bad mothers.
8 / Bad fathers go away.
9 / Bad girls have bad fathers.
10 / Charlene had a good father.

Even her relationships with her children's teachers and the

school principal were based on these rules and transactional patterns. I listened to incredible accounts of Charlene's attempts to rescue her son from the influence of teachers and principals, with no help from Mark. She would blow up in the principal's office, and would beg me to become her son's psychiatrist, which I refused to do.

It was about four months into therapy that I began to be aware of *the five-year-old*. When Charlene abreacted her abuse memories, she acted in a childish manner, changing her speech and facial mannerisms. She always pulled her feet up onto the chair, and wrapped her arms around her shins, with her chin resting on her knees. Sometimes she would not remember the abreaction very clearly.

At first, the five-year-old did not seem to be a distinct alter personality. It was more of an inner state which held the abuse memories, and which she deliberately personified in a metaphorical way, but gradually there was a shift. The five-year-old had never been in control of Charlene's body, and she had never experienced blank spells over the preceding years. She had had a number of episodes of amnesia in her adult life during periods of trauma, such as witnessing a fatal car accident, but this had nothing to do with the five-year-old.

Gradually the five-year-old became more and more distinct, and Charlene started to talk about her as a distinct person inside. She claimed that this was the way it had always been, and that she was just getting comfortable talking about the five-year-old, but I had my doubts. Over the next six months I got to know the five-year-old, and various problems arose, such as competition between Charlene and the five-year-old for therapy time.

With explanations from me of what was going on, Charlene readily accepted that the five-year-old was part of her, but she often talked as if this wasn't the case. She would say that the five-year-old wanted to talk, as though referring to another person. The five-year-old did indeed hold many abuse memories, and these were gradually recovered and dealt with. As the reservoir of dissociated abuse memories was becoming depleted, the five-year-old became less distinct and separate, and gradually the need to talk directly with her was being reduced.

Charlene did leave Mark, with a lot of trouble. After two years of therapy, she was legally separated; employed part-time; no longer suffering from agoraphobia; and had been out of the city for the first time in years, having been too anxious to leave the city for over a decade. We had begun to talk about the possibility of therapy coming to an end.

Then Charlene watched the movie *The Three Faces of Eve* on television. Within three weeks, she had a new personality named Carol who was flamboyant, flirtatious, and sometimes angry. Carol was very similar to Eve Black as portrayed by Joanne Woodward. She called me 'Doc,' liked to make a bit of playful trouble in sessions, and was scornful of Charlene's restricted, anxiety-ridden character. She thought Mark was a jerk. Carol could be called out quite easily, and Charlene was aware that she existed but was amnesic for much of the time during which Carol was out. Carol acknowledged that she had not been in existence for long.

Four other personalities were created over the next few months, including Priscilla, who was prim and proper, with a thorough knowledge of all the other personalities and their characteristics. A fifth personality, Lori, was created solely for the purpose of studying for a course Charlene was taking. The sixth was called 'Number Six' since she didn't have a name: she embodied a childish ability to love others in an idealizing way, as well as a great deal of pain from childhood. The seventh personality was Charlene's mother. The mother introject was hostile, claimed to be possessing Charlene, and wanted her to commit suicide.

I talked with these different characters a little, but not too much. I felt that the five-year-old was a genuine internal state that had existed prior to the therapy, but which was personified and amplified during the course of recovering the abuse memories. The other personalities I felt had been created for the purpose of staying in therapy indefinitely. Their job was providing 'problems' to work on. There were many different disputes and interactions between the different members of the internal psychodrama.

This was very different from classical, genuine MPD, in which the different personalities have existed long before the therapy, have taken control of the body numerous times, and have had well-defined characteristics and functions. Charlene's is the only case I have seen of what is called *iatrogenic multiple personality disorder*. 'Iatrogenic' means created by the physician. Some professionals think that all cases of MPD are like the personalities created by Charlene – theatrical attempts to get the therapist's attention and stay in 'therapy' forever – but such therapy would be no more than a caricature.

We continued to focus on the problems Charlene was having in her daily life, and I made it clear that I was not going to do much 'MPD' work with her. At one point, the mother personality was causing a lot of trouble at home, and Charlene was reacting as though she were having a fight with a possessing spirit. She claimed that her mother was taking control of her body, causing her to levitate off the bed, then making her crash to the ground. At other times, her mother caused various other body contortions and strange statements to be made, all of which highly impressed friends of Charlene's and made them think she needed an exorcism.

Actually, what she needed was to learn that she could live without me. Charlene tended to attribute her improved ability to function to me rather than to herself, and feared she would regress back to the state she was in at the time of her hospitalization if therapy came to an end. She had come to understand quite a bit about how the abuse had affected her perception of others and her relationships, although she was by no means free of all the effects of the trauma. She was driving around the city without difficulty, whereas at the beginning of therapy it was a major ordeal for her just driving to the hospital. Early in therapy she had a severe panic attack every single trip to the hospital, was fearful of wrecking her car, and always took a vomit bag, bottle of water, and sedative pill with her in the car. The water was for dry throat caused by anxiety.

Charlene had established a reasonably healthy relationship with a man who did not physically abuse her, and who was good with the children. This relationship lasted over a year, until she broke it off for sound reasons after careful consideration. She had dealt with substantial harassment from Mark and abuse from the legal system during her divorce, was living in a home she owned, and was working. Her panic disorder and depression were in remission, she was no longer plagued by numerous psychosomatic symptoms, and she remembered and experienced psychological ownership of her childhood. Yet she was frightened to end therapy.

We agreed on a schedule for decreasing the frequency of therapy sessions and eventually stopping them. For the first six months, the sessions had been three times a week, then twice a week, then once a week. We decreased them to once every two weeks, then once a month for a while, then no sessions for six months, and then no more sessions at all. This went smoothly. Charlene has continued to do well, except that she has required low-dose antidepressants, prescribed by her general practitioner, to keep her from getting depressed.

There have been difficulties with the children, and some economic instability, but she has never gotten really ill again. I have had brief telephone contacts with her at a frequency of less than every six months, but no in-person sessions. In another case I might call the patient, or former patient, occasionally, to check whether all the personalities were still integrated, but with Charlene that would be counter-productive because such checks would stimulate more dissociation.

The main lesson I learned from Charlene was to think of the long-term consequences of childhood sexual abuse in broad terms. The abuse doesn't only cause symptoms and psychiatric disorders such as anxiety, depression, nightmares, amnesia, and MPD, but also traps the person in complicated, self-destructive relationship patterns. There is also a significant economic, social, and political component to the long-term consequences of childhood trauma. When there is amnesia for the trauma, and no apparent explanation for why the person has so many problems, it is very difficult to understand the patient empathically or plan a meaningful course of treatment: full recovery requires full recovery of the memories. Not every minute detail has to be remembered and talked about – non-traumatized people can remember only a limited amount of detail about their childhoods, and, in any case, the therapy would take decades if every single detail had to be processed. Given these qualifiers, remembering what has been dissociated is nevertheless an essential part of getting better.

Dissociation is a major way in which human beings cope with trauma. It is true, as the sceptics say, that amplifying a victim's problems by reinforcing a previously non-existent MPD would be harmful, just as making him or her more anxious or depressed for no good reason would be poor therapy. I have included Charlene's story, and made it the second chapter, to illustrate that there is a difference between genuine long-standing MPD and simply making up 'personalities' out of nowhere. Charlene could have stayed in pseudo-therapy for her pseudo-MPD forever, but didn't.

3

The Woman Who Didn't Come Back

In 1987 I got a call from a resident in our Out-patient Department. He had done six months of in-patient work on my ward during the previous year and had had direct contact with MPD cases on the ward. He was aware of the signs and symptoms of the disorder, and was aware that there was a good chance he would see further cases during his training. The resident wanted me to see a woman he had recently interviewed because he suspected she had MPD.

A week later, Mary walked into the resident's office and sat down. She was a brown-haired woman in her late twenties who wore glasses, was at least eighty pounds overweight, and had a tense, suspicious manner. She grasped her large purse tightly on her lap as if it might shield her from us, and she kept her thick winter jacket on. I explained to Mary that the purpose of the interview was to see if I could help the resident understand her problems more clearly, which would in turn help in planning her treatment.

When I reviewed Mary's chart a few days earlier I saw that the resident had taken a thorough history: most of the characteristic signs and symptoms of MPD were recorded in the notes. During an assessment, patients with undiagnosed MPD usually don't say without being asked that they have other people inside them, and it is unusual for another personality to come out spontaneously and tell the examiner that he or she has a different name and age. Diagnosis depends on asking about more subtle indicators.

Most mental health professionals do not make the diagnosis of MPD for two reasons, both of which arise from a lack of systematic training about childhood trauma and dissociation. Most mental health professionals believe that MPD is rare or non-existent; therefore, it does not occur to them that they might meet a case on any given day. Additionally, orthodox psychiatric assessments do not include a careful enquiry for the signs and symptoms of the disorder. In my training, for instance, I was not taught how to ask about amnesia and I did not receive any seminars or formal teaching on the effects of child abuse. This lack of systematic training results in otherwise thorough and competent professionals not considering the possibility of MPD seriously, and not asking the necessary questions.

Having firsthand experience with MPD, the resident was able to ask the necessary questions and put the answers together into a picture that made sense. Mary had taken an overdose and was asking for help with mood swings, depression, and hatred of males: that information alone should raise the question of childhood sexual abuse. The process of diagnosing MPD involves asking general questions that raise a suspicion, then narrowing down more and more to questions that will specifically rule the diagnosis in or out. Recent research shows that a large percentage of people seeking psychiatric help have histories of having been abused as children, so it is necessary to ask in detail about child abuse in every assessment and to try to understand whether the person's symptoms and problems are related to childhood trauma.

Over the previous year Mary had been eating more than usual, had gained weight, and had been angry and irritable. She did not describe the full picture of a clinical depression, though. Her energy and concentration were not impaired, and her sleep was poor, with frequent awakenings, but no worse than it had been for years. She was suicidal at times, but this seemed to be related more to anger than to depressed mood. Certainly, treatment with antidepressants for a partial depression was a possibility, except for the danger of another overdose.

Mary said that, about three times a year, she heard her name being called when no one was there. This experience is not necessarily a psychiatric symptom, and can be completely normal. Several years earlier the voices had been quite active, and she remembered that one was female and strict-sounding, but she didn't want to talk about them. Frequent instances of hearing such voices make the possibility of MPD stronger.

Mary also experienced frequent blank spells lasting one to three hours, and a few years earlier had been blanked out for a number of months at one time. She frequently found herself in places with no idea how she had come to be there, and friends regularly told her about things she had done that she couldn't remember. She often misplaced things and could not find them, and also found things in her apartment that she did not recognize and didn't know whence they had come. She also experienced many 'foggy' states, which she could remember only partially.

Mary said that she must have a 'familiar face' because strangers frequently came up to her and claimed to know her. She recalled one incident in particular in which a strange man insisted he knew her well and called her by her middle name, which she never used. She also got occasional phone calls from people asking to speak to someone with her middle name. During the period she was blanked out for several months, she said, she may have done things that were 'too dreadful to relate.' The resident had learned by checking records at another hospital that Mary was charged with keeping a common bawdy-house during this time.

Mary had had a traumatic childhood. Her father left before she was born, never to be seen again, and her mother remarried when she was five. Her mother and stepfather both abused her physically and emotionally. She said this was too painful to talk about, but mentioned being locked in the basement for forty-eight hours when very young. She denied sexual abuse, but mentioned that she had lost all her memory for ages eight and nine.

Mary said she was called a 'behaviour problem' at school, starting at age seven, and ran away from home quite a few times between ages twelve and fourteen. She married because of being pregnant at age fifteen, and was physically and emotionally abused by her husband, who was twelve years older than her, until she left him in 1986. She also ran away from her marital home several times before the final separation.

According to records, Mary was admitted to a psychiatry ward at age fourteen for being destructive at home and hearing many voices. In a report on psychological testing done at that time, she was described as an 'uncontrollable, dependent, immature, attention seeking, self-centred girl who appears to have little human empathy and a low level of frustration tolerance.' This is a common clinical portrait of an undiagnosed and misunderstood abuse victim. At age seventeen, Mary was admitted to a psychiatric ward again for abusing her daughter, and because she 'awoke' to find herself about to stab her husband.

In light of this information, it was virtually certain that Mary had MPD and that her alter personalities had been active since before age ten: no other psychiatric disorder includes this constellation of symptoms. The voices in MPD occur when the different personalities talk to each other or to the part of the person who is in control most of the time. Often the controlling personality will be able to identify the gender of the voices and give a character sketch of each one, with one being friendly and helpful, another angry, a third accusatory, and so on.

The blank spells result from the amnesia barriers between the different personality states. When one personality has control of the body, another may not remember. These disremembered activities of the alter personalities result in objects being inexplicably missing or present, friends reporting things the person can't remember, strangers seeming to know the person, and the person receiving phone calls asking for other people. In Mary's case, I knew that she must have a personality that used her middle name.

When taking an MPD history, it is important not to mention the term 'multiple personality disorder' while asking about these symptoms. One wants to gather as much information as possible before raising the topic of other people inside, in order to avoid biasing the person's answers (Mary did not spontaneously state that she felt there was someone else inside who took control of her body). The examiner waits until late in the interview to ask specific questions about MPD directly.

In Mary's case, I decided not to ask about other people inside at all, but instead to suggest that she try a relaxation exercise to see if we could recover some of her missing memories. I was sure that, if successful, this would result in contact with another personality state. Although nervous, Mary agreed, and I carried out a simple relaxation exercise, asking her to close her eyes, relax, and feel her body becoming warm and comfortable. She was very cooperative.

After a couple of minutes of relaxation suggestions, I then asked to speak to a part of the mind that remembers what happens during the blank spells. I suggested that it would be just like when Mary has a blank spell out in the world: Mary would be like she had gone inside, like she had gone to sleep, and another part of the mind would be here – awake, eyes open, and able to talk with us. I asked her to open her eyes, and said that, when she did so, another part of the mind that holds the memories would be there. I did not say that this other part of the mind would be personified, feel like a separate person, or have a different name.

Mary did open her eyes. She immediately assumed a much more relaxed body posture, took off her jacket, and put her purse down beside her. She uncrossed her arms, which had been folded over her chest, and put her hands casually on her lap. The expression of her eyes and face were much more assertive and confident, compared with her previously frightened, timid manner, and she also took off her glasses.

This, I learned, was indeed a part of the mind that remembered more than Mary did. We were talking to another personality state that also used the name Mary. This Mary, though, was aware of everything the other Mary did, plus a good deal more. She was aware of the visit to the Emergency Department, the overdose, and the prior conversation with the resident and myself. The second Mary spoke scornfully of the first Mary and her inability to cope with life. She claimed to be much more competent and confident, and said she planned to take over altogether sometime in the near future.

The second Mary did not know all about everything, though, because she also had blank spells and heard voices. I therefore knew that there were other personalities yet to be discovered. As we were just about out of time, I made a deal with the second Mary that she would return for another appointment the next week, in order for us to get to know her a bit better. I got her to agree that she would come if she was in control of the body, or, alternatively, the first Mary would come. It is important to make agreements with all the personalities in MPD work, in many little ways.

It was then time to debrief the first Mary. The second Mary agreed to go back inside so we could do this, and we said good-bye to her. When the first Mary returned, she looked confused and disoriented for a moment. She looked around at her purse, jacket, and glasses in alarm, then quickly put her glasses and jacket back on, and again clutched her purse to herself. I explained that she had indeed had a blank spell and that we had been talking with another part of her mind that held some of the memories.

Mary was so fearful and overwhelmed that I did not explain about MPD, or even mention the term. I did not tell her that the other parts of her mind had separate identities, but instead gave a general explanation about how the mind can block out memories, and how we wanted to find out more about what was going in future sessions. She agreed to come again the next week, and had settled down a little by the end of the session, though she was still upset about having blanked out again.

A week later, the second Mary walked into the office with a confident, assertive stride, and sat down with a triumphant expression on her face. She declared that she had taken control immediately after the first Mary had left the office, and had stayed in control the entire week. Not only that, she had moved, changed banks, and gotten a job. She would not give us her new address or phone number. She mentioned that she had found a bag of drugs in her freezer and flushed them down the toilet, and said she had no idea where they had come from.

After some conversation with the second Mary, she agreed to let me try to contact a part of the mind that remembered what happened during *her* blank spells. I then repeated the procedure I had used with the first Mary: the second Mary closed her eyes for a moment, and suddenly the eyes opened and someone very angry was talking. This turned out to be Eleanor, the personality who used the middle name.

Eleanor was extremely angry because the second Mary had been looking through the freezer and had found her stash of drugs. Eleanor was a dealer who received phone calls at home. She was also angry about the drug deals that got fouled up when the first Mary answered the phone and said the caller had the wrong number. At these times, Eleanor would be listening from the background, but would be unable to take control of the body.

Eleanor knew all about the personality who was a madam and prostitute, but wouldn't tell us her name. The prostitute personality, she said, hated being the least bit overweight: to keep this personality under control, Eleanor made sure to keep the body about eighty pounds overweight. The prostitute personality was so horrified by the extra weight that she went into internal hibernation and never caused any trouble. The two Marys couldn't understand why they gained so much weight, and why they couldn't lose any of it.

Eleanor characterized the second Mary as rigid, strict, straight, controlling, and boring. Eleanor said she would like to get rid of this Mary so she could carry on with her drug life unfettered. When I spoke of the possibility of my acting as a mediator between her and the second Mary, Eleanor was scornful of the idea, because she thought Mary was inflexible. She did acknowledge, though, that if negotiations proceeded to her benefit she would be interested.

I learned something about both the MPD and the function of obesity from Eleanor. In many abuse victims, I have found that excess weight plays a specific role in the person's life. Often it acts as a combination of insulation and a repellant to prevent males from making sexual approaches. This is necessary because of the fears created by the childhood sexual abuse. At other times, the fat serves to reconfirm the person's perception of themselves as ugly and unattractive (abuse victims of normal weight also feel this way about themselves). This negative self-image is itself a long-term symptom of child abuse. The consumption of food also seems to be an attempt to fill up an inner emptiness and soothe the pain.

This general function of obesity in abuse victims is amplified and modified in MPD patients, in relation to the complexities of the personality system. Thus, for instance, a non-MPD prostitute might deliberately put on weight to try to get off the streets, though her pimp would beat her for that. A prostitute with MPD might use the same strategy but she would have one personality that did the eating, another that turned the tricks, and a 'straight' personality who was amnesic for both the eating and the prostitution. These different roles might be divided up among a number of different personality states.

Eleanor did not feel like talking very much, and spontaneously went back inside, whereupon the second Mary re-emerged and said she also did not feel like talking very much. The session ended shortly thereafter with an appointment made for the next week. Mary never came back, and I never saw her again. We were unable to get a forwarding address or new phone number, and so could do nothing but wait until she contacted us.

Had I done something wrong? Had I gone too fast? Should I not have talked with Eleanor, or should I have spent more time with the second Mary? I didn't know. I wasn't able to learn any particular lesson from this experience, in terms of how to engage a person with MPD in treatment. I was sorry I couldn't meet the second Mary again, even just to find out how she was managing with her plan to completely take over.

Two years later I got a phone call from a psychiatrist who contacts me once in a while to ask for advice about her MPD cases. She wanted to know how to integrate personalities, never having done it before, and said she was working with a woman I had met a few years earlier. I didn't recognize the patient's name, then the psychiatrist mentioned that I probably knew her by another name: the patient was Mary, who had had a legal name change.

Mary had done a great deal of intensive work in therapy, including the recovery of extensive memories of childhood sexual abuse, and was now ready for the integration of several of her personalities. She was functioning well and supporting herself. Mary turned out not to be the woman who never came back. She was able to enter treatment with another therapist and get better.

Mary taught me several lessons, the first of which was humility as a therapist: I cannot be the best therapist for everyone. Also it is clear that, at some points in their lives, people may not be ready to begin the work of therapy. For Mary, with her problems and at that time in her life, all I could do was plant the seed of future therapy with several alter personalities, and say goodbye to her in my imagination, since I never got to say goodbye to her in person, or to wish her well.

4

A Case of Polyfragmented MPD

MPD is the fragmentation of the psyche into dissociated personality states that mistakenly believe themselves to be separate people. In some individuals this process is taken to an extreme degree, called polyfragmentation, in which there may be hundreds of separate states. Some of these psychic structures may have no name or age, yet still be experienced as separate identities.

It is impossible to have hundreds of fully formed personality states in one person because there isn't enough lifespace in one lifetime. In a polyfragmented patient, there will usually be a relatively small number of more fully formed personality states that have been responsible for the bulk of the person's experience. Often the personality fragments will hold a single memory or feeling, and many may never take executive control of the body.

Polyfragmentation seems to involve two processes. One is the usual formation of an alter personality which becomes relative full-bodied. Alter personalities, even when relatively fully formed, are still restricted in comparison with the entire personality of which they are a component, but they are more substantial than the fragments formed by the second process. The second process seems more like a memory-filing device in which memories are broken down into small pieces and stored under filing labels consisting of names and ages.

It is important not to devalue personality fragments: no

matter how minute, each fragment is part of a puzzle that cannot be put together without all the pieces. Some therapists set up an internal apartheid in which certain personality states are ranked as full alter personalities, while others are demoted to the status of mere 'fragments.' This error can cause resistance to therapy, internal conflict, and acting out. Besides, today's fragment may become tomorrow's alter personality when the structure of the personality system shifts, or when what appeared to be a fragment reveals its full range of memory, experience, and feeling. The distinction between alter personalities and fragments is imprecise, not very important clinically, and really just shorthand to aid case discussions. The main point of the distinction is to counter the incredulity aroused by patients said to have huge numbers of 'personalities.'

I met Pam, a woman who would prove to have polyfragmented MPD, within the first week of starting work at Charter Hospital of Dallas. She was a twenty-six-year-old single woman who had been admitted to other hospitals thirteen times in the previous six years for borderline personality disorder. These admissions had varied in length, but several had lasted three months and included extensive periods of time in wrist and ankle restraints. Pam had had a serious cocaine problem in the past but had been clean in terms of substance abuse for the past three years.

I first met Pam when she was in the quiet room on the General Adult Unit. I heard a lot of noise and looked in to see what was going on. I saw Pam cowering in the corner, sitting with her knees drawn up, her arms protecting her head, and her head tucked between her knees. She was agitated and fearful, didn't know where she was, and was screaming, 'No! No! Don't hurt me!' As I approached a little closer she talked to me as if I were her father.

Suddenly this behaviour stopped; she looked around in a confused fashion, and asked who I was and how she had gotten into the quiet room. It was evident that Pam had MPD and that a frightened child alter had been in executive control. Careful inquiry revealed a classical history of partially remembered childhood trauma, ongoing blank spells, auditory hallucinations, and other signs and symptoms of MPD. Interestingly, she also gave a textbook history of rapid-cycling bipolar disorder.

Prior to each admission for borderline personality, Pam had experienced a distinct period of hypomania lasting four to seven days during which her energy was increased; mood elevated; sleep decreased; libido increased; thoughts, actions, and speech sped up; and judgment slightly impaired. This hypomania was always followed by a sudden transition into a profoundly depressed state which would have met criteria for a clinical depression except that the duration was often less than the required two weeks. Most admissions were preceded by intense suicidal ideation, and on a number of occasions she had called a crisis line and held a loaded shotgun, muzzle in her mouth, while dialing the phone.

Pam had experienced at least four of these episodes per year for the past ten years, and had had her first clinical depression prior to age ten: none of these episodes had ever been diagnosed or treated.

She was transferred to the Dissociative Disorders Unit, and we began to explore her personality system. Within a week, an alarming pattern of behaviour had developed, which persisted unabated for a month. Pam had four identified personality states: her host personality, who suffered from bipolar disorder and borderline personality disorder; a frightened child state who did nothing but fearfully abreact abuse episodes and could not be engaged in conversation; a helper personality who identified itself as 'the Friend'; and a growling, spitting, self-abusive, head-banging state.

Pam would switch into the child or the self-abusive state almost without warning. She would experience sudden onset of an intense headache, clutch her head, bend over, then fall to the floor. Sometimes she would be able to stagger to the quiet room before switching; sometimes it would happen in the hallway or in her room. Staff would come running to hold her down, but often she had pounded the wall or floor so hard that an X-ray was required and there was severe swelling or bruising. She was transferred to a medical hospital in a neck brace several times after running head first into the wall, but was always all right.

The self-abusive alter personality would yell 'Die!' over and over, and would spit, growl, and try to bite, but could never be engaged in conversation. This alter would stay in executive control for about one minute, rarely more than two minutes, then would suddenly go back inside. Switches in both directions were preceded by seizure-like, intense clonic muscle contractions of most of her muscle groups; then, a sudden release, a swoon would occur, and a slightly dazed host personality would return, or the spitting alter would come out in a rage. These episodes happened two to four times per day and were exhausting staff and co-patients.

Another aspect of the phenomenology of these switches was also seizure-like in nature: we discovered by observation that, if the angry state went back inside, it would be prone to spontaneous re-emergence at any time. However, if we aggressively called the angry alter out again right away, we could establish a refractory period. Sometimes two switches were required, sometimes three: we always knew that we had entered a refractory period because the headache would instantly dissipate. If we were not in a refractory period, Pam still felt an intense generalized pressure in her head.

The refractory period would last about twenty-four hours. Next we learned that if we deliberately induced several switches to the angry alter prior to the end of the refractory period, we could restart the clock at time zero, and were safe for another twenty-four hours. We therefore contracted with the host personality to have her lie down, be physically restrained by staff, and have the angry alter called out. We attempted to augment this strategy with hypnotic suggestions for the angry alter to go to sleep; this technique seemed to extend the refractory period by a few days, but the effect was always temporary.

The Friend could not give us any useful information;

although he had a helpful attitude, he could maintain executive control for only a brief period before spontaneously relinquishing it. We were therefore stuck in an impasse, and were seriously considering transferring Pam to a state hospital for chronic custodial care. There did not seem to be any productive way to establish a working relationship with any of the alters, and none of them appeared to have any knowledge of anyone else in the system except for the Friend, who knew about the other three.

Pam's EEG was normal, and a neurology consultation yielded an opinion that she had a dissociative disorder, and was not likely to respond to anticonvulsants. I nevertheless seriously considered a trial of carbamazepine, an anticonvulsant medication which can also be helpful in bipolar disorder, and in modulating rage attacks in non-epileptic patients.

Without much hope that anything would come of it, I decided to do a sodium-amytal interview. Sodium amytal is a barbiturate medication which is given by vein and has a general anaesthetic effect. It is the 'truth serum' of television dramas, but is not, in fact, a truth serum. Memories recovered under sodium amytal can be accurate, distorted, or fantasies, and it is not always easy to make a clinical judgment as to which is occurring. The purpose of this sodium-amytal interview was a 'fishing expedition' to see if anything would turn up.

Within five minutes of starting the sodium amytal, I asked Pam to close her eyes and gave her brief relaxation instructions. I then asked if there was another part of the mind that knew about things, that we hadn't talked to yet, and that could come and talk now. Much to my surprise, Pam opened her eyes, an expression of childish exuberance burst out on her face, she grinned broadly, and said, 'Hi!'.

Taken aback, I asked, 'Who are you?' Still exuberant, she shouted, 'I don't know!,' followed almost immediately by, 'Midge!'

I couldn't tell whether this alter was an artefact of the sodium amytal, whether it had been in existence before the interview, whether it had made up the name Midge on the spot, or whether I was on the right track with this line of investigation, and was getting into a pre-existing alter personality system to which access had been previously blocked.

Since all our other efforts had led to an impasse, I decided to proceed with the interview as though I were talking with a pre-existing alter personality. Whereas Pam was somewhat subdued and somber much of the time, without a wide range of feeling, Midge was a talkative and excited young adolescent. Her manner was boisterous and enthusiastic. She knew all about the four identified alter personalities; she also said she had been paying a little attention to what had been going on in the hospital, but not a great deal, and was also aware of other people inside.

I asked a number of preliminary questions about other personalities Midge knew, and enquired as to whether she had any suggestions about how to deal with the angry state. Unfortunately she didn't. However, within a few days, Midge had established herself as part of Pam's life in the hospital. She frequently took executive control, became oriented to the ward, and gave herself the project of decorating Pam's room with drawings, bits of writing, postcards, and posters. She didn't like Pam's clothing and strongly objected to her smoking.

We very rapidly gained entry into a polyfragmented personality system without any further sodium-amytal interviews. Pam proved to have 335 different personality states, each with a name and age, and she produced a large chart of all of them, which she kept on her wall in her room.

Because it was impossible to deal with all the personality states directly in therapy, we asked Pam to group them into teams. The members of each team shared a common theme or characteristic. For instance, one group consisted of characters who were paranormal or mythological in nature, including past-life intrusion alters and entities that could fly above the hospital by astral projection: these personalities produced bird's-eye-view drawings of the hospital.

Other groups consisted of rebellious teenagers, frightened

children, alter personalities holding certain types of memories, and alters responsible for adult functions. Central to the system were two beings Pam did not regard as alter personalities. Sarah and Rebeccah were spirit helpers of a transcendental nature who lived inside Pam, talked to her, guided her silently, and partially controlled her personality system. They could intervene to prevent a suicide attempt or in other emergencies, but usually preferred to stay remote in the background and work indirectly.

Pam did not consider Sarah and Rebeccah to be part of her, and insisted that they could never be integrated, but would always be there to help her. They were indeed very helpful in the therapy, providing guidance, reassurance, and information about the personality system. It took a few months for the entire personality-system map to be completed, and most of the information on which it was based was provided by these two spiritual beings.

We set up a system in which each team had an internally appointed team leader who would be the spokesperson for the team. Only the team leader would take executive control, and all work by that team would be funnelled into the therapy through the leader. This system was necessary to provide structure, to plan sessions, and to avoid a therapy that went on for decades. Imagine how long the psychotherapy of a family of 335 conflicted people might take! It was clear that we could not treat all these states as separate entities requiring attention.

Pam agreed to this plan wholeheartedly and carried it out very efficiently. Within a short time of obtaining a system map and engaging a number of key alter personalities in therapy, the sudden switches to the angry state stopped, and internal comforting of the scared child by older personalities settled down her behaviour.

Pam exhibited a number of different behaviours over the course of her hospitalization which required limit-setting interventions. For instance, she had a baby alter personality that would take control in the day room or the hallway, lie down on the floor, curl up in a foetal position, suck her thumb, and call for a bottle. Other personality states informed us that this baby had been neglected as a child, and had had to wait a long time for a milk bottle. They also advised us that the infant needed to drink from an actual milk bottle in the hospital in order to be soothed.

Rather than comply with this suggestion, we assigned other alter personalities to soothe the frightened, upset children inside, and to rock them and given them internal imaginary milk bottles, if necessary. To have engaged in an actual feeding with a milk bottle would have been profoundly regressive, and would have undermined both Pam's ability to function as an adult and her self-respect.

Some of the paranormal alters wanted to spend hours with the therapist, engaging in entertaining discussions of various metaphysical topics and descriptions of astral-projection voyages. We set rigid limits on this kind of conversation, although sometimes not rigid enough.

Over the next month Pam worked at an amazingly fast rate and was ready for discharge. She was no longer actively suicidal, and had an out-patient therapist who would see her, with intermittent joint sessions with me. Shortly after discharge, though, tragedy appeared on the horizon: Pam's mother was reported missing, and Pam was fearful that she had committed suicide. Police were advised, but for a week nothing turned up, until, finally, Pam was informed that her mother had been found hanging in a barn at a farm owned by friends of the family. Because of her mother's long history of intermittent depression, general emotional instability, and previous suicidal ideation, it was evident that it was a suicide. There was no question of foul play.

Over the next two months the therapist and Pam did a tremendous amount of grief work. We expected her to fall apart, to blame herself to a pathological degree, to become depressed, or to simply dissociate her grief and not deal with it. To our surprise, she worked very hard, really experienced her mourning, and worked through it at a pace which meant she was neither dwelling on the grief excessively nor avoiding it. She was ready to carry on with the gruelling work of MPD therapy.

Within a month of her mother's suicide, Pam began to discuss another issue that was troubling her: her father was already living with another woman, and intending to marry her. Pam resented her father for this behaviour, which she thought in very poor taste. She became incensed when her father's financée signed a birthday card for her, 'Mom.' We identified with Pam's feelings, and wondered how her father could be doing this.

At this point in her therapy, Pam began hearing new voices and experiencing blank spells. Sarah and Rebeccah, despite their supposed status of knowing all about everything, didn't know what was going on. This meant to me that they were not transcendent spiritual beings, but helper alter personalities with an extensive but incomplete knowledge of the personality system.

We decided to ask to speak to one of the voices, a somewhat belligerent and sarcastic male voice. Pam closed her eyes, and a new alter personality named Bob took executive control. Bob informed us that he had come into existence about two years earlier to help Pam deal with life. He was rather vague about what he was supposed to help with, or how. When we asked Bob about Pam's mother's suicide, he amazed us by explaining that her mother was not dead. Pam had been having a great deal of difficulty dealing with chronic marital discord between her parents. Wanting to help, Bob had reasoned that if he made Pam believe her mother had committed suicide, she would be spared these conflicts. He therefore put these delusions into Pam's mind, and made her believe that her mother was actually another person, her father's new girlfriend. During this period Pam had been over to visit her parents many times.

Bob agreed with us that, although his motivation was good, his strategy was backfiring: Pam was getting more upset about her father's fiancée's behaviour than she had previously been about her parents' fighting. Bob agreed that we should explain the whole thing to Pam; we asked him to go back inside, called

Pam out, and delicately explained everything to her. We asked Bob to confirm out loud inside her head that everything we were saying was true, which he did.

We expected Pam to fly into a rage, become very depressed, or have some other dramatic reaction. Instead she shrugged the whole thing off as a sort of internal prank, said she was glad her mother was alive, and thought there wasn't any need to talk further about it all.

Pam's therapist was exasperated, amazed, resentful, and perplexed, as was I, although I was doing only a small fraction of the therapy. The suicide, the grief, and the grief work had been *completely* convincing, congruent, and authentic. It never occurred to us for even an instant that the mother might not have committed suicide. The accounts of visits to the father and his new girlfriend were detailed, rational, and also congruent at all possible levels – from cognition to feelings, to body language. Clearly, for Pam the suicide was a reality.

Soon, tragedy struck again. Pam was diagnosed as having inoperable lung cancer. She named her doctor, and described the type of cancer she had, her chemotherapy, and her pain. She wore a scarf over her head, having experienced substantial hair loss, including loss of her eyebrows; however, once deceived, we were cautious this time. A check with the social worker in the Oncology Department revealed that Pam was not registered there. Now someone inside was making Pam believe she had cancer, and was shaving her eyebrows! We wanted to continue working with Pam, but an angry alter personality began making death threats against the therapist, and we decided to stop the therapy. She has been lost to further follow-up.

What did I learn from Pam? Besides the value of sodium-amytal interviews and how to manage polyfragmented MPD, I learned that very detailed, congruent memories can be completely fabricated. This made me wonder about the truth of other memories and realities we deal with in therapy.

The usual clinical criteria for deciding whether memories are real or false is their internal consistency, plausibility, stability over time, congruence at all levels, and response to psycho-therapy. Pam's grief met all of these criteria. I learned that absolutely convincing memories and apparently authentic therapy dealing with them can be a charade. The charade has a purpose, and is helping the person deal with a problem of some kind, but the traumatic events never happened.

I have also worked with one other MPD patient who had a cancer, including surgery for it, but who was never registered at the hospital at which she alleged she had received treatment. In this case there was no possibility that she was actually treated at another hospital, and her 'terminal cancer' went into spontaneous remission after a prayer healing. In that case, it was easy to discern what she gained from the fictitious cancer in her immediate personal life. I also consulted on the tele-phone to a therapist who was, in turn, consulting to a priest who counselled a non-MPD woman with terminal cancer for nine months before he realized she didn't have cancer. This woman had hair loss and appeared ill.

Pam and these two other women are not curiosities. Their minds work by the same mechanisms and principles as those of other people with MPD; therefore, all MPD memories are subject to doubt. This is particularly true of detailed and elab-orate Satanic ritual–abuse memories, which can involve sacri-ficing five or ten babies on Satanic altars, the babies having been deliberately bred through impregnation of the patient by her father.

I was once consulted by a sane, rational woman who knew that much of what she was remembering could not be true: among other things, she remembered having her head cut off with an axe. I learned from Pam that the mind is a myth-maker. The mythic narratives can be rational, ordered, logical, and recalled as occurring in the real world within the limits of Newtonian physics. These false memories are not 'dreams.' There is nothing psychotic about them. The only difference between such false memories and real memories is the fact that the events never happened.

False memories do not have to be sociologically implausible

or be in any way fantastic. It was perfectly possible that Pam's mother had killed herself. This is also true of Satanic ritual-abuse memories: they have the quality, once the memories are fully recovered and dealt with in therapy, of being rational narratives. It is not possible to tell clinically that the events never happened, and they seem as real as independently ver-ified trauma memories, such as incest witnessed by a sibling or mother, or confessed to by the father. The ritual–abuse memories seem fantastic and implausible only if one makes an assumption that such cults could not actually be operating in North America. If one makes an assumption that Satanic human-sacrifice cults could actually exist in North America, then the ritual-abuse memories seem real. To me this is a disturbing problem. Are some, most, all, or none of the cult memories real? How do you tell clinically? Does it matter clinically? These difficult as yet unanswered questions I deal with in a forthcoming book, entitled *Satanic Ritual Abuse.*

We were able to verify by Pam's internal account that the mother's suicide never happened, which was confirmed when the therapist spoke with the mother on the phone on the pre-text of a casual inquiry about how things were going. I realized that not just the remote past, but the immediately perceived reality of an MPD patient can be highly plastic. Pam could look at her mother, visit with her, talk with her, and think she was talking to another woman. Such distortions in MPD patients are similar to the body-image distortion experienced by people with anorexia nervosa, the only difference being that Pam was distorting her mother's body image rather than her own.

There must be a fundamental dissociative mechanism at the basis of some cases of anorexia nervosa, I think. I wonder if there is a dissociated inner state in these patients that could be contacted through a sodium-amytal interview?

Did we do anything wrong in our treatment of Pam? Was there something I would do differently in the next case? I don't think so. It would be counter-therapeutic to obsessively doubt every memory in every therapy. I would still try a sodium-amytal interview if the therapy was stuck to the degree that

Pam's was, and out of control behaviourally. Perhaps we disclosed Bob's revelation to Pam too quickly, or perhaps we pushed too fast elsewhere in the therapy: I don't know.

It is evident that we failed Pam somehow, and that she had to push us away in order to get out of therapy. The death threats did not seem idle, and she knew from previous limit-setting that they would result in discharge from therapy. Is Pam dangerous to the public? I don't know, though there is no specific reason to think so since she has no history of assaulting anyone but herself. Will she ever complete her therapy with someone else? Would she have been better off without our making the diagnosis of MPD? I can't answer any of these questions.

We did accomplish one thing: we negotiated successfully with an alter personality who had been deliberately causing Pam's rapid-cycling bipolar disorder, and the alter agreed to stop doing so. The bipolar disorder appeared to be another unreality in Pam's life. She had a textbook history of a biologically driven manic-depressive illness, except that it didn't really exist. She created a perfect clinical picture of a disorder she had apparently never read about, didn't have, and which had never been diagnosed. Only long-term follow-up in a sustained therapy would reveal whether the mood disorder was successfully treated when understood as a dissociative disorder. The prior hospitalizations were confirmed by medical records, including the borderline diagnoses, the severe suicidal ideation, and the extended period of time in restraints.

I assume that some terrible ongoing trauma was driving Pam and that she couldn't bear to become aware of it, but I don't know what it was. Perhaps in her case it's for the best that she not remember, at least for now.

5

A Psychic Helper

I have always been interested in paranormal phenomena and extrasensory perception. Although ESP is a universal aspect of human experience, it has been suppressed by the intelligentsia in the twentieth century, and is not a subject of mainstream psychiatric discussion or research. The paranormal is regarded as unscientific within contemporary academic psychiatry.

Since the paranormal is a pervasive aspect of most or all human cultures, the suppression of this range of human experience has resulted in psychiatry's losing touch with a large portion of psychological reality. This is so whether or not ESP experiences are real: if ESP is real, then psychiatry, and academia in general, have suppressed study of both the psychology and the physics of the paranormal; if ESP is not real, then only the psychology of ESP has been banished from the mainstream.

MPD patients like Jennifer taught me about the relationship between trauma, dissociation, and the paranormal. In the nineteenth-century hypnosis, dissociation, childhood trauma, and ESP were linked together, and studied and thought about intensively by Jung, Janet, Binet, Richet, William James, Frederick Myers, Freud, Breuer, and others, although Breuer and Freud barely touched on ESP, and James and Myers tended to leave out the trauma. The careers and writings of these leading figures overlapped, and were directly linked to spiritism; experiments in parapsychology; the founding of societies for study of the paranormal; and a large body of clinical, theoretical, and experimental literature.

All four of these facets of the human psyche were suddenly banished in the late nineteenth century in conjunction with Freud's repudiation of the seduction theory. Freud decided that the incest being reported to him by his female dissociative-disorder patients must be fantasies, which created a problem for him: if the trauma never happened, why did his patients have their symptoms and pseudo-memories? To solve this problem he abandoned hypnosis as a treatment technique, de-emphasized dissociation in favour of repression, continued to ignore the paranormal, split with Jung, and veered away from the psychological reaction to real severe trauma as the key to psychopathology. In order to suppress the understanding of one component of this interrelated set of phenomena, he had to suppress interest in all four of the major components, which in turn made it necessary to split with Jung, who continued to be intensely interested in dissociation and the paranormal.

Although this is a thumbnail, simplified sketch of the history, the true and important point is that there *is* a history. We are currently in the late phases of a historical period in which four pervasive aspects of psychopathology have been banished from mainstream study. Child abuse and dissociation are currently struggling to be accepted into mainstream psychiatry, against resistance, although much headway has been made in the last five years. Whereas hypnosis continues to be of fringe interest but is academically respectable, ESP is still viewed as frankly unscientific. The paranormal will be the last of the four to re-enter mainstream psychiatry, and this transition will be stimulated by MPD patients. It will be at least another five to ten years before ESP begins to be referred to regularly in the *American Journal of Psychiatry*, for instance, whereas dissociation is gradually becoming a regular topic in this flagship journal of American psychiatry.

Considerable research data I have published support a simple generic *analogy* for the relationship between the four components of the dissociative quartet. I am not proposing a genetic *model*; rather, I am using genetics for illustrative purposes. Actually, though, genes for dissociation and ESP, and their activation by trauma, are probably more likely to exist than are genes for specific mental disorders such as schizophrenia or depression.

According to my model and data, speaking analogically, the genes for dissociation and the paranormal are closely linked to each other on the same chromosone. Although either gene can be activated alone, resulting in either a pure dissociative or a pure psychic phenotype, and although either or both genes can be activated endogenously, any extragenetic factor that activates one tends to activate the other, since they are linked. Severe, chronic childhood trauma is one such factor.

What are the predictions of the model? First, neither dissociative nor paranormal experiences are inherently pathological, and both can occur in individuals with no trauma histories or psychopathology. However, highly psychic individuals tend to be highly dissociative: operationalized though imperfect definitions of psychic and dissociative experiences are provided by the Dissociative Experiences Scale (DES) and the Dissociative Disorders Interview Schedule (DDIS) referred to in the introduction. Highly psychic individuals and high scorers on the DES should have higher rates of childhood trauma than non-psychics and low DES-scorers. The most traumatized diagnostic group, MPD, should have more psychic experiences and higher DES scores than other less-traumatized diagnostic groups, according to the model. This is exactly how the data go.

Another way to look at it is that trauma opens a window to the paranormal. This window is usually closed during normal development in our culture owing to ideological hostility to the paranormal: the dissociative fragmentation of the psyche in response to childhood trauma interferes with the closing of the window. One would predict that some people with MPD whose psychic windows were kept open by trauma will cease having psychic experiences after integration, while others who are endogenously psychic will continue to report ESP phenomena post-integration.

Jennifer was one of the people who taught me about MPD and the paranormal. I met her in 1986 when she came for an appointment on referral from her family physician. She was described in the referral letter as being very troubled, and experiencing periods of missing time. As she walked in, I noticed that she was very skinny, with straight, thin, medium-brown hair; blue eyes; and a not very attractive face. Her somewhat bedraggled, victimized manner, combined with a street toughness, suggested the stereotype of an abused wife or someone who had had a rough childhood, yet there was a sadness and softness in her eyes.

Jennifer described a life in disarray. She was twenty-two, single, unemployed, and currently living with her divorced older sister, who had two young children. Jennifer had grown up in a chaotic alcoholic family with much yelling, fighting, slamming of doors, throwing of things, slugging and hitting, and a father who was a nasty drunk. She was sexually abused from an early age by her father, a stepfather, and several other boyfriends, uncles, and older boys. As adolescents, she and her sister were wildly promiscuous, with reputations that spanned a large area in rural Manitoba, including the small town they grew up in.

Substance abuse began early, but was limited to alcohol and marijuana. Jennifer had been living in the city since she was seventeen, having moved there partly to get away from the family, and partly to get away from her reputation as a readily available sex object. In the previous few years, the promiscuity had settled down, as had the drinking, but she had been unable to work steadily, partly because of recurrent blank spells lasting up to a week in which she would be absent from home and work.

The blank spells had continued to occur right up to the time I met her, and were causing a serious problem for Jennifer's sister, who was relying on her to babysit. Jennifer suspected that she might be using drugs or partying a lot during the period of missing time, and wanted the blank spells to stop. At first she denied ever hearing voices or being aware of someone else inside, but then, with reassurance and indirect questioning, it became clear that she thought admitting to either of these would make me conclude she was crazy.

She knew quite a bit about an entity inside her that she said was helping her in her life. His name was Jonathan and he was not a human being. Rather, he was a spirit being of some kind who lived in a parallel dimension, but knew how to enter into her mind and this world when he wanted to: there was no way anyone could keep Jonathan pinned down, she said. He was his own man and did what he wanted. There was no way I could make him talk to me if he didn't want to come out, she said.

It was evident that having Jonathan inside gave Jennifer some sense of power, freedom, and control in her life. When she described his psychic powers, a shine of narcissistic grandiosity illuminated her face, animating her features with a glow related to both the radiance of mania and that of charismatic Christianity. Individuals in a high manic state have an altered complection and radiate a readily observable glow of pathologically intense, euphoric energy; in contrast, in the depressed phase of their illness, their complection is conspicuously much more sallow, dull, ill-looking, and unilluminated. Similarly, charismatic Christian preachers exude a forced, artificial energy which is cerebral in nature, originates from nervous plexes in the head and upper chest, and is dissociated from the deep spontaneous levels of their being: the religious fervor and the sexuality of charismatics are disconnected from each other.

The energy Jennifer radiated when describing Jonathan's psychic powers was clearly an attempt to compensate for an underlying feeling of worthlessness, dirtiness, and ugliness, and these fundamental feelings in her psyche were undoubtedly attributable to her childhood trauma. It was easy to contact Jonathan directly, and only a simple request was required to elicit a switch of executive control. Not knowing this the first time I asked for Jon, as Jennifer usually called him, to come out, I decided to use a relaxation-style hypnotic induction to facilitate the switch. I described what I would do, then asked Jennifer to sit as comfortably as possible in the recliner, and close her eyes.

Before I could begin the relaxation instructions, Jennifer exclaimed, 'Boy, am I relaxed!'. Seeing that there was no need for a further hypnotic induction, I simply asked to talk to Jon.

Jon opened his eyes, sat up, and said hello. His manner was distinctly different from Jennifer's – he was much more confident, almost cocky; his posture and mannerisms were much more assertive; his voice was a bit gruffer and more masculine; and his speech conveyed a no-nonsense quality. He was serious in manner, whereas Jennifer tended to be more nonchalant and unengaged.

Jon confirmed that he was not actually a human being, but he wouldn't divulge what he actually was, intimating that this was a transcendental secret. He did indeed come from another dimension, and was involved in Jennifer's life as a protector and observer. He sometimes used his psychic powers to intervene directly in Jennifer's life without her knowing, and would do so to steer her out of danger, or bring her some small good fortune. He offered to demonstrate his psychic powers to me if I was interested: these included precognition, clairvoyance, telepathy, and telekinesis, and he could also make objects materialize and dematerialize.

In another culture, Jennifer might have had a defined social role as a medium, priestess, or shaman, but in our culture she had no social function, nor did Jon. Jon served only personal, psychological purposes within Jennifer's life.

In the second session with Jennifer and Jon, Jon began to disclose a little more about his interests and activities. One reason he was in Jennifer's body, it turned out, was that he was sexually interested in women. He needed a human body to inhabit in order to pursue his relationship with his girlfriend, which he did during the blank spells. Jon had a girlfriend whom Jennifer also knew, but Jennifer thought their relationship was purely Platonic. Jon thought that Jennifer would not be able to handle the knowledge that Jon was using her body to have lesbian sex, so he kept her amnesic for this part of his behaviour.

When I asked Jon if he would let Jennifer remember my

conversation with him, he agreed to that, but said he would selectively maintain her amnesia for our discussion of his sex life, which he did. When I called Jennifer back, she was aware of my conversation with Jon, including the new information that he was responsible for the blank spells. She was now aware that he went out and partied with her female friend, but she did not know about the sex. Jennifer said she was glad that Jon had let her remember this, and she was awed by his ability to control the amnesia barrier, which she saw as an aspect of Jon's impressive range of psychological and paranormal powers.

Jennifer said that Jon could demonstrate his psychic abilities to me if I was interested. Although I wasn't sure if it was therapeutically helpful, harmful, or irrelevant to pursue this, my curiosity got the better of me, and I agreed to a psychic experiment. Jon came back, and said that he would read my mind over the next week and would put a message on a piece of paper he would cause to materialize inside one of the books on my bookshelf. When he came back the next week, he would tell me which book I could find the message in, which would contain personal information only I could know.

The next week, when Jon returned, he said that he had conducted the experiment successfully and, with a confident swagger, he walked over to my bookshelf to pull out the book with the message in it. Although I usually kept my office door open, and he could easily have come in person to insert the piece of paper and the message on it, I was intrigued to see what would happen. Jon pulled down a book and leafed through it to find the piece of paper, which was not there. Alarmed, he said that he must have put it in another book by mistake, and he proceeded to concentrate psychically on the books to cue into the correct one.

The outcome of the experiment was that Jon could not find any message. He became almost panicky while looking through more books, his air of masculine bravado disappeared completely, and his shoulders drooped. He had the sheepish, defeated manner of a tough guy on a school playground who has just been stared down by an older girl. I felt sorry for him, and immediately realized that I had made a mistake in agreeing to the 'experiment,' since I had set Jon up for humiliation. He suddenly announced that he had to leave, and in an instant Jennifer was back in executive control.

Jennifer was not the least bit disturbed by the failure of the experiment, and her faith in Jon's psychic powers was unshaken. She said he was angry at me, and that he might not ever talk to me again. Since I had obviously made a treatment error, I didn't confront Jennifer about her perception of what had happened, and we moved on to other topics.

Jennifer said that she and Jon had been talking a lot during the previous week, and that he had agreed not to blank her out anymore. He had also agreed to schedule his time out in such a way that it did not interfere with the babysitting duties, and as a result things were running more smoothly on a day-to-day basis. Jennifer did experience a brief blank spell when visiting her female friend, but was not concerned about it because she knew that Jon was always looking out for her. I assumed that Jon had selectively blanked Jennifer out during a period of lesbian sexual activity, and did not make any specific comment to Jennifer.

I saw Jennifer only one more time, although she called me on the phone a few times. Over the next couple of months, she did not have any further extended blank spells, but she said that Jon was very hard to contact, and seemed to be in a bad mood a lot of the time. It appeared that, as a brief therapeutic intervention, my contact with her had been helpful to some degree, although I had erred in agreeing to the demonstration of Jon's psychic powers.

Setting aside whether or not ESP is ever real, or whether Jon had any real psychic abilities, it was obvious that he functioned as an alter personality. One of his tasks was to compensate for Jennifer's deeply negative view of herself, and to give her life some power, freedom, and transcendent meaning. Such a need and such a coping mechanism should not be 'confronted' or 'tested.' Jon could be understood as an autohypnotic illusion created to provide Jennifer a sense of higher meaning in her life: she must be special if a special being like Jon took such an interest in her.

Jon was also a guardian spirit, and in this role he was much needed, since Jennifer had grown up so unprotected and traumatized. As well, he was an intrapsychic device created to facilitate lesbian sexual contact, about which Jennifer would have been too conflicted. Jennifer's experience of heterosexual sexuality was almost entirely abusive, or consisted of trauma-driven acting out, but Jon's existence allowed her to experience safe, lesbian intimacy, nurturing, and sexual arousal, which was a good thing, although she was amnesic for it. Since Jon was male, he could view his behaviour as heterosexual, and believe that he was simply using a female body out of necessity.

Jon was involved in Jennifer's life primarily as a psychic guardian, and his use of her body for sex was incidental, according to his own view of the situation. This arrangement provided several layers of fail-safe protection. Jennifer could have psychologically safe sex with a woman without being lesbian, which was necessary since she viewed herself as exclusively heterosexual, and believed that homosexuality is 'sick.' One layer of protection was the amnesia; the second was that it was not she who was having the lesbian sex, but a discarnate entity: her body was simply Jon's for use, and Jennifer was not the agent of the behaviour. A third layer was that the sex wasn't really homosexual because Jon was male. To preserve this complex defensive structure, it was necessary for Jon to be transcendently powerful, in control, and not subject to censorship by Jennifer. This perception of him was an undoing of her perception of the all-powerful male abusers from childhood, who had now been transformed into a benign guardian spirit. The transformation was not complete, because Jon was still a male who used Jennifer's body for his sexual pleasure, without regard for her feelings and without her willing participation, although he did so from the inside rather than the outside, and in a way that was pleasurable for the organism rather than traumatic.

Jon was created partly out of identification with the aggressor, and he often behaved in a very controlling fashion. Until Jennifer could see all of this in therapy, she would not be able to heal, and would not be truly empowered.

If Jennifer had been able to engage in therapy, and if I had not made that key treatment error, how would I have handled Jon's claims of having psychic powers? I would have told him that there was no need for him to demonstrate his psychic abilities, and that we could leave any such demonstrations to the future after the work of therapy was completed. I would have validated him as a helper and protector, so that he did not feel the need to demonstrate his paranormal power to me to be accepted and valued in the therapy. I would have been more sensitive to the fact that Jon needed his identity of transcendent spirit because he was afraid that, without it, he would never be accepted and loved by Jennifer.

Jon's attempt to demonstrate his ESP to me was an attempt to be accepted. I should have understood this rather than being misled by my curiosity, and I should have known that the humiliation of a failed attempt would uncover the underlying humiliation he felt about his lesbian activities and the childhood sexual abuse. I'm sure Jon was ashamed that he was unable to stop the abuse in childhood, and I'm sure he was very worried that Jennifer would reject him if she found out about his sex life.

If Jon's paranormal abilities were real, they would not be lost when the psychological issues were worked through in therapy, at which time they would be integrated into Jennifer. Then, in the future, as a healthier and more healed organism, she could elect to participate in any kind of ESP research she wished, without having her decisions complicate her recovery.

The fact that paranormal abilities are entangled with numerous complex defence mechanisms and trauma issues does not imply that they are illusory – though they may be – anymore than Jon's sex life, which was equally entangled in Jennifer's trauma history and MPD, was illusory. The fact that ESP serves a defensive function is not decisive one way or the other in relation to the reality of ESP. Real ESP could be used to cope with trauma as easily as real wrist-slashing, alcohol abuse, or binge eating and vomiting.

The paranormal experiences of MPD patients need to be dealt with in therapy in the context of the whole person, and his or her life, needs, and defences, just like any aspect of the person's psychology. The ESP should be respected, whether it is real or illusory, and should never be scoffed at, joked about, or dismissed as unscientific. Failure to handle the ESP sensitively and therapeutically will hurt both the patient and the therapy.

Do I think that Jon really had paranormal powers? I doubt it. Do I think he was really a discarnate entity from another dimension? No. I would like to meet such entities if they exist, and would like to observe objective demonstrations of such powers if they are real, because both would make the universe more alive and mysterious. As a therapist, I must be careful not to let these magical wishes become a source of countertransference error, as they did in my brief work with Jennifer. The more common error in psychiatry, though, is to dismiss the paranormal out of hand as unscientific, a response which entrenches the defences and prevents therapeutic exploration of the psychological meaning of the ESP.

6

A Woman with Unusual Spells

When I was working as the medical director of the Anxiety Disorders Clinic in our Department of Psychiatry, I received an unusual referral letter from a family doctor, accompanied by a consultation report on the patient from a neurologist. The patient was described as a thirty-three-year-old separated woman who suffered from 'attacks': I was asked to assess whether these were panic attacks, episodes of acute anxiety.

What was unusual about the letter? The woman, Marie P, had been experiencing spells and attacks of various kinds since adolescence. She was diagnosed as suffering from epilepsy at age fifteen, and was treated with two different anti-epileptic medications up until age thirty-one, at which time she stopped them on her own. After she stopped the medication, her seizures surprisingly also stopped.

Despite her seizures disappearing, Marie was still having unusual spells that the family doctor thought might be panic attacks: the neurologist didn't think they were seizures. What were the spells like? In his letter, the neurologist said that Marie's boyfriend, Tom, had witnessed them, and that, according to Tom, the attacks occurred at least two or three times per week, and more frequently when Marie was under more stress.

Whenever Marie got upset, she would go to her room to lie down. A few minutes later, the boyfriend would hear a noise, and would go into the bedroom. There he would find Marie thrashing around, talking, and expressing fears about her previous boyfriend. Tom would hold her down for a few minutes while she thrashed and kicked, then Marie would come back to herself and behave normally, never able to remember anything about what she did during these spells.

Marie also had spells during the night. She would wake up agitated and frightened, and would try to run out of the bedroom. Tom said that she would speak only in French, didn't recognize anyone in the house, and acted very frightened and childlike. Marie didn't remember anything about these attacks either. In addition, she would sometimes blank out for brief periods during the day, and would come to in another room, sometimes with bruises on her arms and legs.

The referral letter described spells that didn't seem to be panic attacks or seizures. What was going on, then? When Marie came in for her appointment, I asked a series of questions and learned that she did, in fact, have panic disorder. She had classical panic attacks and was developing increasingly severe agoraphobia. Because of her fear of having a panic attack away from home, she had been going out of the house less and less often during the previous few months, but the panic attacks were distinct from the spells for which I had been consulted.

Besides amnesia for states in which she behaved very differently from normal, Marie had other dissociative experiences. She had periods in which she felt unreal, and others during which she went off into a trance or dream, and couldn't hear friends talking to her. Large parts of her childhood she couldn't remember; as well, she had a history of childhood abuse.

Marie's alcoholic father beat her daily from age four to age fifteen, a which time she left home. She was raped by an older brother at age ten, and remembered threatening to kill her father before she left home. Her father frequently threatened to have her put in an insane asylum while she was growing up, and told her that she was possessed by the Devil. Shortly after she left home, she married an older alcoholic who physically abused her until the marriage ended twelve years later.

With this information, I scheduled a second session for hypnosis. I explained to Marie that, with hypnosis, I might be able to get in contact with a part of her mind that remembers what happens during the attacks. I suspected that Marie had been repeatedly sexually abused as a child, and that she had a French-speaking child personality who was the victim of the abuse, but I didn't tell Marie this. Marie had not learned to speak English until her family moved to Canada when she was eleven. I suspected that the child personality was unaware of the passage of time since childhood, and was waking up spontaneously at night, not knowing where she was and not recognizing anyone. I arranged for a French-speaking nurse to sit in on the next session.

Marie came back at the appointed time. She was a pleasant-looking French woman of medium height, with short dark-brown hair, dark-brown eyes, and a worried manner. She smiled occasionally – a warm, but nervous smile – and was concerned that something strange or frightening might happen during the hypnosis. I explained again that hypnosis involves only talking, and that all I do during hypnosis is help her to concentrate and focus her attention while, at the same time, relaxing. I assured her that it was a safe procedure, and that the nurse and I would make sure she was all right.

With the reassurance, Marie lay down on a mattress on the floor, and the nurse put a light blanket over her. Taking several minutes to help her get relaxed and comfortable, and to repeatedly reassure her that she was safe, I gradually began to blend in suggestions that she would have a spell just like the ones at night. I suggested to her that she would go off to sleep, and that, in a little while, another part of her mind would wake up and be able to talk with us. I said that this would be the part of the mind that remembers what happens during the spells at night.

This illustrates the curious logic of hypnosis and MPD: I was asking in English to speak to a part of the mind that remembers what happens during the spells at night, but that part spoke only French.

Despite the logical problem, after more relaxation and safety suggestions, Marie opened her eyes. An immediate, dramatic change took place in her posture, body language, facial expressions, and conversation. Marie now spoke only French, withdrew to the corner of the room, and huddled there, frightened and wide-eyed. When we asked her what she was frightened about, she named her brother, uncle, and father, and said she was afraid her brother was outside the room, and was going to come in and hurt her.

With the nurse acting as translator, I explained that she was safe now, that she was in hospital, that I was a doctor, and that we wouldn't let her brother hurt her. I said that he wasn't outside the door, or even in the hospital. Marie seemed to believe this, and became less frightened and more relaxed. The first thing she wanted to know was how she had got to the hospital. I explained that her mother had brought her while she was sleeping, a necessary fabrication at the time. To begin explaining the complexities of MPD to this frightened child personality at this time would have created more fear and confusion.

I explained casually that I just wanted to ask a few questions about where she lived, and where she went to school. Marie explained that she was eight years old, told us where she went to school, and went on to describe repeated sexual abuse by her brother, father, and uncle. Eight-year-old Marie acted her age. She sat in a childish position, asked naïve questions, and had an open, childish manner. The nervousness, worry, and tension that characterized adult Marie's manner had all melted away. The *Gestalt* of her face had changed from that of a care-worn woman in her thirties to that of a young girl who, when she was not frightened, appeared spontaneous and relaxed.

I talked with little Marie for a while and then told her that it was time for her to go to sleep again, and that I would talk with her again soon. She asked for reassurance several times, wanting to know that no one was going to come into the room and hurt her. She then closed her eyes, and, with further hypnotic suggestions, adult Marie opened her eyes. Before adult Marie came back, I suggested that adult Marie would be able to remember as much of the session as felt safe, and that it would be good if she remembered at least a little.

This is what happened: when adult Marie was back, she was able to remember much of the time when little Marie was in control of the body, but it seemed like a dream to her. Taking this as a cue, I explained that it *was* like a dream, that part of her was dreaming about the past as if it were in the present. I also told her that she had been abused by family members when she was a child, and she said that she could remember saying that under hypnosis.

I explained to Marie that the 'spells' at night occurred when this part of her mind woke up. Since this dream part of the mind thought it was a long time ago, it naturally didn't recognize anyone, and spoke only French. Since the dream mind thought the abuse was going to happen again, during the spells Marie was frightened and upset. A part of the mind was waking up, but still dreaming at the same time.

Marie accepted this explanation readily. When she returned for the next session a month later (Marie cancelled a couple of times in the interim), she reported that the spells had stopped completely. However, she wasn't interested in any more hypnosis; instead, she wanted to talk about the flashbacks that had been troubling her.

Over the previous four weeks, Marie had been experiencing the sudden return of traumatic memories. One of these occurred when she saw a woman she hadn't seen for a long time. Marie remembered an attempted rape that had taken place in this woman's home more than a decade earlier, but when she confronted the woman about it, the woman denied it. This event made Marie extremely angry. In fact, she had been experiencing such violent feelings and impulses during the flashbacks that she didn't want any more hypnosis, because she was very afraid of losing control.

We scheduled another session for six weeks later, because Marie didn't want to come again before that. This proved to be the last time I saw Marie. She was still having flashbacks, but this time was willing to be hypnotized, and eight-year-old

Marie was easily contacted. She clearly remembered our previous conversation, and understood that she was in the hospital, that the abuse had happened a long time ago, and that there was nothing to be afraid of now.

I explained to eight-year-old Marie that most of the time she was sleeping inside, and that she had been doing so for a long time. I asked her to look at her hands and see that they were no longer a little girl's hands, but a grown-up's. I explained that, when she woke up at night and was frightened, it was really safe, because the brother, father, and uncle were far away, and there had been no abuse for a long time. Little Marie confirmed that she hadn't woken up since the last time we talked.

Adult Marie again remembered the conversation with her child alter personality, and again accepted the explanation about dreaming. But she didn't want any more therapy, and never came back again. Attempts at follow-up contact were unsuccessful. Did I do something wrong in this case? I don't know for sure. Would I handle a similar case differently now? I don't think so. Actually, in one sense the sessions were very effective in a short period of time, since the spells stopped and Marie had a rationale to explain what was going on.

The trouble was with the flashbacks. It seemed that a reservoir of rage had been tapped into, and that Marie's dissociated anger was beginning to emerge spontaneously. This is what often happens when you 'take the lid off': you can't get it completely back on again. Because she was so fearful of becoming violent, Marie couldn't risk finding out more about what was locked away inside her. She traded 'spells' for flashbacks.

I wonder how much violent crime, especially sadistic sexual crime, involves the sudden re-emergence of dissociated violent feelings and traumatic memories? A good deal, I suspect. Does this mean that Marie is a danger to society? I don't think so. She has never committed a violent crime, and I have not heard about her from other physicians or police in the four years since I saw her. But she has untreated MPD. I suspect that eight-year-old Marie could quite easily be integrated with adult

Marie, with permanent cure of the nocturnal 'spells,' but the difficult part of the therapy would be recovering and dealing with the rage.

So far in my experience it has been unusual to contact an alter personality, offer treatment, and have the patient decline. This has happened only a few times. I'm not certain what it was about Marie that scared her away from therapy; all abuse victims carry a great deal of anger, unless they have been able to deal with it effectively, which Marie hadn't. Not everyone who has been a victim of childhood abuse needs therapy, but Marie probably does. I hope that some day she will be able to find a therapist she can work with, and who can work with her.

7

A Woman in a Man's Body

There are two adult psychiatry wards at St Boniface Hospital. I worked on one, but was occasionally consulted on cases admitted to the other ward, which is one floor below. This is how I met Walter, a young man in his late teens who had been admitted in a suicidal crisis: I was asked to confirm the diagnosis of MPD and to make suggestions for treatment.

Walter had been involved with psychiatry continuously since his preschool years. From age four to age seven, he took an antidepressant for hyperactivity, and from age seven to age sixteen methylphenidate, an amphetamine sold under the trade name Ritalin. Although he appeared to be normal at birth, Walter's development was slow after he had a serious episode of meningitis at age eight months. The hyperactivity was thought to have resulted from the meningitis.

Psychological testing done at age ten years showed Walter to be of average intelligence, but he exhibited a great deal of inconsistency and variability in his performance on different tests. He was said to have bizarre thoughts, and to be in a state bordering on psychosis. These findings are not unusual for a dissociative child tested by someone with insufficient knowledge of dissociation. At the time the testing was done, in the 1970s, there was little awareness of dissociation and no systematic knowledge of how dissociative children or adults score on standardized psychological tests. Nevertheless, it was clear that Walter was neither mentally retarded nor intellectually gifted.

Throughout his childhood and adolescence, Walter was shy, socially awkward, not well accepted by other children, and without close friends. He was physically and emotionally abused by his alcoholic father, but there was no history of sexual abuse. He had one brother two years older than himself. He had been involved with the 'wrong kind of friends' for a while at age sixteen, and had gotten drawn into drugs, alcohol, and shoplifting at that time, but this behaviour had stopped.

Although he had received much counselling over the years, Walter had never had any psychiatric diagnosis other than hyperactivity. The hyperactivity had settled down by the time he stopped taking medication at age sixteen, although the fact that he used street drugs and alcohol for a year at this time suggests that he may have been trying to self-medicate for incompletely resolved hyperactivity.

The crisis that resulted in Walter's being admitted was complicated. He had just dropped out of a university course the previous week, but the reason for his having done so wasn't clear. The main problem was another personality named Cindy who was 'freaking him out.' Cindy had been in existence for a long time, but had been fully formed and active for only the previous four years, and especially for the previous two.

When I talked with Walter, he described himself as dumb, ineffectual, very low in self-esteem, not very good-looking, and lonely. Cindy, by contrast, was intelligent, physically attractive, warm, and competent. She tended to be somewhat arrogant, conceited, sarcastic, and controlling. Walter described her as a superwoman of high intelligence who could do many things he couldn't, and who instructed him in life.

Cindy was jealous of Walter. She didn't like his having intimate relationships with other people, especially girls or women, and she found such relationships 'intimidating.' Walter had had a girlfriend for the past year, with whom he had discussed a possible engagement, but Cindy had damaged the relationship by making his behaviour inconsistent, and by interfering with his sexual performance.

For the previous two years, Cindy had been engaging in long

erotic phone conversations with a number of different men who knew nothing about Walter. One of these, Peter, was a friend of Walter's. Peter had written letters to Cindy, which Walter had shown to ward staff. Cindy was represented to Peter as being Walter's sister, and was said to be sexually abused by her father and kept locked up a lot of the time. Peter had recently insisted on meeting Cindy, and as a result Walter had disclosed that he and Cindy were actually the same person. Cindy had been taking executive control without identifying herself in order to have phone sex with Peter.

Also, Walter had disclosed Cindy's existence to his parents, who were in a turmoil about it. He had done this partly because of his close, Platonic relationship with his brother's girlfriend, who had known about Cindy for several years, and who urged him to tell his parents about her.

Besides Walter and Cindy, there were several imaginary figures that the brother's girlfriend also knew about. Walter had a son and Cindy had a daughter, both of whom lived at secret addresses. Walter and Cindy confirmed that there were no other alter personalities, and both reluctantly agreed that the children were imaginary.

Because there was no memory barrier between Walter and Cindy, none of the other features of MPD, such as blank spells, people telling Walter about things he had done which he couldn't remember, finding objects present or missing which couldn't be accounted for, or hearing voices, was present. Walter and Cindy talked with each other, but both knew what was going on and didn't experience 'voices' in the usual sense.

Cindy was easy to contact. A simple request to talk with her was all that was required. When she came out, Cindy did not seem much different from Walter except for her voice. She spoke quietly because, according to both Walter and Cindy, she had been involved in a car accident several years previously and had had to have surgery on her larynx; this had never actually happened. Cindy agreed that, as she got used to talking with people directly, rather than mostly over the phone, her voice would normalize and become indistinguishable from Walter's.

Cindy said that she was taking over control more and more, and that she would like to dominate Walter completely. Her attitude had an almost sadistic quality. Cindy spoke scornfully of Walter and his inability to cope with life, and she felt no guilt about the way she tried to drive other women away or interfere with Walter's relationship with his girlfriend. At the same time, she claimed to have a warm, protective relationship with Walter, and to be the only one who was always there for him. She was quite possessive.

Walter similarly spoke in glowing terms of Cindy as loving and caring, but then complained about how controlling and possessive she was, and how she caused him trouble in his sex life.

Cindy said that she had been present inside Walter since the moment of conception, but that she was relatively undeveloped until about age seven. At that time, she took on a more definite form in order to serve a protective, soothing function. Cindy claimed responsibility for making the hyperactivity go away. She said that Walter was always teased and ostracized during school, and had few friends, but that she tried to help him feel better about himself.

Cindy described how she gradually fell in love with Walter's friend Peter, and started taking executive control of the body in order to have actual physical sex with him, in addition to the erotic phone calls. She felt that she was female and heterosexual, while Walter felt he was male and heterosexual. This is one of the functions of opposite-gender heterosexual alter personalities: if the person is bisexual or homosexual, but feels uncomfortable about it and can't admit it, creation of a heterosexual opposite-gender personality provides a solution to the conflict. By having Cindy engage in 'heterosexual' sex with Peter, Walter could get the closeness, attention, and affection, and also the homosexual contact, without being homosexual.

Another strategy is to create a same-gender homosexual personality, which is common in MPD. In this instance, though, the person might feel uncomfortable about having a homosexual alter personality, whereas having a heterosexual personality of the opposite gender might be rationalized as more 'natural.' All of these strategies depend on cultural stereotypes of what is acceptable sexual behaviour. Cindy was very angry about her surreptitious sexual life being revealed, but was prepared to continue a relationship with Peter as herself.

Walter is one of the few cases of dual personality I have seen. Such cases were apparently more common in the nineteenth century – at least, most of the cases reported then had only two or three personalities. In the last decade, the average case has more than ten named personalities and personality fragments. Walter is also the only case of MPD I have encountered with absolutely no amnesia. One would think that these features would make the therapy less difficult and prolonged. Unfortunately, Walter never got into a consistent therapy with someone who was prepared to work with both him and Cindy. We had no openings in our clinic, but I stated in my consultation that I would be prepared to offer ongoing consultation if a therapist was found. Three years after seeing Walter, I received a written request from an agency in the community to provide therapy for him, but again couldn't do so.

After I talked with Walter, I made a number of different recommendations for therapy. I said that the therapist should work with both Walter and Cindy to negotiate more mutually beneficial ways of handling life together. Both of them agreed that this would be a good plan, and both were willing to compromise and make concessions for the common good. I said that rather than confronting Walter with the allegation that Cindy was an illusory fiction, the therapist should 'go with' the idea of two separate personalities: confrontation would stimulate resistance and uncooperativeness. Like many protectors, Cindy was fearful that I wanted to get rid of her, and that I devalued her role and the help she provided.

I recommended that the therapist repeatedly suggest that Cindy's voice become normal fairly quickly, as this would allow the two of them to switch executive control without anyone on the outside noticing what was happening. I suggested meetings with the family, the brother's girlfriend, Peter, and Walter's girlfriend to gather more information, educate them about MPD, and solicit more support and understanding. It was also important for Walter to develop better independent living skills and to continue with his studies. Suitable structured programs and living situations were recommended. As is always the case, the therapy of the MPD would involve a great deal of work on general problems, skills, and coping strategies. Walter would need to learn how to function in such a way that he no longer needed to be two people, but he currently lacked the ability to do this. To focus solely on taking away the MPD would be destructive because it would leave him unprotected and unable to function. I also said that Cindy's role as a helper and protector should be validated repeatedly, and that she should be enlisted as a collaborator in the therapy. Integration should not be discussed much initially, I said, because that would provoke Cindy's fear that the plan was to get rid of her. Integration would occur in time, when the conflicts were resolved and Walter no longer needed her. I also recommended that the therapist remain neutral with respect to Walter's final sexual orientation, which could be heterosexual, homosexual, or bisexual. This would still be an issue in post-integration therapy, and might not be resolved for some time. The problem with the MPD was that, while providing short-term solutions, it postponed resolution of the conflicts. I said that hypnosis would not necessarily be required in the treatment because there was no amnesia.

Despite an unequivocal diagnosis, a simple personality system, a clear plan of therapy, and willingness of both alter personalities to participate in the therapy, no therapist was found. Why? I don't know for sure, but based on my experience there were probably a number of reasons. One is that it is hard to find psychotherapists for any disorder in Winnipeg. Private psychotherapists' fees are too high for most MPD patients to afford, and psychiatrists, whose fees are paid by the government health care system in Canada, are all booked up. Further, most people who do psychotherapy do not treat MPD.

This problem will continue in North America for at least the next decade. More and more cases of MPD will be diagnosed, and the number of cases will run farther and farther ahead of the number of available treatment slots. Besides being a victim of childhood abuse and MPD, Walter is also a victim of inadequate social resources.

I had no way of finding out, but I wondered about the role of Walter's meningitis in the development of his hyperactivity and MPD. I wondered how many hyperactive children dissociate because their brains are disordered, and as a means to cope with the problems experienced at school, with friends, and at home as a result of the hyperactivity. Having attention-deficit disorder, being hyperactive, and not fitting in are a significant childhood trauma in themselves. Walter had experienced the additional difficulties of growing up in a home with an abusive, alcoholic father. I wondered whether Walter was truly hyperactive, or whether this was an incorrect diagnosis, applied to unrecognized symptoms of child abuse. I hope he will eventually find a therapist.

8

Talking with a Dead Grandmother

I assessed Joan when I was in northern Manitoba doing consultations for the northern medical service. She was a white woman in her mid-thirties who was married to a man who worked in an alcohol rehabilitation centre. She herself worked as a bookkeeper for a small business. They had been in the North for many years, but were thinking of moving to Winnipeg when their two children reached high-school age in a few years. The marriage was solid, and the children had no behavioural or psychological problems.

Joan was referred by a friend who had attended a workshop of mine. She had a number of problems, including panic disorder with early onset of a mild degree of agoraphobia, excessive use of alcohol, difficulty sleeping, and a feeling that there was someone else inside. Over the previous year she had begun using liquor to try to stop the panic attacks, and in order to get to sleep; by the time I saw her, she was becoming discouraged enough about the alcohol abuse and anxiety to be considering suicide, though she was not clinically depressed.

Joan was a slight, well-groomed woman with a very nervous manner. She looked pale and distraught, with tense facial features and a fidgety manner. After she had explained about the panic attacks and alcohol, I asked her why she had told her friend about having other people inside. She said that this was just a feeling she had, and that the anxiety seemed to be coming from someone little inside. She was not hearing voices or experiencing any ongoing blank spells, but had had periods of missing time in her teenage years. Not really expecting to encounter full alter personalities, I suggested that, with some light hypnosis, it might be possible for me to make contact with any other separate parts of her mind inside, to which she agreed.

Joan appeared to go into a hypnotic state quite easily. She became relaxed and calm, the tension left her body, and she looked like she was in a trance state as she lay on a couch with her eyes closed. Following a simple request to talk to any separate parts inside, I was able to speak directly with a ten-year-old child inside who said that she was frightened and that grown-up Joan didn't know about her. After Joan came out of trance, I explained to her that I was able to speak directly with another part inside, and that this part seemed to be representing herself when she was ten years old. I suggested that she come to Winnipeg for further assessment and treatment on an in-patient basis.

Joan was treated to stable integration on our unit in five weeks, and to the best of my knowledge has remained integrated for six years without recurrence of panic disorder or problems with alcohol. How was this done?

Joan was a very hard-working psychotherapy patient who did not act out or become distracted by problems and issues on the unit. I have learned that in-patient treatment of MPD becomes more complicated and less productive the more the patient becomes embroiled, legitimately or not, in disputes with the nurses, complaints about the treatment team, rivalries with other patients, and other side issues. Patients who have stormy in-patient courses, with many volatile, angry interactions with staff, get less work done. They may have a poorer long-term prognosis, but I don't know that for a fact.

Self-mutilation on the in-patient unit is a slightly different issue, and is not necessarily a sign of manipulative acting out, or correlated with interpersonal difficulties. Joan was not involved in any of this kind of behaviour, and could have been treated entirely as an out-patient had she lived in Winnipeg. She worked in a focused, committed fashion.

Joan's personality system was simple and easy to map out, consisting of only four personalities: Joan, the host personality, who was responsible for virtually all of the adult lifetime; a lively, uninhibited teenager; a child Joan; and Joan's dead grandmother. I will describe only the work with Joan and the grandmother, which was the bulk of the therapy. The therapy was conducted by me, a co-therapist, and a hospital chaplain.

As her personality system was simple, so was Joan's childhood trauma relatively mild compared to those of most people with MPD. Her relatively light trauma history, absence of serious acting out, simple personality system, good social and interpersonal function, and stable and supportive family life made for a good prognosis.

During her childhood, Joan's parents died in a car accident, so she was brought up by her maternal grandmother, who was now inside her as an alter personality. The grandmother had been very strict and puritanical, was completely against teenagers wearing makeup and dating, stated repeatedly that boys and sex are dirty and dangerous, and restricted Joan to the house. She used to hit Joan frequently, and would make her stand still for long periods as a punishment.

The child alter personality held feelings of loss and abandonment, and was the victim of much of the abusive behaviour, while the adolescent personality embodied the healthy rebellion against the grandmother.

The grandmother alter literally believed herself to be the grandmother's spirit, and said she had stayed around after her death to keep Joan in line, and to prevent her from wearing makeup, being promiscuous, or getting into trouble. Joan also believed that this was literally her dead grandmother inside her, whereas she accepted a psychological model of the other two personalities once she became acquainted with them.

At one point we asked the grandmother about biographical information she should have known if she was actually the grandmother, and it was clear that she had only as much knowledge of her life as Joan had. We simply noted this, and did not comment on it in therapy.

What we did was more or less couples therapy with Joan and her dead grandmother. We worked with them as if they were literally two separate people who had unresolved issues between them. After establishing co-consciousness between the two, which was quite easy to achieve by a combination of request and suggestion, we had them engage in a therapeutic conversation. Joan would express her grievances against the grandmother; the grandmother would scold her for being a rebellious child, and would remind her that she was doing everything for Joan's own good; Joan would soften her resentment a bit, but then point out that she was in fact now grown up and happily married; and so it would go.

The outcome of the work was that Joan acquired a greater understanding of her grandmother's intention to protect her, thanked her for her efforts, and pointed out that her work was in fact successful since the adult Joan was not promiscuous, had a good husband, and did not wear too much makeup. The grandmother admitted that she had gone a bit too far sometimes, especially with the physical abuse, and was able to give Joan some of the credit for doing well in life.

Joan learned from her grandmother that her own mother had gotten pregnant out of wedlock, and understood that there was good reason for her grandmother to be so worried about boys. As the therapeutic rapprochement between patient and grandmother was being completed, the co-therapist and chaplain began to discuss with Joan how integration would be achieved. Although integration of the other two alters into Joan made sense to her, she did not believe that the grandmother could be integrated, since she was a discarnate spirit and needed to go to heaven.

The solution to the problem worked out in collaboration by the two therapists, Joan, and the grandmother was to have a prayer session to help the grandmother let go of her attachment to the earthly plane, and pass on to a life in heaven. This session was conducted by the therapist and chaplain together as a combined psychotherapy session and prayer ceremony.

With formal goodbyes, thanks, and good wishes, the grandmother agreed that her job of protecting Joan on earth was completed, and that it was time for her to take care of herself, and move on to an existence in heaven. The grandmother reported seeing friends waiting for her in a light up above as she was leaving the body, and then was gone, never to return.

How should we understand this case? Was this really the grandmother's spirit, or 'just' an alter personality? The fact that the grandmother couldn't remember simple details about her life not known to Joan, but which she should have recalled easily, would suggest that she was not actually the grandmother. But there is a problem: if the *lack* of such knowledge implies an alter personality, the *presence* of such knowledge should imply a discarnate spirit. One argument implies the other.

What if the grandmother had known many details of her life not known to Joan? This would not prove anything, because the information could have been communicated to Joan years ago, and lost through normal forgetting, or active dissociation. Lack of such information could be explained in terms of some difficulty having to do with an actual spirit's intrusion into the physical plane or with the transfer of information to our world. In the end, I think, it is a matter of faith. There is simply no objective criterion or test that can be applied.

The same logic applies to demon possession and alter personalities that claim to be demons, of which I have met many. Those I have met have all turned out to be frightened children, paternal introjects, or other psychological entities originating within the person. However, there really is no true technique of discernment. If a 'demon' writhes in response to holy oil, this does not prove it is a demon, since an alter personality identified as a demon should behave in this culturally prescribed fashion. If an entity departs in response to an exorcism, that also does not prove it was a demon, because an exorcism might simply be the culturally appropriate integration ritual for this particular alter personality and patient.

Was the prayer ceremony with Joan's dead grandmother an exorcism? No, because it was not coercive. The success of the ceremony has no evidentiary weight in deciding whether the grandmother was an alter personality or a spirit. I think the key question, from a psychotherapeutic point of view, is whether the therapeutic work gets done. For the purpose of therapy, the ontological status of the entities is a secondary consideration. If the work had not been completed, I doubt that the grandmother would have agreed to the ceremony, and she could not have been permanently forced out by prayer or exorcism. Since the work had been done, coercive exorcism was not required.

I personally believe that this was not actually the grandmother, yet conducting the therapy *as if* she was actually a discarnate spirit was the correct way to proceed. In another patient, it wouldn't have been.

It follows from this reasoning that exorcism might be a therapeutically and culturally correct intervention in some cases. The most common problem we see in the dissociative-disorders field, owing in part to selection bias and the fact that exorcism successes do not come to us, is failed exorcisms that have alienated the demons and made them hostile to therapy. My experience with demons is that they must do a great deal of therapeutic work before they are ready to be integrated, and I have not yet met a demon I believed actually to be one. Joan and her grandmother, though, taught me to be open and flexible about these spiritual matters.

The secularization of demon possession and spirit intrusion has been taken too far in the last two hundred years. Psychiatric psychotherapy and spiritual interventions have become dissociated from each other, with the result that exorcisms are done in ignorance of the person's psychology, and that psychotherapy has become exclusively secular, excluding a wide range of human experience and depriving itself of important sources of healing power.

Therapist, exorcist, and prayer healer should learn to work together within a conceptual framework which allows for a full range of theological beliefs, while protecting the therapy from wild extremes. Perhaps in some cases, coercive exorcism is the most practical option: if we can coercively admit people to hospitals on an involuntary basis when required, why can't we be coercive psychotherapeutically once in a while, using exorcism? The important thing is not to overutilize or abuse any given mental health intervention, whether it be commitment, involuntary intramuscular medication, psychotherapeutic confrontation, or exorcism.

I think we reached the right balance in treating Joan and her dead grandmother to stable integration. The credit for this treatment success does not go to me, since I did only a small bit of the therapy.

9

A Chemical-Dependency Problem

Kenna was twenty-three years old when she was admitted to my ward at St Boniface Hospital and assigned to me. She had been admitted to the psychiatry ward at another hospital in the city a number of times, and was followed by her family physician as an out-patient with a diagnosis of borderline personality disorder. She had come to our Emergency Department this time simply because she happened to be in the area when she experienced a wave of greater-than-usual depression and suicidal ideation.

Kenna's MPD was very easy to diagnose, even in 1986 when my diagnostic skills were not as sharpened as they are now. She had a classical history of childhood trauma, voices, blank spells, somatic symptoms, substance abuse, and other features of the disorder. She was amnesic for most of the twenty-four-hour period immediately prior to hospitalization, and wasn't really sure why she was so depressed and suicidal.

When I asked if I could try to talk with a part of her mind that remembers what happens during the blank spells, she agreed, and a switch occurred, marked by a closing of the eyes, a nodding of the head, then an opening of the eyes, and a change in manner. Whereas Kenna had been quiet and depressed, this new part of her was slightly hostile and angry, and not at all depressed. On questioning, the alter identified himself as a male, and said he was aware of Kenna, and of coming to the hospital. He didn't want to provide much information beyond that, and said he wanted to be discharged. I also met a second Kenna who was aware of the host Kenna, but who was separated from her by a one-way amnesia barrier.

After three days in hospital, Kenna was no longer acutely suicidal and asked to be discharged. She was not interested in follow-up at my hospital, and I did not see her again for two years. In the summer of 1988, she was referred to me by her family doctor for diagnostic evaluation for MPD and possible therapy. The referral letter described ongoing blank spells, suicidal ideation, and depression.

When Kenna came into my office, she looked much the same as when I had first met her, except that she was very sad and demoralized. She was tearful, felt overwhelmed by life, could see no hope for the future, and was obviously clinically depressed. Both before I met her and while I worked with her, Kenna had trials of a number of different antidepressants, which usually seemed to help some. Probably the most effective medication I prescribed her for depression was trazodone, which was also helpful for her chronic headache.

Besides her recurrent clinical depressions, Kenna also suffered from insomnia, panic attacks, migraine headaches, and asthma. She had been treated with intravenous medications for both migraine and asthma in emergency departments on many occasions. She was prone to bronchitis because of her respiratory problems. She had been in the intensive care following overdoses, but had never cut her wrists. She abused alcohol, but did not use street drugs, and there was a question as to whether she abused prescription opiates and benzodiazepines. There was suspicion that her migraine was not always genuine, and that she sometimes used it was a way of getting intramuscular opiates.

Kenna was living a socially isolated life in an apartment, had no boyfriend, and had conflicted relationships with her adult siblings and mother. She was working as a retail clerk. As I talked to her again in 1988, she described being tired, discouraged, and suicidal. She remembered part of the three-day admission in 1986, but appeared to have no direct knowledge of other parts inside, other than several voices she heard. She had frequent blank spells lasting hours usually, but sometimes a whole weekend.

During the three years I worked with her, I never did much memory work with Kenna, had only a sketchy knowledge of her abuse history, and did no abreactive work with her. She talked about some of her abuse in a factual fashion, but without intense feeling, and reported disturbing flashbacks she experienced outside therapy, but no alters ever relived trauma in my presence, or came out to reveal trauma secrets to me. In fact, the bulk of the therapy was supportive in nature, without any active MPD work being done.

Over the course of the three years, I would estimate that about one-quarter of the therapy time was devoted to active MPD work, which included the integration of five or six alters, direct contact with five or six more, and the listing of about an additional ten by name. Most of the work was devoted to current relationships, medication management, and support.

Within six months, Kenna's mood was dramatically improved without antidepressant medication. She was experiencing headaches less often, was sleeping well, was not having panic attacks, and had integrated a number of alter personalities. This was not achieved easily, and included unplanned sessions in the Emergency Department on several occasions. Suicidal alter personalities had to be dealt with by firm limit setting, active reframing of their intentions, vigorous efforts to establish co-consciousness between them and Kenna, and much internal communication and negotiation by the alters between sessions.

Once the suicidal crises were solved and this first group of alters integrated, however, Kenna's approach was to leave well enough alone. Now that she understood the concept of MPD, she felt she could tolerate the occasional blank spell without being worried about it, and she was always certain that she did not want to uncover further childhood trauma.

In 1989, Kenna met and began dating a twenty-five-year-old computer salesman, with whom she set up residence after a few months. At first the relationship went well, and she was not symptomatic in terms of depression, anxiety, substance abuse, or dissociation. I saw her only every few weeks for general discussion of how things were going. She still had recurrent problems with her asthma, especially when the pollens came out in the spring, but her headaches were minimal.

Then the relationship began to go sour as the honeymoon phase of the romance came to an end. Kenna's prior borderline diagnosis was not wrong, it was just not understood in context. When her stress level was minimal, her social support adequate, and her physical status stable, Kenna was not particularly 'borderline': she was not volatile, stormy, or unstable internally, behaviourally, or in her relationships. However, when her stress level increased, the clinical picture changed dramatically.

As the relationship deteriorated, there was a great deal of arguing, yelling, door slamming, storming out, threats and accusations of infidelity, and increased drinking, and eventually the boyfriend was thrown out. He continued to want the relationship, and would come around at all hours, alternately threatening and pleading. Kenna would alternately accept and reject him, pulling him back into a relationship with sex when she needed him for emotional reasons, for money, or to help out in some way. There was much unreasonableness and exploitation on both sides.

As the relationship went downhill, Kenna's depression, anxiety, alcohol use, and blank spells increased. As I discussed the situation with the angry male alter personality I had met in 1986, I became aware of how explosive and rageful he was during these periods of high stress, and I knew that Kenna's risk of suicide was considerable.

One night I got a call from a physician on call for psychiatry at another hospital, asking for help. Kenna and her boyfriend were in the Emergency Department. Kenna was in four-point restraints on a stretcher, with both wrists and ankles secured by leather straps. She was growling, shouting that Kenna was going to die, and had not been affected by an injection of haloperidol. This had been going on for over an hour.

Realizing that this was the male alter personality, I asked the physician to wheel her stretcher over to the phone and hold the phone against her ear, which he did.

I then said, 'Raymond, what's going on?'

Raymond proceeded to explain how angry he was at the boyfriend, and how he had come out and threatened to kill him, whereupon the boyfriend had driven Kenna to the Hospital. Raymond was now doubly enraged at being tied down on the stretcher by a doctor who didn't even know who he was, and who kept calling him 'Kenna.'

I made a deal with Raymond. I pointed out that, unless he settled down, the doctor was going to give him another injection and admit him to hospital, which would make him very angry, and would also be a nuisance for Kenna. I said that, if he agreed to go back inside, and stay inside until our next appointment, I would explain the situation to Kenna and tell the doctor to untie her, and she could go home. After negotiating unsuccessfully with me to be untied before he went back inside, Raymond agreed to this plan.

In a moment, I was speaking to Kenna, explaining that Raymond had been out and what had been going on. She asked the doctor to talk to me again. The physician on call said it was the most amazing thing he had ever seen, and that he had no idea how I did that. I explained what I had done, he untied Kenna, and she went home. The next day I had to give her two milligrams of benztropine intramuscularly to counteract the akathisia and neck dystonia she was still experiencing as side-effects of the haloperidol. Akathisia is a restless, agitated feeling in the legs, and an inability to sit still, and dystonia is a form of abnormal prolonged muscle contraction.

Over the rest of 1989 and the early part of 1990, Kenna behaved like a severe borderline. She was angry, suicidal, and manipulative; experienced intense migraine headaches; had frequent panic attacks and almost continuous generalized anxiety; was often clinically depressed; and could be very irritating and demanding. Throughout this period, though, I had occasional contact with pleasant and cooperative alter personalities.

One evening I spent an hour on the phone with Kenna, against my better judgment, before driving to the Public Safety Building to fill out forms to have the police pick her up and take her to our Emergency Department, where she was admitted. It was during this period that I learned something about MPD and substance abuse, and also about the staff on the inpatient ward.

I was prescribing anti-panic doses of benzodiazepines for Kenna, and was having difficulty coordinating prescriptions with the family physician, as Kenna would get a prescription from him, then an overlapping one from me. In order not to be tricked by her and to keep track of what was going on, I had to spend considerable time on the phone with the family physician, and corresponded with him as well. Because she was on welfare at this point, we were able to have only one drugstore fill her prescriptions, since welfare authorized payment to only one drugstore, and we were also able to track her prescriptions through the triplicate program, since she was receiving opiate-containing medications for her migraine.

With this careful monitoring, we were able to control Kenna's pattern of getting overlapping prescriptions. However, she had a variety of strategies for getting duplicate prescriptions from the same doctor – namely, me. On a number of occasions I had to prescribe an extra supply of benzodiazepines: once, the medications simply disappeared; another time, they disappeared during a blank spell; once, her sister flushed them down the toilet; another time, she came out of a blank spell with her purse missing; yet another time, her angry estranged boyfriend stole them – the list went on. Given that I had decided to prescribe high doses of benzodiazepines for panic disorder, which is accepted practice, I couldn't simply refuse to replace the missing medication, because of the risk of a withdrawal seizure and the certainty of emergence of extreme anxiety. As a result, I was led to question the prescribing of any medication at all. A similar dilemma applied to her acetaminophen with codeine: was she experiencing genuine headache, or was this simply a ploy to obtain drugs?

A decisive factor for me – something I had observed over a

period of years – was that Kenna had sustained periods, as long as six months, during which her external stressors were minimal, and her social supports were good; during these periods, she never took or requested any medication of any kind. Therefore, it did not appear that she had a primary substance-abuse problem. Both the family physician and I were highly suspicious of being manipulated, and I discussed our concern with Kenna repeatedly, but we both concluded that, on balance, she had genuine symptoms, and actually got symptomatic relief from the medications.

The problem became a crisis when she was admitted to hospital in the fall of 1989, having come through the Emergency Department, with suicidal ideation. During this admission, I received consultation opinions from both a neurologist specializing in migraine and a substance-abuse specialist with extensive knowledge of dissociative disorders. The neurologist thought she had genuine headache, and agreed that, during periods of high stress, prolonged treatment with opiates might be unavoidable. Whether or not the headache was clearly migrainous in nature was uncertain, but not relevant to management. Trials of a variety of non-opiate medications had not been effective for the headache, and she had received intravenous medications for acute headache at different emergency departments from many different physicians over the years.

I took the view that Kenna's primary problem was stress-evoked symptoms, for which she desperately sought symptomatic relief using her repertoire of borderline behaviours. Neither the borderline behaviour nor the drugs were the main issue, and both disappeared as clinical problems when her overall state improved. The chemical-dependency expert agreed with prolonged treatment with opiates during the hospitalization, despite the risk of the miperidine actually inducing headache in its own right.

When her headache was severe, Kenna was nauseated, and could not take opiates by mouth. I therefore prescribed 100 milligrams of miperidine intramuscularly, three times a day. This is a typical post-surgical dose I had seen many times in medical school, and it was reviewed by both the neurologist and the chemical-dependency specialist.

There was much overtly angry opposition and criticism from the ward staff, who were absolutely convinced that she was manipulating me for drugs, that she was a primary substance abuser, that I was being deceived, and that what I was doing either verged on or was over the border of malpractice. There were numerous angry discussions of Kenna's treatment at team meetings.

I reviewed with the staff a number of the relevant facts of the case, and of my overall practice. For instance, although she certainly could be seen as a substance-abusing borderline within the time frame of this admission, her longitudinal history did not support this view. I reminded ward staff of the two consultation opinions, to no avail.

I explained the rationale for an non–*pro re nata* (p.r.n.) fixed-interval medication regime. I explained that non–p.r.n. regimes are the best way to manage chronic pain, because they reduce the negotiating between patient and nurses for medication 'as needed,' and hence the acting out, manipulation, and anger. Fixed-dosage regimes also remove the re-emergence of symptoms when p.r.n. dose intervals are too long, and remove the necessity for displaying symptoms in order to be rewarded by nurses with another dose. Fixed regimes also interrupt the anxious expectation of return of symptoms, and thereby help to de-escalate the symptoms. This explanation was met with a rejoinder that migraine headache is not a form of chronic pain, and this logic applies only to long-term pain or cancer patients. My reply that the principles were the same, even if the duration of treatment was only weeks, did not appear to be the least bit persuasive.

Staff argued that Kenna would come to the nursing station, requesting her next dose of medication, but did not appear to be in any pain at the time. They said that, to them, this was evidence that she didn't really have a headache, and only wanted drugs. I then explained that this is exactly the observation one wants reported by nursing staff in an effective pain-management regime: the entire point is to have regular dosing that controls symptoms, without re-emergence of symptoms prior to the next dose. I pointed out that this observation could, therefore, not be used as an argument in favour of a diagnosis of primary substance abuse. The rejoinder was a repetition of the view that she didn't look like she had a headache.

Staff argued that Kenna would become addicted. I assured them that she would be tapered off opiates prior to discharge, but was not believed, though this is what actually happened. They then stated that she could not possibly have a real headache, because she continued to smoke and sit in the noisy, bright dayroom while complaining of headache. Anybody with real migraine, they said, would not smoke, and would lie down in a quiet, dark room.

My answer was that she smoked because she was addicted to nicotine, and that this was, in fact, her only true primary chemical dependency, and I said that it did not matter whether the headache was common or classical migraine, or a mixed migraine-tension headache, or a pure tension headache; what counted was the intensity of the symptomatic distress. Additionally, not all headache is exacerbated by light and noise, or relieved by quiet and dark, as Kenna's wasn't. I pointed out that, when she had a headache at home, she didn't dim the lights.

This discussion was not carried out in a calm, professional manner; rather, the tone was angry, indignant, hostile, and accusatory, with clear, overt angry expressions on staff faces. Kenna was aware throughout how angry staff were at her, and that they thought she was just manipulating me for drugs, not because I said anything to her to that effect, but because of her own observation of the ward staff.

I pointed out that, even if there was disagreement about the opiate prescription, as I was not prescribing this regime as part of my standard practice, it could not be attributed to my general overprescribing of opiates or my being easily manipulated by MPD substance abusers. I pointed out that in a large number of MPD admissions, including prior admissions for Kenna, I had never prescribed intramuscular opiates, or anything other than short courses of acetominophen with codeine, and I reiterated that I would not prescribe in this way on an out-patient basis. Again, my explanations were to no avail.

As I considered whether the staff might be right, I kept in mind the pervasive hostile countertransference of a large percentage of ward staff to my patients and my work, and I realized that this high level of countertransference distortion could well be determining the reaction to Kenna. I was also aware that, when she was in a decompensated state, Kenna could be very demanding and irritating.

Then, one weekend during this admission, Kenna had an asthma attack. I was not aware of it until I came to work on Monday morning. She was taken over to the Emergency Department, and the emergency physician diagnosed asthma, and started a course of intravenous steroids. Since she was still symptomatic on the Monday, and since she required an IV for a few more days for the steroids, I decided to switch her opiate from intramuscular miperidine to intravenous morphine. I also consulted Internal Medicine about ongoing management of the asthma attack, and the best way to taper her off the steroids. I did not anticipate the ensuing reaction from ward staff or the Internal Medicine physicians.

The Internal Medicine resident said that this was not a genuine asthma attack, and that Kenna was simply manipulating to get steroids because they were making her euphoric. She also said that the IV should be stopped, and that Kenna should get oral steroids with a rapid taper. When I pointed out that she had never been able to tolerate oral prednisone due to gastric irritation, even when she had no headache, and that her nausea would prevent her from taking either the steroid or the opiate, this was dismissed as more manipulation on Kenna's part.

What really disturbed me was the resident's manner. She spoke about Kenna with a smirk, talking about her as a bad, manipulative person who wasn't going to fool the resident. The resident's invitation was clearly for me to participate in her hostile, dismissive, mocking attitude towards the 'borderline' patient. This attitude on the part of Internal Medicine, of course, suited the psychiatric ward staff perfectly. It was now obvious to them that Kenna was also a steroid abuser.

I pointed out to ward staff that the Internal Medicine resident had only a minute amount of experience in the diagnosis and management of acute asthma compared with the emergency physician, and that I was following the recommendation of this more experienced physician to the letter – again to no avail. Kenna's asthma subsided, and I discontinued the steroids as planned; she was switched to oral opiates, and tapered off those, then discharged on no opiates.

After this admission, I received an update on benzodiazepine prescriptions filled for Kenna during the preceding two months, and learned that, during the course of the admission, she had paid cash for a lorazepam prescription from another family doctor she sometimes saw. When I brought this to Kenna's attention, she said she was amnesic for it, and denied ever having consciously double-doctored.

I therefore asked to speak to an inner self-helper personality of Kenna's who usually knew much, but not everything, about what was going on, and she revealed that another personality I knew had gotten the prescription. I then asked to speak to this alter, Stacey.

Stacey was usually slightly hostile with me in a playful fashion, and was prone to temper outbursts if she did not get her way. She readily admitted to getting the extra prescription, and also to taking the missing medication at various times in the past. I had not been able to get cooperation from Stacey during the admission, and had had to impose various restrictions on her occasional angry behaviour.

Stacey admitted that she also sometimes made Kenna's headache worse, including during the previous admission, and said that the reason she did so was because the drugs calmed her down, helped the pre-existing headache, and took away some of the internal psychological pain. When the pain wasn't so bad, she didn't have headaches as much, and she could get by without medication. She completely denied ever influencing the asthma, said that all alter personalities experienced the asthma, and denied getting any kind of psychological effect from the steroids. She was angry at the Internal Medicine resident and the ward staff for their attitude towards the asthma.

Stacey agreed that her angry behaviour was often provocative and irritating, and her attitude was fairly sociopathic, in that she didn't much care about the effect of her behaviour on others. However, like all the alters I met, Stacey cares genuinely for her nephews and nieces, and is always very concerned about any mistreatment they receive.

I concluded that the treatment of the substance-abuse problem, in Kenna's case, must be the treatment of the stress-related exacerbation of psychiatric symptoms, the MPD, and Kenna as a whole. I thought back to the efficiency with which an MPD intervention solved the problem with Raymond at the Emergency Department, and I concluded that a similar treatment paradigm would eventually lead to resolution of the difficulties that came to a head in the in-patient unit. This would be a very different approach from that advocated by the ward staff.

The diagnosis of borderline personality disorder functions primarily as a rationalization for hostile countertransference acting out by psychiatrists and other mental health workers. Because Kenna was a bad borderline, she must be manipulative, a sociopath, and a liar who would do anything to get drugs, and I must be getting exploited for miperidine, steroids, and benzodiazepines. This being the case, the best 'treatment' was to take Kenna off all her drugs and discharge her, the sooner the better.

The body language and attitudes that go along with this countertransference are knowing smirks, mockery, superiority, rejection, and sadism. The primary stance is that the borderline 'isn't going to pull anything off around here.' This attitude is communicated in myriad subtle and obvious ways, while being rationalized and disavowed, as it was in Kenna's case.

Kenna has not completed her MPD work and is still at risk for further embroilment in destructive in-patient admissions.

10

A Woman Who Decided
Not to Remember

Terry was the first advanced-degree professional with MPD I met. Since then, I have met five physicians with MPD, among a variety of other professionals with the disorder. Terry came on referral from her internist because of periods of missing time, and was aware of my work with MPD, and the possibility that that might be her diagnosis.

She was functioning well at her job, with a minimum of switching, and none of her colleagues had ever suspected she had serious mental health problems. The same was not true in her marriage, which was very unstable. A number of alters interacted with her husband in an inconsistent fashion, including one who was very sexual, one who was angry and rejecting, and one who was the calm professional. Her husband, by her description, was a self-absorbed, insensitive narcissist, and probably unfaithful.

Terry didn't feel personally secure enough to risk a separation, and was therefore locked into an unsatisfactory marriage. She derived most of her pleasure in life, self-esteem, and sense of identity from her work, which she discussed in an animated fashion. She was obviously gifted at her work and very creative. She wrote technically interesting poetry that was intelligent and moving. As well, Terry was poised, attractive, and well dressed, in not-too-conservative business attire. She had ash-coloured hair, aquiline features, and striking eyes.

Terry remembered absolutely nothing of her childhood before

age ten, except for two brief snapshots of events that did not
appear to have any particular significance. Otherwise her
amnesia for childhood was dense and complete. Most people
with MPD have extensive but incomplete amnesia for childhood, although complete blocking out of the first ten or more
years is not rare. I have also encountered this form of amnesia
in women who did not appear to have MPD, but who had many
post-traumatic, depressive, and psychosomatic symptoms.

Terry had a disconcerting personality system. There were
about five different Terrys, who were amnesic for each other
and were difficult to distinguish from one another. There were
subtle differences in facial *Gestalt*, tone of voice, and personality style between them, and careful questioning confirmed that
each was amnesic for conversations with the others within the
same session. Each Terry denied that there were any other
Terrys, and insisted that she was the only one who existed.
There was a distinct switch with eye roll, eye closing, and head
nod, during the transition from one Terry to another.

Each Terry had a different perspective on work, the marriage, and life in general. At times the amnesia seemed to slip
a little, and one Terry would acknowledge that 'she,' referring
to one of the other Terrys, handled certain aspects of life. It
was perplexing to observe clear switching and intrasession
amnesia, combined with such a high level of denial. I spent
time enquiring of each Terry about her amnesia, about why
she couldn't remember walking in and sitting down, about
coming out of blank spells not knowing how she got to her
present location, and pointing out inconsistencies and gaps in
her information. These efforts were responded to with statements about having a poor memory or dismissals of the
amnesia as inconsequential.

The first few sessions had a humorous, jousting flavour to
them as we sparred back and forth about how the Terrys understood what was going on, and how they disbelieved my suggestions about there being different parts inside. I steered the
conversation towards a discussion of how we might work
together, what the point of therapy might be, and what the

goals and conceptual framework of therapy might be, without establishing a common ground.

Terry thought that I was rigidly fixated on one way of doing things, that I was inflexible, and that I was unwilling to make a treatment contract on her terms. She wanted to start a therapy without defined goals or methods, just to see how it went, and didn't want me to impose a preconceived structure on our conversations. My view was that she wanted to visit me and have interesting, unstructured conversations without a clear treatment plan, and that although this might be mutually pleasant, it didn't justify payment of physician's fees by the government. I had the feeling that 'therapy' would be no more than a government-subsidized intellectual conversation.

One reason I felt this way was that Terry insisted her husband not know she was seeing me. She couldn't give a clear rationale for her insistence on this arrangement, other than the fact that her husband would get angry, belittle the therapy, yell at her, and try to get her to stop coming. Although that might have been an accurate assessment of his reaction, I felt uncomfortable about a therapy based on this kind of secret, both because the perpetuation of secrets is rarely healthy for abuse survivors, and because it gave our therapy relationship a clandestine quality.

It turned out to be a moot point, because Terry did not engage in long-term therapy. The key factor in this outcome was Terry's decision that she did not want to remember. I reviewed with her the almost complete certainty that the purpose of the amnesia was to hide childhood trauma, that this might include sexual abuse, and that there were likely parts of her hidden behind the amnesia barrier who remembered the trauma. She accepted the concept of 'parts' hidden behind the amnesia barrier as a plausible postulate, although she still denied the existence of parts that took turns being in executive control during her adult life. Terry did not want to remember for several reasons: she felt that she was under too much stress in her married life, and that she did not have a husband who could support her emotionally during the recovery of her trauma memories. Also, she was concerned that uncovering the memories would upset her somewhat precarious equilibrium, and result in her losing her job. If this happened, she would then be financially dependent on her husband, and even more locked into the marriage.

The most important reason, though, was that Terry did not want to remember being abused by either of her parents. Her relationship with them, although long distance, was relatively nurturing and stable, and she did not want to lose that. She felt that if one or both of her parents had abused her, and she remembered, she would hate them. It was the prospect of hating her parents, and losing her positive image of them, that made Terry decide not to remember.

We discussed her options over several sessions, and concluded that we would not do any memory work. She still wanted to come to see me just for conversation, but I declined, as I declined her suggestion that we meet occasionally for coffee. After eight or so sessions, I never saw Terry again.

I thought that Terry made the right decision. Although in theory it might have been best to launch into a full MPD treatment with a goal of memory recovery and integration, for Terry, at this stage in her life, and in her personal and social situation, that would have been a bad decision. She needed to keep both her denial and her amnesia intact. She appeared to be functioning at a high level in her job, and there did not appear to be a realistic prospect for significant change in her marriage.

Although she sometimes felt suicidal, she was never close to acting on these feelings, and she was not experiencing severe post-traumatic symptoms. No alters were acting out destructively. Therefore, she was right to leave well enough alone, for now and perhaps forever. Terry reminded me of another woman I treated as an in-patient for depression. This woman remembered nothing at all before age fourteen, responded fairly well to an antidepressant, and was discharged back to her family doctor for medication follow-up, and to her therapist for support and counselling. I advised the therapist to leave the amnesia alone for now, a plan with which the therapist was in wholehearted agreement.

This second woman was taxed beyond the limit of her coping skills by an ongoing hostile divorce, financial problems, acting-out teenagers, lack of social supports, and her own fatigue. She did not have the energy or stamina for active memory work.

Many factors in a patient's life represent reasons to leave dissociated memories alone. A patient might have had several heart attacks, or suffer from an untreatable cancer, end-stage obstructive lung disease, or advanced AIDS. Another might be too enmeshed in an ongoing abusive relationship; yet another might be using too many street drugs too often, with all the associated trauma and danger that goes with a street life.

Terry was the person who first taught me that it is some-times best not to remember. This principle applies intermit-tently for varying periods of time in all MPD therapies: it is an essential consideration in the pacing of any active uncovering therapy, whether the person has MPD, dissociative disorder not otherwise specified, or pure psychogenic amnesia.

11

Request for a Sex Change

I received a consultation request from a family doctor, asking me to assess the suitability of a twenty-five-year-old man for a sex-change operation. Since I had had little experience with transsexuals, I thought this would be an interesting case to assess, even if I couldn't give a definitive opinion.

We gave Ted the Dissociative Experiences Scale and the Dissociative Disorders Interview Schedule when he came for his assessment, and he had a classical MPD profile. He also had a long and complex psychiatric history, which began with his first suicide attempt prior to age ten.

Ted had been physically and sexually abused as a child, and still had much of his childhood blocked out. He had had a diagnosis of schizophrenia for years, and was being treated with injections of antipsychotic medications, which were helping perhaps a little. He had been in hospital numerous times, had been treated with ECT seven or eight times, and said that his former psychiatrist used to give him ECT 'whenever the voices got bad.'

His first suicide attempt occurred when he tried to drown himself in a reservoir, and his first psychiatric hospitalization was before age ten. As an adolescent, he was involved in numerous break-ins, thefts and fights, and was caught by police several times. He had not proceeded on to more serious crime, fortunately.

Among his many psychiatric problems, Ted had an atypical

eating disorder which waxed and waned over the years, and in fact he had probably had frank anorexia nervosa as an adolescent. His eating habits were irregular, and he experienced intermittent binging and vomiting. Additionally, he suffered from recurrent depressions, abused alcohol, and was uncertain about his gender identity.

When I first met him, Ted was very masculine in appearance. He wore a baseball cap, jeans, and an old shirt, spoke in a deep voice, and had masculine mannerisms. He said he felt male, that he was heterosexual, and that his sex life during his brief marriage had been satisfactory. However, there were times, he said, when he felt more female and wanted to have a sex-change operation.

Besides hearing voices in his head, Ted experienced recurrent periods of missing time and many other signs and symptoms of MPD. He said that, sometimes when he was talking on the phone, he would be talking in a feminine voice, and that his psychiatrist had once commented on this. He also liked to cross-dress during the periods of time when he felt more female.

Ted felt that there was a more female aspect of him that wanted to be in control, and he said that there was often an internal struggle between himself and this more female part. Surprisingly, he wasn't completely against the idea of a sex-change operation, although he himself did not feel female. He said he had been cross-dressing for years, and that this had caused problems with his wife.

I asked Ted if I could talk to the more female aspect of him, and he replied that although that would be okay with him, 'it doesn't just come out like that.' I told him that perhaps if I helped him to relax it would be easier for the more female part to come out. He agreed to this, and I did a brief relaxation induction of a light trance, then asked if there was a more female part of Ted that would be able to come out and talk.

Ted opened his eyes, looked dazed and disoriented, and sat quietly, without saying anything. I was able to engage the newly emerged female part in conversation quite easily, and she identified herself as Deborah, didn't know who I was, and didn't remember coming to the hospital. I had the distinct impression that Deborah was not a genuine alter personality, and that she was exaggerating her degree of disorientation, and I suspected from her hesitancy and manner that she had just made up the name Deborah on the spot. She seemed too exaggerated in her effort to act demure and feminine. I didn't comment on these impressions of mine to Deborah, however.

Deborah said she lived with Ted in an apartment, and gave the correct address. She said that she wanted to get rid of Ted, and wanted to have a sex-change operation to get rid of the genitals, so that she could be in complete control. She was obviously using trance logic, because, on the one hand, she talked about Ted as a physically separate roommate, and, on the other, she wanted to get rid of his genitals so she could be in control.

Deborah had no doubts that she was female, and she described the war between herself and Ted as a battle to the death for control of the body. It appeared that she might prefer suicide to losing. She said that, when Ted was in control, she just went away, and that she didn't like that. I thanked Deborah for talking to me, said I would talk to her again, and asked Ted to come back.

Ted returned, amnesic for the conversation with Deborah. Over the next few sessions I saw him, I explained to Ted that I had been able to talk with Deborah, that she viewed herself as female, and that she wanted to take over control. I told him that I would not recommend surgery until this problem of the warring selves inside was resolved, and I offered him a trial of psychotherapy to work on his problems.

I saw Ted only a few times, at scattered intervals, because he was unable to come to appointments regularly, could not focus on any particular tasks in therapy, and wasn't motivated to work effectively on his problems. His day-to-day lifestyle was chaotic, with an irregular sleep schedule; various encounters with a variety of seedy characters; intermittent stormy contact with his ex-wife; and erratic visits to a number of different doctors, social agencies, and clinics.

Over the next year, Ted's female alter personality changed her name to a new first and last name, which were variants on Ted's name, and I met her once outside the hospital, at which time she was in drag. She recognized me and came up to talk briefly, expressing dissatisfaction with Ted's genitals and a desire for a sex-change. It was transparently obvious at a glance that she was a biological male. Deborah said she had been in continuous control of the body for months.

Another time I happened to be listening to a radio talk show while driving in my car, and recognized Ted's deep, male voice asking a question of the guest, so I knew that switches of executive control were still going on, and over the next couple of years I received several letters from doctors and therapists asking for information about Ted, and inquiring as to whether I could take over his treatment. He did not appear to have made any treatment progress at all.

My brief contact with Ted made me wonder how many undiagnosed men with MPD have had surgical sexual reassignment. Quite a few, I suspect. I am aware of one published case in which male alter personalities in the background were extremely unhappy about the surgery, and claimed to have been awake without any analgesia throughout the operation. This was a case in which the MPD was diagnosed after the reassignment was complete. I couldn't understand how someone with active MPD could pass through the psychiatric-assessment phase of reassignment; I could understand the MPD being missed, but not the presence of serious psychopathology.

It is probably the case that men with undiagnosed MPD who received sex-change surgery have female alter personalities who have gained continuous executive control, and successfully suppressed the male alters. This was Deborah's goal. This does not mean that the gender identity of the entire organism is exclusively female, however.

Since I have very little clinical experience with transsexuals, I can't offer any meaningful opinion, but I would like to do a research project screening transsexuals for dissociative disorders. I wouldn't be surprised if as many as 10 per cent of transsexuals screened for surgical reassignment have undiagnosed MPD. I wonder whether dissociated male ego states could be uncovered in a higher percentage of transsexuals with aggressive history-taking, hypnosis, and sodium-amytal interviews. I suspect, though I can give no real opinion, that such screening should be a standard part of the clinical assessment of both transsexuals and transvestites.

Given the availability of substantial research about MPD in the psychiatric literature, I suspect that failure to diagnose MPD prior to surgical reassignment will be grounds for successful lawsuits over the next decade.

I saw another transsexual for diagnostic assessment who was farther along in the reassignment process than Ted, and who illustrated other aspects of the problem of undiagnosed dissociation in this population.

Grace was a tall, willowy, well-dressed, feminine, and attractive woman who had been reassigned chemically, and who had full breasts, but she could not proceed to surgery because she was HIV positive. She was stuck with her male genitalia, but had a solid female gender identity, exclusively male sexual partners, and no ambivalence about her sexuality. However, she was not mentally stable, and never had been. Again I wondered how she had gotten through the psychiatric screening, since she had a long history of overdoses, unstable mood, a chaotic lifestyle, and drug use.

Grace spoke openly and freely about her past and her childhood trauma. She was born with the name Robert in southern Texas, and was anally raped for the first time at the age of four. It was at the moment of that first anal rape that Grace appeared, and she had been in executive control ever since. She was very defensive about who had been in control of the body prior to the rape, and didn't want to talk about it.

Grace talked at length about her 'dark side,' which she had to struggle against and which sometimes overpowered her. When this happened, she would have rage attacks, get into a fight, attempt suicide, or act out in some other way, including assaulting her lovers. Grace made a point of emphasizing that everyone has a dark side, and made considerable effort to downplay the seriousness of her dark side.

She was also very evasive about hearing voices, stating that she was not crazy, and never had been. On careful circumstantial and indirect questioning, though, she would admit to having conversation with the dark side out loud inside her head, and said that when the dark side spoke, she did not feel that it was herself talking. I was unable to get a clear history of amnesia occurring independently of her extensive drug use, which included cocaine, but there was suggestive evidence that she might have experienced occasional blank spells independently of the influence of drugs and alcohol.

When I asked Grace about the possibility of my speaking with the dark side, she was completely against that, saying that it couldn't just come out; that it couldn't talk; and that, if it did, it might be out of control, which would get her in trouble. I was therefore not able to come to a conclusion about what kind of dissociative disorder Grace had.

There was an unusual feature to her case, which was the reverse of the usual pattern in MPD. Usually, an alter personality is created to experience the trauma and keep the memory of it a secret on the inside, while the host personality remains amnesic. In Grace's case, it seems that Grace was created at the time of the first anal rape to instantly become the host personality, and that she had full memory of all the trauma. The original host personality, Robert, seemed to have been locked inside ever since.

I wasn't sure if Grace was distorting the psychiatric history a bit in order to maintain control. I suspected that her ascendancy in the personality system might have taken some years to develop, and that in childhood there had been a period of dispute similar to that between Ted and Deborah.

If a sodium-amytal interview was a part of the screening process for reassignment, in Grace's case I would specifically have asked to speak to Robert at some point in the interview. I would predict that Robert holds the anger from the trauma, but is amnesic for the actual events, while Grace holds the information component of the memory.

If this is an accurate assessment of Grace's psychology, would surgical reassignment be cruel or helpful? I don't think it is a straightforward question to answer. Presumably, pre-surgical treatment with estrogens, besides developing breasts and other secondary sexual characteristics, helps to suppress the male alter personalities even more completely. I wonder if this is also the mechanism involved when heterosexual male sex offenders are treated with estrogens. I wonder as well if the female hormones differentially suppress the offender alters in offenders with undiagnosed MPD.

The assessment and treatment of transsexualism, transvestism, and male sexual crimes has much to learn from the dissociative-disorders field. I remember doing a history and physical on the only female-to-male surgically reassigned transsexual I have ever met. Her supposed phallus, constructed out of full thickness abdominal skin and fat, was grotesque, though she showed it to me proudly. Her symptoms included a variety of 'hysterical' symptoms, visual hallucinations, substance abuse, and borderline personality disorder. Another case of undiagnosed MPD? The possibility never crossed my mind back in medical school, but I did wonder how she ever got through the psychiatric screening.

There are undoubtedly many non-dissociative transsexuals who have normal psychological profiles, and who adjust well to surgical reassignment. The point here was to focus on the treatment failures, at all stages of the reassignment process, and to suggest that careful assessment of childhood trauma and dissociation might reduce the percentage of unsuccessful cases. Such assessment could also ensure that individuals with otherwise undiagnosed dissociative disorders receive proper treatment for their underlying childhood trauma.

12

The Evil One

I have met many demons, devils, evil characters, representatives of Satan, and Satan himself in the course of my MPD work. All of these entities turned out to be alter personalities, and none was actually a discarnate spirit. Many of the cases with demon alters were Satanic ritual–abuse cases, but as such entities also occur in non-ritual cases, one cannot conclude from the existence of a Satanic alter personality that there has been Satanic ritual abuse.

In a study of 236 cases of MPD from around North America, published in the June 1989 issue of the *Canadian Journal of Psychiatry*, I found that 28.6 per cent of cases included an alter personality identified as a demon; clearly, such personalities are an everyday part of MPD work. In fact, demon possession is not rare in the general population: 0.6 per cent of a sample of 502 people in the general population reported having been possessed by a demon, and a further 0.6 per cent were unsure about having been demon possessed. As well, 0.2 per cent reported being possessed by a dead person and 1.0 per cent being possessed by another living person. These findings appeared in the June 1992 issue of the *Journal of Nervous and Mental Disease*.

It is not possible to understand the nature of the human mind without thinking carefully about demon possession, which is one example of a universal human experience. I assume that all cultures have recognized some form of possession by spirits, dead ancestors, totems, animal souls, or other external entities. These experiences are one of the main foundation stones for the psychology of MPD, which is a secular variant of possession created as a response to chronic childhood trauma.

How can one determine if an entity is an alter personality or a demon? This question would be dismissed as irrelevant by the vast majority of psychiatrists and psychologists, and regarded as unscientific. The Evil One taught me otherwise.

In fact, the question of the reality of demons has been disregarded by mainstream psychiatry on the same basis as childhood trauma, dissociation, hypnosis, and the paranormal were dismissed in the late nineteenth century. Serious enquiry as to whether one is in the presence of a demon is considered by mainstream psychiatry as unscientific on the basis of *ideological prejudice*, not science. The reductionist, atheistic bias of modern psychiatry which dismisses the reality of demons is just that, reductionism. It is not science.

One of the key strategies of the mechanistic-reductionist philosophy that dominates twentieth-century medicine is to define the reductionist model of medicine as *the medical model*. This is a clever, though unconscious, strategy because it implies that all other models of medicine are non-medical: reductionism has claimed a monopoly, in effect, over medicine, and has borrowed the prestige of science to cloak itself in an aura of power, sobriety, and rationality.

Actually, it is an open scientific question whether demons exist. Why, scientifically, should demons not exist? Why is it scientifically impossible for demons to exist, in a universe characterized by black holes, neutrinos, nuclear fission, and the Lorentz contraction? I see no reason at all why discarnate spirits should not actually exist, other than the reductionist insistence that all mind must be an epiphenomenon of brain. Scientifically, demons might or might not exist: the pseudo-scientific attitude of the twentieth-century intelligentsia has been to legislate that demons do not exist, to ridicule anyone with a different attitude, and to politically suppress other viewpoints. This has nothing to do with true science, and every-thing to do with suppression of free scientific enquiry. Galileo was put under house arrest by the Catholic church for saying that the earth went around the sun. In the late twentieth century, the orthodox scientific establishment ostracizes anyone who considers the existence of demons to be a serious scientific problem, though it lacks the totalitarian control to implement house arrest. In both cases, what is going on is orthodox dogma suppressing free intellectual enquiry.

The lesson of the Evil One is that the existence of demons is a real psychological problem which cannot be solved by insistence, dogma, or suppression of alternative viewpoints. In fact, many mental health professionals and theologian-counsellors practising in North America believe in the reality of demons, and regularly treat people for demon possession. This form of medicine has not died out in our culture; it has just been repressed politically and ideologically by the dominant intelligentsia.

I have talked with a number of Christian therapists who believe they are capable of *discernment*. Discernment is a technical term referring to the determination of whether a demon is present, and it involves classical tests such as invoking Jesus in the presence of the demon, use of holy oil and prayer, and challenging the entity as to its true nature. Actually, none of these tests can ever function as a true method of discernment: contemporary Christian therapists who try to do exorcisms vastly underestimate the technical difficulty of true discernment. Why?

I have learned from MPD patients and the literature on demon possession that such tests yield false-positive diagnoses of demon possession in dissociative-disorder cases. Since a demon alter personality will react to such tests in the culturally prescribed manner, just as a demon is supposed to, it will be mistaken for a demon by exorcists on that basis.

Similarly, exorcism is not a test for demon possession, because a demon alter personality may be integrated or suppressed by an exorcism, giving the illusion that it was an external entity and was successfully expelled. In other words, an exorcism could be a culturally appropriate psychotherapeutic intervention for some forms of dissociative disorder, or for demon alters in some cases of MPD.

Reciprocally, failure of an entity to depart after an exorcism does not prove it is psychological in nature; the entity might be a true demon, and the exorcism might simply have failed. Logically – that is, scientifically – it is impossible to use any currently known test for demon possession except to confirm a prior theological bias. Even if a demon is expelled and enters another person or animal, or even if paranormal phenomena such as levitation or poltergeist-like activity occur, an explanation can always be offered on the basis of telekinesis, suggestion, and other non-demonic mechanisms.

I met the Evil One for the first time well into Elly's psychotherapy, which was conducted entirely on an out-patient basis to stable integration. Elly's Evil One is one of a number of alter personalities by that name I have met in different patients. I have also met various other demons with such names as Satan, the Dark One, the Satanist, Damien, and Beelzebub. The majority of demons are child alter personalities under ten years of age, and the rest are usually under twenty years of age.

Elly was a married twenty-five-year-old physiotherapist, living with her husband and two dogs in a house in Winnipeg, when I first met her. She had a physiotherapist alter who was amnesic for her sexual abuse: this alter had quite a bit of trouble functioning at work, especially with male patients, while she was recovering memories. Elly was about five foot six, slim, and very muscular and athletic from distance running and weight training.

When I first met her in consultation to her therapist, who was based at a community clinic that served sexually abused women, Elly was extraordinarily tense, agitated, and alarmed. She sat hunched over in the chair, her straight blonde hair hanging over her face, wringing her hands, tapping both feet very rapidly on the floor, and visibly sweaty. At the same time, she looked and sounded tranced out and far away.

Elly didn't know what was wrong, except that she felt a terrible and intense anxiety welling up from inside. As I enquired further about what was going on, it became clear that she had a dissociative disorder. She felt that something inside her was trying to come out, and was very afraid of what it was. As well, she gave a classical MPD history of blank spells, child abuse, voices in the head, sudden changes of mood and behaviour, and the impression that her thoughts, feelings, and actions were often controlled by something outside her, or forced into her from outside. She would often experience being a detached observer of her body's behaviour, while not experiencing herself as the agent of that behaviour.

Within a few sessions, several alter personalities had come out to talk, including a frightened child who had been hiding in a closet inside. It became clear that the anxiety Elly was experiencing was a result of the closet door having come open: Little Elly, age five, was afraid that someone had come to get her to abuse her some more, and her anxiety had been flooding into Elly.

There was also a male teenage personality, Jed, who was a helper and protector, and who came out to do tomboyish things, such as riding bicycles, driving trucks, sports, playing with the dogs, and fixing things. And there was a personality called the Protector, who kept track of what was going on with the other alters, knew about all the incest, and tried to soothe Little Elly when she was too frightened.

Elly was amnesic for the other alters, Little Elly knew about the Protector only, and Jed and the Protector knew about everybody. As we worked with these alters, sharing the memories, taking care of Little Elly and bringing her out of the closet, and convincing Jed that he was in the same body as Elly, Jed and the Protector started to mention another presence they sometimes felt inside. They called it the Evil One. Bit by bit, as Jed and the Protector cautiously explained more to us about the Evil One, we learned that the Evil One had been inside for a long time, was very big and strong, threatened to kill the other alters, and wanted to take over forever. It was difficult for Jed to talk to us about the Evil One at all, because the entity listened all the time, and would get very angry about any disclosure of information by Jed. Several times Jed was beaten up inside by the Evil One, and told us that his face was bruised and swollen.

Fortunately, when the Protector was out, the Evil One was amnesic and unable to listen. This meant that we could keep Jed out of trouble while gathering more information about the Evil One. Elly herself knew only a tiny bit about the Evil One, so we didn't have to ask her much about him. All four alters were completely convinced that the Evil One was a demonic entity, and that they were possessed. They experienced the entity's presence inside as palpably evil, and said they could tell he was demonic on this basis. Whenever the Evil One was around, Jed and the Protector felt a cold chill going up and down their spine.

The Evil One was very angry at us, and told Jed many times that he would violently assault us if he ever came out in session. We couldn't engage the demon in indirect conversation using Jed as an intermediary because the Evil One refused to talk, and would beat Jed up whenever we tried to use Jed as an internal messenger. We therefore devised a strategy for bringing the Evil One into therapy which worked well, and which illustrates how to deal with discarnate entity alters.

Elly was a devout churchgoer, so we invited several people from her church to help us in a special extended session, which we planned out in advance with the Protector. We explained to the Protector that we did not think the Evil One was actually a demon, but rather a very angry, hurt alter personality who was carrying a lot of the pain and rage from the abuse. Our plan was to contact the Evil One directly, and to work with it on this basis.

With full agreement from the Protector, but without prior consent from the other alters, we used the technique of voluntary physical restraints. Elly came to the special session expecting a combined therapy-prayer ceremony; we called out the Protector, then took the Protector into another office in which a rollaway bed had been set up for physical restraint. The Protector lay down on the bed, and we strapped her down with wrist and ankle restraints and sheeting.

Before calling out the Evil One, the church members said a prayer, asking for spiritual help and guidance from God and Jesus, grace, and divine protection for Elly while the Evil One was being contacted. They specifically refrained from defining the Evil One as demonic. The church members repeated aloud that the entity held much of Elly's pain and anger, and said that the anger needed to be released to Jesus, who would take it for Elly and cleanse her. The vocabulary and language of the prayer were orthodox, genuinely felt, and not at all forced or artificially ecstatic.

I then shifted verbal control over to myself and began a hypnotic induction, combined with an explanation as to what we were doing, and how we wanted to make friends with the Evil One, and get to know him. I asked for the Evil One to be present, and Elly's body tensed, strained violently against the restraints, and contorted with anger. The Evil One opened his eyes, and began cursing us, and threatening us. He was definitely angry!

I was surprised at how quickly the Evil One admitted his true nature. It took about twenty minutes of discussion and direct insistence that destructive, violent behaviour was unacceptable, for the Evil One to become calm, and admit that he was actually a boy. I remember this frightened child alter personality, the former Evil One incarnate, saying, quietly, 'I don't want to hurt anyone.'

The Evil One agreed that it would be much better to integrate with Elly and not have to bear the pain, fear, and anger alone, and that it would be much easier being accepted rather than feared and rejected by the others. The Evil One agreed to let Elly come back so that we could explain the proposed integration, and the true nature of the Evil One to her, which we did.

Elly readily agreed to accept the Evil One into herself, so we proceeded with the integration ritual. With concurrent prayer and thanks by the church members, I conducted a hypnotic integration ritual in which the Evil One permanently joined together with Elly: this ritual was conducted out of restraints, with intense emotion on Elly's part and tears of relief afterwards. The integration of the Evil One has held for several years now, and all the other alters have been integrated as well.

A primary strategy in MPD psychotherapy is to make friends with the persecutors, whether they be adolescent males, angry adult women, demons, or Satan himself. It is essential to correct the cognitive errors of the host and child alters, who view the persecutors as Evil, terrifying, destructive, and alien. In fact, much of the persecutors' behaviour *is* destructive, and needs to stop, but their essential nature is not evil. Actually, this may also true of demons, since they are fallen angels. My assumption is that demons are fallen angels who can be rehabilitated, which is where I and many Christian fundamentalists part ways.

I personally don't believe that Evil existed in the universe prior to the evolution of the human cerebral cortex, although I am willing to consider the possibility that human evil can be paranormally *exteriorized*. Of course, evil can be dissociated, and experienced as discarnate on a secular, psychological basis. Whatever the theology, the spiritual and secular-therapeutic objectives should be the same: to heal and integrate the dissociated anger and pain.

Defining demonic alter personalities as actual demons reinforces the dissociation, and perpetuates the problem, even if the alters are temporarily suppressed by an exorcism. Exorcists should be much more careful in their differential diagnosis than is often the case, because the costs of a false-positive discernment of demon possession can be very high.

In our treatment of Elly, we integrated psychotherapy and prayer into a single ceremony which brought great power to the intervention. A secular psychotherapy alone would not have mobilized and harnessed all of Elly's internal resources: atheists might view this as maximizing the placebo effect, or as aligning strategically with the patient's belief system. There is no need for the psychotherapist participating in such a collaboration to be Christian or believe in Jesus.

Could a formal exorcism ritual ever be the best intervention? I think it could. We use forceful interventions at various levels in the mental health system already. These include involuntary hospitalization, involuntary intramuscular medication, and judicial orders for psychiatric assessment and treatment. Physicians who must participate in drug rehabilitation and have their urine checked to retain their licences are recipients of coercive secular treatment.

Why should coercive spiritual interventions not be permissible? An exorcism is the spiritual equivalent of holding a violent in-patient down, and giving him an injection of haloperidol. If coercive haloperidol is acceptable, why should coercive exorcism be banned from the mental health field? Only because of prejudice, and only because *all* spiritual interventions have been banished from twentieth-century psychiatry. 'Religious counselling' is tolerated in contemporary psychiatry, but basically regarded as a minor adjuvant intervention that does not touch the core of the mental illness. Prayer is not supposed to have any direct effect on the brain abnormalities presumed to be the basis of schizophrenia and manic-depressive illness, for instance. It is clear that psychiatrists far outrank chaplains inside hospitals. Like all coercive mental health interventions, exorcism should be used sparingly, and only after a careful differential diagnostic assessment that takes dissociative disorders into account. At present, many MPD patients are misdiagnosed and given ECT and antipsychotic medications within the mental health system. Within the theological system, many are treated with harmful exorcism.

The proper state of affairs would be for exorcism to be thought about carefully as a potential coercive intervention to be used in cases in which other voluntary interventions have failed. It should be used only with the consent of the host or another responsible personality, and only when exorcism is consistent with the patient's theology. I have seen coercive exorcism of self-destructive entities by a Christian mental health professional work very effectively and rapidly on a short-term basis as a crisis intervention, and I view such interventions as a less restrictive alternative than chemical restraint. I have also seen attempted exorcisms destroy a treatment alliance and waste two months of hospitalization. I haven't yet met an actual demon, although I have met and worked with the Evil One.

13

Checking with the Expert

I get asked to do consultations by a wide variety of mental health professionals working in numerous different agencies, for many different reasons. Some professionals need their client to be seen by me to get an official psychiatric diagnosis of MPD because the system they work in is not accepting the diagnosis, or is interfering with treatment. Others do not require confirmation of the diagnosis, but instead want help with the therapy, and sometimes the referring person suspects MPD but isn't sure.

Martha's therapist asked for a consultation because Martha, a woman in her early fifties, had asked for one. Martha was a widow who worked as a legal secretary, and she had been in therapy with several different people over the previous five or so years. She was aware of her personalities and diagnosis, but wanted to see the expert to have the diagnosis validated. I saw her four times over a period of a month in 1988.

Martha had four different personalities. The host personality, Martha, had been active for about two years, and had been in control most of the time for the previous year. She was an adult, competent, coping personality who went to work and took care of things in life. She was intelligent, imaginative, and had a good sense of humour. Originally created in childhood, Martha had been dormant for almost fifty years until reactivated to cope with current stresses in life.

Martha's legal name was Betty Ann. Betty Ann was the same

age as Martha, but she was depressed, suicidal, unable to cope, and didn't like Martha's having taken over. At the same time, she couldn't deal with life and felt like giving up. Betty Ann had been suicidal enough to come to the Emergency Department once, seeking help, about a year previously, but she had never been admitted to a psychiatry ward at any time in her life.

Betty Jean was five years old. She stuttered, was scared and tearful, always thought people were going to laugh at her, and didn't want to take control of the body at all. Betty Jean was aware that Betty Ann had grown up, and she felt she had no role to play now, so she just wanted to stay inside.

Chuck was about five or six years old. Like Betty Jean, he was aware of Betty Ann's ageing, felt he had no function now, and was content to stay inside and never be in control of the body. Chuck was happy-go-lucky and confident.

The memory barriers between the different personalities were a little bit complicated. Martha knew all about everyone. Betty Jean knew about Martha, but Betty Ann didn't know much at all about her. Betty Jean just knew that she experienced a lot of blank spells owing to Martha being in control. Betty Ann was not aware of the ongoing internal existence of Betty Jean, and did not have a clear understanding of her having existed as a separate personality in childhood; nor did she know about Chuck; and Betty Jean, Martha, and Chuck knew one another.

Martha was dealing with severe stress at the time I saw her. She had had a series of chemotherapy treatments for Hodgkin's disease, a form of cancer, which was in remission; suffered from arthritis; and was in danger of personal bankruptcy because of legal bills and lost work time. She was in the process of what turned out to be a successful malpractice suit against one of her doctors. Her husband had died in a car crash in the late 1960s, and she had brought up her children by herself, not all of whom were yet fully financially independent.

Betty Ann was born in trying circumstances. Doctors were planning to do a hysterectomy on her mother for uterine fibroids, a common benign tumour of the uterus, when they discovered a foetal heartbeat. Her mother was advised to have an abortion on the grounds that there wasn't enough room for the baby to grow. The doctors told her mother that she might die from the pregnancy, and that her child would likely be crippled or deformed, but she decided to continue with it. This information was all supplied by Betty Ann's mother.

After the birth, Betty Ann's mother was so weak that the hysterectomy could not be done for two years. During this period, her father was nearly bankrupted by the expenses of child care and a nurse for his wife. Betty Ann felt that her parents were always angry that she was conceived, and that she did not die in the womb, or after birth. Also, she felt that they had wanted a boy. As a child, she had been laughed at for trying to be a boy, and also laughed at when she tried to be a girl, because of her gangly appearance.

Betty Ann grew up on a farm. At age three she was sexually molested by a hired hand, who took her in the barn, stood behind her, and used her hair and head to masturbate himself, leaving his ejaculate in her hair. Betty Ann was blamed for this by her parents. She didn't really know what the man was doing and wasn't very traumatized by it. She just remembers feeling that she was disgusting and unworthy of living because of her parents' reaction. After the assault, Betty Ann's long curly hair was all cut off, and a fence was put up around the house. She interpreted both of these events as punishments directed at her.

Because there were a lot of migrant workers in the area each summer, Betty Ann's parents made her and her sister cut their hair short, wear only overalls, and pretend to be boys each summer, for years after the sexual assault. Betty Ann was called 'Chuck' in public all summer for years.

Betty Ann was also called 'Betty Ann' and 'Betty Jean' interchangeably as a child. She remembers her mother shouting at her as she went off for her first day at school, reminding her to call herself 'Betty Ann' at school. This is the only case I have encountered in which the names of the personalities were deliberately chosen by the parents, although the parents didn't know they were contributing to the formation of a multiple personality disorder. Betty Ann responded to specific role demands in childhood by creating distinct personality states, which endured into her fifties. The only time personality states are deliberately created and named by parents, according to the information we are getting from MPD patients in North America, is in cults.

In Satanic and other types of cults, apparently, personalities are deliberately created to carry out certain ritual tasks, to hold post-hypnotic instructions, and for other purposes I describe more fully in my forthcoming book *Satanic Ritual Abuse.*

Martha was not sexually abused by her parents, and was never involved in any cults. She did remember emotional abuse, though, in addition to being blamed for the sexual assault. At age five, she was put out on the porch by her mother for a prolonged period of time in the middle of the night as punishment for crying. The next day she was diagnosed as having measles and a middle-ear infection. Martha was created at this time to cope with the pain, fear, and trauma of being put out on the porch when ill. She was probably feverish, and might even have been in delirium at the time.

I have met a number of alter personalities who were created to deal with the stress of illness and hospitalization, and have always wondered how much the fever, social isolation, sensory deprivation, and direct effects of illness on the brain might contribute to the dissociation. It would be interesting to study the mental state of non-MPD children and adults in delirium, to see how dissociative they are, and whether there are transient changes in identity.

Delirium is often accompanied by full or partial amnesia for the delirious period upon recovery: this dissociative feature of delirium is probably caused by the physical disease process. DSM-IV contains an example of delirium not otherwise specified resulting from sensory deprivation, and classical delirium is described as including memory deficit, so it is clear that the relationship between organic and psychosocial causes, delirium, and dissociation is complex and requires further study. Dementia is subclassified in DSM-IV as occurring with delusions, depressed mood, hallucinations, perceptual disturbance, behaviourial disturbance, and communication disturbance, so there is no reason why an organic form of dissociation could not exist as well. One of the most fascinating things about MPD is that it makes you think about illness, and about life in general, in new ways.

The exact time of and reason for Betty Jean emerging as a separate personality was not clear. She did not seem to have played a specific role in childhood, and seemed to have alternated executive control with Betty Ann quite freely for a few years. As Betty Ann grew older, closer to ten years in age, Betty Jean stopped coming out, and has remained inside ever since. But she was quite easy to contact during the sessions I had with Martha, as was Chuck.

Martha was also aware of a personality split occurring at the time of her husband's car accident, which she witnessed from a second car that was following behind on the highway. It appeared that Martha was reactivated for a short period of time to help Betty Ann cope with this crisis.

Besides being very imaginative and interested in literature and the arts, Martha was psychic. She has experienced many different psychic phenomena during her life, which she thinks are real. At one point her daughter, who she adopted at age six, appeared to have a dissociative disorder with paranormal overtones. The daughter was hospitalized and had to be physically restrained. She started to curl up in a foetal position, baby-talk, and act in a very regressed manner for extended periods of time, and would thrash around and become very difficult to control. At one point she started praying to Satan during these episodes, for all of which she was completely amnesic.

Around the same time her daughter was most disturbed, a black cat inexplicably appeared on the third floor of their home when all the doors and windows were locked. Once Betty Ann found a lighted candle burning on her daughter's bed when her daughter, who later claimed she had nothing to do with it, was out of the house. All family members repeatedly heard human footsteps on the third floor when there was no one there, and the dogs used to bark down the basement stairs with their hair raised, again when no one was there.

There was poltergeist activity in the form of electrical motors suddenly burning out, the telephone not working repeatedly, and the phone ringing two or three times and there being only a dial tone when someone picked it up. Of course, none of these events was necessarily supernatural, and each could be explained by many different natural mechanisms, especially when there were two people with recurrent amnesia living in the house. However, when the daughter improved psychologically, all these other phenomena also stopped, except for the footsteps on the third floor, which were still heard occasionally.

Martha believed that these were all real supernatural events. I have discovered through clinical experience and research that people with dissociative disorders frequently experience numerous extrasensory and paranormal phenomena. These include mental telepathy, clairvoyance, telekinesis (means moving objects with the mind), contact with ghosts and poltergeists, and possession states.

Why should people who have been abused as children, and who have complex dissociative disorders, also be psychic? In one sense, it doesn't matter if the psychic experiences are real; real or not, this is an important unanswered question in psychology. There is something about the human mind we don't understand, an aspect of experience which has been banished from mainstream psychology and psychiatry. MPD patients force us to think about the paranormal, and to try to fit it into our theories about and understanding of the mind.

Psychic and extrasensory experiences are so characteristic of people with MPD that they statistically differentiate MPD from other diagnostic groups such as schizophrenia, panic disorder, eating disorders, and temporal-lobe epilepsy. I have met many people with experiences similar to Martha's, and all of them have considered their experiences to be real. They may all be wrong, but there is some reason why psychic experiences are linked to childhood trauma and dissociation.

The ability to dissociate and the ability to have extrasensory experiences are closely linked – I mean psychologically, not genetically, although they could also be linked genetically. I think that the ability to have frequent complex dissociative experiences can be latent in the absence of serious child abuse, and that it often gets activated when there is childhood trauma. Being psychic is not so closely related to having been abused as a child, but this range of human experience is also prone to activation by trauma.

The gift of second sight, as it used to be called, is often activated culturally or spontaneously in the absence of childhood trauma. However, when such an individual is also abused as a child, then he or she creates MPD as a survival strategy, and as an adult has both MPD and psychic experiences. This results in psychic experiences differentiating MPD from other diagnostic groups with much lower rates of childhood physical and sexual abuse. Non-psychic, non-dissociative abuse victims may develop other psychiatric disorders, but not MPD.

The relationship between paranormal experience, dissociation, and child abuse is something psychologists and psychiatrists should study. A whole dimension of human experiences is simply left out of modern academic psychology, although it is universally present in religion, folklore, mythology, and literature. Martha and others like her have taught me to think clinically about the paranormal in a way which is not skewed by the ideological biases of twentieth-century psychiatry.

This is what Martha did for me. What did I do for her? I did see her the four times, and listened to her accounts of her inner landscape and her guardian spirit with great interest. Although guardian spirits were largely destroyed during the industrialization of Western society, people with MPD, among others, keep this spiritual tradition alive. Some MPD patients think they can tell the difference between their personalities, which they accept as psychological in nature, and guardian spirits, which they never experience as part of the self, even when the MPD has been treated to stable integration. Are they correct, or simply not integrated? I don't know.

Returning to what I did for Martha, it was something very simple: I filled out a permanent disability form for her, based on her multiple personality disorder, which was accepted by her insurance company. With the successful lawsuit, her disability, and a government pension beginning at age sixty-five, Martha was set for life financially. Without the disability she would have been homeless and destitute, would have had to go on welfare, and would have had to live in the core of the city in a small apartment.

Instead, Martha lives in a modest rented farmhouse just outside town with several of her children, many pets, and a large vegetable garden. She is busy, but not stressed, and genuinely happy. She has elected not to try to reach integration, and has accepted the fact that she will have occasional blank spells when Betty Ann takes over, and insists she not remember. She has also explained her MPD to close friends, who can now understand what is going on, and can fill her in on what happened during any blank spells. She sees a therapist once a month, primarily for support and not for active therapy, and feels that, at her stage in life, and in her life situation, this is an excellent outcome.

Martha wrote me a long letter, saying that she was happy and had regained her zest for life. She no longer has to worry about how to function at work with recurrent amnesia, or how to 'explain' sudden lapses in her work performance. She does not have to worry about her MPD being discovered at work, and her then being fired, all the financial stress is gone, and her cancer continues in remission. Her arthritis is fairly severe, but she can still garden and go for walks.

For this woman who supported herself and her children for many years, it is an early retirement well earned. The insurance company is to be commended for its rapid decision to support the claim. Cynics might comment that Martha wanted to see the expert only to get her insurance form filled out. As far as I'm concerned, that would have been fine, even if it had been her sole motivation, which it wasn't. Martha's is the best outcome I have seen in a case of MPD not treated to integration.

14

Flash and the Destroyer

Margaret was referred to me by a private-practice psycho-therapist for diagnostic assessment for MPD and treatment recommendations. She was a thin, pale woman in her early twenties, with straight brown hair and a fearful, pinched, with-drawn manner. She was not aware of any child abuse in her past, but was plagued by many different symptoms of anxiety, depression, dissociation, and substance abuse. These did not seem to fit any specific pattern, partly because she was such a vague historian – there were many large amnesic gaps in her life, several of them lasting a couple of years.

The focus of attention in the first assessment was a child alter who would come out in session and be fearful and quiet. The therapist triggered the emergence of the child alter by accident one day when she touched Margaret on the arm as a comforting gesture. It turned out that touching Margaret always caused a dramatic startle reaction, followed by immedi-ate emergence of the child state.

The therapist was unsure if this was MPD, assumed there must be some kind of trauma history, and didn't known how to proceed. The child alter didn't talk much or do any thera-peutic work, although she was obviously very fearful. The therapist had been trying to engage the child alter in conversa-tion with limited success: she had drawn out some words, and the alter now knew her and wasn't as afraid of her as initially, but there was no real progress.

I talked with Margaret, and she agreed that I could touch her in order to bring the child out, which I did. The inner child didn't know who I was, where she was, or why she was in my office, but felt fairly safe because the referring therapist was sitting beside her. I discovered that her name was Maggie, and learned that she was five years old. She knew who Margaret was but wasn't aware of everything Margaret did.

I agreed to see Margaret for several more sessions with the therapist, to try to figure out how to proceed in therapy. Within two more meetings, we had agreed to transfer the treatment to me, since the therapist felt she did not have sufficient skill in MPD therapy. Margaret said she would be much more comfortable working with a man, a change from dealing with traumatized women who want a female therapist and hate men.

Within several months, Margaret provided me a map of a complex personality system which was highly structured and detailed. It consisted of two 'communities,' each arranged in a circle, with two small circles joining the two larger circles. Within each of the two communities, there were three sets of alters Margaret called 'families,' and within each family there were three sets of paired alters she called 'sisters.' The families were arranged in concentric circles within the communities.

The two smaller circles in-between the two larger circles were observer personalities overlooking each community, one called Guide and one called Observer. 'Observer' is one of the names frequently met in MPD personality systems, and 'Guide' is also fairly common. These two entities held a record of all the life experience of all the alters in their respective communities, and also communicated with each other. At the beginning of therapy, however, the two communities were completely amnesic for each other.

It took about six months to get Margaret's community fully identified, and it wasn't till the end of the first year that the second community was mapped out. The therapy was very complicated, with innumerable double binds and acting out, but with much interesting and hard work mixed in. At the end of three and a half years of out-patient therapy, when Margaret gradually stopped seeing me on her own initiative, she had made no overall progress, although for a brief period she had been fully integrated.

Margaret is the only person I have treated to apparent full integration who has gone on to a complete relapse of the MPD, and little or no improvement in her overall function. I still don't understand why this happened. Her case illustrates many principles and lessons of MPD psychotherapy.

Margaret was the first person I met who suffered from Rip Van Winkle Syndrome. This informal, unofficial syndrome, which may have been coined by Dr George Fraser in Ottawa, is what occurs when an alter wakes up who has been asleep inside for many years, unaware of the passage of time. I had this experience with one of Margaret's alters, who spontaneously took executive control in session one day. Tonie believed that she was in Vancouver in the summer of 1982, and was incredulous when I suggested that she was actually in Winnipeg in the early winter of 1988.

After considerable discussion and explanation, all of which had no effect, I asked Tonie to look out my office window, which she did. There she saw a winter landscape with snow, a frozen river, leafless trees, and visible exhaust from cars.

Tonie was astonished and exclaimed, 'That isn't Vancouver!' I was able to work with her from this point on, since her denial was no longer intact. She had irrefutable experiential evidence that what I had been saying was true, and that she had missed a large block of time as a result of having been asleep inside.

Tonie described a number of conversion symptoms she had experienced intermittently over the years – most prominently, a recurrent paralysis of her left arm which had sudden onset and was often accompanied by the appearance of a red area on her left forearm, with some loss of sensation as well. Tonie said that she consulted several doctors about this paralysis, and that one had suggested she might need surgery to release pressure on the nerve in her elbow (the ulnar nerve). She had been prescribed a number of medications for this symptom, including a diuretic.

Tonie was a party girl who fit the classical stereotype of histrionic personality disorder. She liked to party, dance, and be wildly seductive, but never actually formed a sexual liaison with anyone: this was taken care of by other alters. She had no idea why she suddenly came to in unknown locations, then was gone again, but was not concerned about her loss of time. One might say that she had *la belle indifférence* for her amnesia. However, she was bothered by the intermittent paralysis, and the uncomfortable sensation in her arm that often went along with it.

It was not until I made contact with a second Tonie, called Tonie-Adu, that I was able to understand the symptom. Tonie-Adu was a twelve-year-old mute, who looked at me with a haunted, frightened expression. Tonie had made her mute because she had been screaming continuously since Margaret was twelve, at first in the real world, then inside Margaret's head. Tonie was able to make Tonie-Adu mute in terms of use of the vocal chords, but was not able to shut off her screaming inside, which had been going on continuously for ten years.

When Margaret was twelve, Tonie-Adu was sleeping with a young man named Andrew, who was a member of a biker gang. One day, Tonie-Adu was with Andrew when a gang fight broke out; during the fight, she was attacked by two opposing bikers, dragged off behind a building, and raped. When they were finished raping her, Tonie-Adu returned to where she had last seen Andrew just in time to watch him being shot to death. As she kneeled over the body, blood still flowing from his mouth and chest, Tonie-Adu screamed, 'Andrew! Andrew!' over and over so many times that it slurred into 'Adu' – hence, her name.

When the two rapists grabbed Tonie-Adu to drag her off, they grabbed her on the left arm at the spot where the red area appeared over the years in conjunction with the paralysis. Subsequent work with Tonie-Adu resulted in resolution of her conversion symptom, cure of her muteness, healing of her trauma, and integration with Tonie, who was not stuck in endless abreaction of the past. I assume that Margaret is at ongoing risk for recurrence of these symptoms, because the formerly integrated alters are dissociated again.

Margaret had many layers of dense protection against her different trauma memories, organized in many different ways. Tonie-Adu was one example. Another was an anger-escalation sequence she had created inside involving Flash, the Destroyer, and Margie, a three-year-old victim of paternal incest.

If someone on the outside was starting to act aggressively towards Margaret, she was at risk for switching to Margie, so the Destroyer feared that Margie would get hurt. There would be a switch to Margie, followed immediately by a switch to the Destroyer, who was a very aggressive, angry male alter. The Destroyer would take care of the situation by intimidating and driving away the potential perpetrator. However, if the situation was particularly threatening, there would be a blinding flash of light inside the head, followed by a blank spell.

When Margaret came out of the blank spell, the outside person would be gone; or Margaret would be in a different location; or there would be evidence of violent behaviour by Margaret, such as furniture thrown around, and a bruised person lying on the floor.

By getting to know the Destroyer, I found out that when the flash of light occurred, an alter named Flash came out. Flash was even more angry and aggressive than the Destroyer. Over a period of a month or two I was able to establish contact with Flash, and piece together the childhood origins of both Flash's name and the internal flash of light.

Flash was created during childhood pornography that Margie was forced to participate in. He would sometimes come out when the body was three years old, throw a temper tantrum, and ruin the pornography filming for the day. The flash of light inside was a memory of the photographic floodlights. Margaret had been given intravenous drugs, oral drugs, and alcohol prior to the pornographic filming, which was the basis of a needle phobia contained in one of the other alters. This history also explained a post-traumatic reaction Margaret once had to the lamp in another therapist's office – the shape of the lamp reminded Margie of the pornography lamps, and she reacted as though the therapist were a pornography producer come to sexually exploit her.

It took another year after meeting Margie to finally get in contact with another alter who was involved in pornography at about age six. I first heard about Violet from the other alters in her family; they warned me to stay clear of Violet, not to go near her room, and never to open the door to it. Violet was locked in a room inside Margaret, and that was where everyone wanted her to stay.

The other alters told me that there was something extremely disturbing and frightening going on inside Violet's room, and also mentioned one other peculiar fact: Violet and her room always smelled of Pinesol. Margaret had always had a post-traumatic, hyperaroused reaction to Pinesol as well, without knowing why.

After much discussion and negotiation, it was finally agreed that I could open the door to Violet's room, and talk to her; to do this, it was necessary to first ensure that the other alters in the community had gone to sleep or gone away to a safe place, which they did. With adequate hypnotic preparation, I opened the door and asked Violet to come out. She quite easily told me what was going on in the room, and wanted to know if I was one of *them*, meaning one of the pornographers.

I explained to Violet that I was a doctor from the hospital, and that I had come to take her to the hospital so that she didn't have to stay in that room anymore. After discussion of this possibility over a few sessions, with Violet going back into the room between sessions, we finally formed a plan. I would come from the hospital while there was filming going on, enter the room on the pretense of coming to get Violet, and then we would leave together, and escape back to the hospital.

Inside the room, there were adults, and boys and girls of various ages, making hard-core pornographic films. Pinesol was used to clean the studio on a regular basis because the children would often vomit from fear, or from the drugs and alcohol they were given. Violet described in detail the sodomy, fellatio, cunnilingus, and other acts the children were forced to perform on adults and each other. She was very happy when the escape was successful, and she was able to sleep at the hospital.

Entering internal landscapes is a commonly used technique in MPD psychotherapy. At times, the therapist will stay in the present while an alter reports back on its mission to rescue other alters, destroy castle walls, disarm internal computers, rebuild architecture, create safe places, or carry out other missions. This is all part of the fantasy-proneness component of high hypnotic and dissociative capacity. It is not the foundation of either the disorder or the therapy, but is an interesting component of both.

Often when MPD patients are described as 'suggestible' by mental health professionals, the term is used to suggest they are weak-minded, gullible, hysterical, and easily influenced. Actually, the suggestibility of MPD patients is a powerful asset which they can use to great benefit in the therapy. Suggestion can go both ways: towards regression, dependency, and the sick role, or towards health, responsibility, and recovery. Violet illustrated the positive use of fantasy and suggestion in therapy.

Margaret's system contained several alters who appeared to be psychotic, while the other community included an alter who claimed to have a car, separate identification, a separate residence, separate friends, separate bank accounts – all without Margaret's knowledge. I was unable ever to verify that this was the case, but the alter's claims seemed to be believable.

There was always doubt about the reality of the stories Margaret told. For instance, one of her alters had a clear memory of aliens coming into her apartment, impregnating her, coming back some months later to remove the foetus, then returning years later to show her the half-human, half-alien child they were raising among the stars. This alter was mortified when I raised the possibility that the aliens were possibly not literally real: she cried profusely, and said I had ruined the therapy and her chances of recovery forever by doubting her.

Margaret made this claim before I had heard about the current epidemic of UFO abductions. I did not realize, when I heard Margaret's story, that thousands of people in North America have similar memories. Many of these people probably have complex dissociative disorders, but many appear to be otherwise normal. The only lesson I learned from Margaret in this regard is that expressing doubt damages the treatment alliance: whether failing to express doubt reinforces a delusional disorder, I don't know. One's view of this issue will hinge on whether or not one believes in the reality of UFOs, alien abductions, and related phenomena.

If the abductions are real, it would appear that the human race is being used as breeders, with amnesia for the human participation implanted hypnotically by the aliens. Other alters of Margaret's told me that they had been ritually abused in Satanic cults, and that these cults used women as breeders of babies for sacrifice. According to the current folklore in the dissociative-disorders field, these cults practise mind control and the creation of amnesia, much like the aliens do. Margaret taught me that there is a connection of some kind between UFO abductions and the use of women as breeders for Satanic cults. What is the connection? I don't know.

In thinking about what was real in Margaret's stories, and what fantasy, it was not easy to determine where to draw the line. I don't want to make the kind of mistake 'good Germans' did who looked the other way and pretended Auschwitz didn't exist, if there is a Satanic Third Reich active in North America today. On the other hand, I don't want to be the dupe of mass hysteria and urban legend. What to do? What to believe? I don't know.

Margaret was an extremely difficult person to work with. She was demanding, blaming, manipulative, angry, and always threatening suicide. She projected negative feelings onto me and everyone she came into contact with, and did so with great self-righteousness and at high intensity. Her perception of mundane daily events, or what happened in therapy sessions, was incredibly distorted. I sat in on several sessions with various agencies involve in her life in one way or another, and her later accounts of these sessions were astonishing. At times, it was almost as if she was describing an entirely different meeting, attended by different people.

Despite an immense amount of hard work, Margaret never really gained any understanding of how her behaviour alienated other people. At the end of three and a half years of therapy, she was still complaining bitterly about intensely abusive behaviour inflicted on her by other people, when the events were actually quite neutral, reasonable, had occurred several years previously, and had been witnessed directly by me. A minor infraction in therapy on my part would result in an alter not talking to me for six months.

In the context of this stormy, perplexing behaviour, the psychotic alters told me about the abuse they had experienced at the hands of their father. The 'psychosis' was actually a highly disturbed, perpetually abreactive state that wasn't psychotic at all. Margaret's father, by her account, besides being an incestuous paedophile and child pornographer, was a drug dealer.

For a period of time when the family was in British Columbia, Margaret's father used to take her along when he went to drug deals in the mountains. This was when she was about twelve. The father, his friend, and Margaret would drive back into remote country in a truck, meet with the drug contacts, talk with them, then murder the people with knives and shotguns. Margaret would help them bury the bodies, then both men would have intercourse with Margaret. Afterwards, they would sit down and have a beer and sandwiches, and then they would all go home. The psychotic alters were the ones created to be there during these times. All of this trauma was abreacted, and the alters integrated.

The psychotic alters had a separate group of friends who supplied them with hard drugs, which they used to dampen down their unending abreactions.

Another group of alters had a private language which they spoke inside, and wrote in her journals. I read several incomprehensible poems written in this language, which I'm sure a linguist could easily establish was confabulated and devoid of the linguistic properties of a real language. Others alters kindly provided me translations of these works, and I pointed out that, in order to participate in therapy, these alters would have to learn English. I made a technical error of integrating this group of alters before they had done any real therapy work.

Margaret also had an alter who was a transcendent non-human mystical being named Cosmos. Cosmos was disdainful of the therapy, since it occurred on the lowly cosmic plane of planet Earth, but was nevertheless very helpful. She was highly skilled at sending out internal vibrations, and energy which soothed, calmed, and healed the frightened children. Cosmos was particularly helpful in assisting Tonie-Adu to stop screaming, so that she could come out and talk, and in calming the needle-phobic alter.

Actually, Margaret did not stay in therapy for three and a half years, strictly speaking. Although Margaret was the host personality when I first met her, she abandoned executive control for most of the therapy, because of perceived insensitivity and bad therapy on my part. For three years I was blamed bitterly for destroying Margaret, thereby making real therapy and recovery impossible. None of the other alters would take any responsibility for finding or helping Margaret. She appeared for a while at the time of integration, in order to participate in the integration ritual and to do a tiny bit of preparatory therapy, but that was all.

Extensive discussion with the alters never shifted their view that I was solely responsible for Margaret's departure, and solely responsible for engineering her return. A few attempts I was persuaded to make in this direction using hypnosis were unproductive. I learned that this kind of long-term abdication of responsibility is a bad prognostic sign, as is extreme distortion in perception of everyday events, and massive overutilization of projection. Although in many ways Margaret worked hard in therapy, she was never able to overcome these pervasive characterological problems.

Another problem in the therapy was Margaret's artificial

concept of what integration involved. Because of a variety of external pressures which were actually self-imposed, Margaret felt that she had to be integrated quickly by a certain deadline. Over a period of two months in the second year of therapy, we integrated all her alters through voluntary, hypnotically assisted integration rituals. The integration lasted three weeks.

In this aspect of the therapy, I simply erred: I colluded with Margaret's unreal concept of integration and did not set adequate limits on her demands for rapid integration. Her failure to stay integrated was entirely my fault, according to Margaret, because of mistakes I made in my attitude towards her external stressors.

Margaret was the kind of patient who, in the nineteenth century, was called a *grand hysteric*. Her dissociative performances were virtuoso. For instance, she went into a catatonic coma once, and was monitored in ICU for three days. I was called over to the other hospital she was in, after she was transferred to the medical ward upon waking up, and reviewed the chart, which revealed that the ICU doctors had no idea what was going on.

One of the alters in Margaret's family filled me in on what had happened. This alter had the interesting ability to 'pull everyone in,' as she called it. Whenever the stress level got too high, she would simply pull everyone in, put them to sleep internally, and render the body catatonic to outside observation. She usually did this at home alone, and lay down in bed before doing so. The catatonia would last a few hours, or up to a day at a time.

On this occasion, the alter and the Destroyer were having a fight for executive control, while Margaret was walking home from the grocery store. The fight got to such a heated pitch, and the Destroyer was so close to winning, that the other alter felt she had no choice but to pull everyone in, resulting in the body's collapsing on the sidewalk, an ambulance being called, and an admission to ICU.

The last year and a half of therapy following the failed integration continued in the same vein, with Margaret blaming me for her problems in life, and her continued involvement in chaotic, self-destructive relationships, active substance abuse, alleged ongoing Satanic-cult involvement, and inability to function at school, at work, or in relationships.

Despite all these poor prognostic indicators, I continued to feel that Margaret was potentially treatable, and that I was missing something. She gradually phased herself out of therapy, and I heard from her intermittently until I moved to Texas. It was about a year after the end of the therapy that it occurred to me that I was probably only aware of half her system. For an intuitive reason I can't articulate, I suspect that Margaret had two more communities for which she was amnesic, each with its families and sisters. If this is so, I hope the sisters some day find a therapist they can work with.

Margaret taught me that I am unable to treat everybody with MPD. Whether some people are inherently untreatable or not, I don't know. Perhaps Margaret will some day find someone who can help her recover, perhaps not. Possibly she is involved in too much ongoing self-destructive behaviour to recover at this stage in her life, or possibly she is a victim of cult mind control I never understood.

Perhaps the next revolution in psychiatry will provide a conceptual framework and therapy techniques which can help people like Margaret more effectively than the classical MPD psychotherapy of the late twentieth century. I hope so. When such work is being done, I hope that the pioneers will not be overwhelmed by hostility from orthodox psychiatry. While creating an orthodoxy of our own, we should remember our treatment failures.

15

Electro-shock Treatments

The way in which electro-convulsive therapy, or ECT, is depicted in the movie *One Flew Over the Cuckoo's Nest* is a distortion; the character played by Jack Nicholson returns from having being given the old form of treatment, called unmodified ECT, which is administered without a general anaesthetic, with sutures on each temple, when ECT doesn't involve any incisions. The Hollywood image of ECT as a grim, barbaric, destructive treatment given to control behaviour problems is both true and untrue, as Eleanor would teach me.

It is true that ECT was grossly overprescribed in the past, and given to people with many different diagnoses, many of which do not respond to ECT. Psychiatry has probably created more bad publicity for itself by indiscriminate use of ECT than by any other error. At the same time, it is also true that ECT, properly prescribed, can be a kind, humane, and very effective treatment for serious depression. I saw an old woman who could not eat, drink, or mutter more than a few words transformed after four ECT treatments into a cheerful woman with a hairdresser's appointment. Without ECT, she would have required tube feeding and an IV.

Many of the patients who are most angry about ECT, and vocally critical of psychiatry, are upset about the long-term memory loss they feel they suffered as a result of the treatment. The scientific literature on ECT does not support the existence of any serious long-term memory impairment from

ECT, although there are definitely short-term problems that last a month or so, and subtle subclinical deficits detectable only by psychological testing that may last longer.

Because the scientific literature does not identify any objectively demonstrable serious long-term effects of ECT, psychiatrists tend to perceive patients who make such claims as complainers, compensation neurotics, or ideological enemies. They blame the problem on the patient and the illness, rather than on the ECT. The patients then become more hostile, convinced that psychiatrists are lying, and become committed to an antipsychiatry political position. Eleanor taught me that both sides are right, and both sides are wrong.

Eleanor was self-referred with a diagnosis of MPD that had been made two years earlier. Never married, she had worked as a legal secretary for almost twenty years, despite repeated hospitalizations and sixteen years of intermittent involvement with the mental health system. A slim, tall woman, she appeared younger than her forty-one years. At the time I first met her, she was still taking lithium and an antidepressant for her long-standing diagnosis of bipolar mood disorder, or manic-depressive illness. She had been treated with a single course of ECT for depression about fifteen years earlier, with a good response.

It was unclear how Eleanor got a diagnosis of bipolar mood disorder, as opposed to unipolar depression. She certainly did not have any history of clear mania, or even what sounded like possible sustained hypomania. By contrast, I have assessed other women, such as the polyfragmented MPD case described in chapter 4, who had undiagnosed classical bipolar histories. Another woman I assessed was on lithium and an antidepressant for her supposed bipolar disorder, but it was easy to establish that she switched into 'mania' every day when she arrived at work, and switched back to 'depression' at the end of the work day.

This woman had an energized, happier alter who was the one who went to work, and a full complement of classical signs and symptoms of MPD. She had experienced true clinical depressions, but never a period of sustained mania, and never a period of hypomania lasting more than twelve hours. There are undoubtedly many cases of undiagnosed MPD being treated for atypical bipolar disorder, rapid-cycling bipolar disorder, cyclothymia, bipolar Type II disorder, and other variants of these diagnoses.

In some undiagnosed MPD patients, lithium seems to have no effect; in some, it causes an unpleasant constriction and blunting of all feelings; in others, it modulates the extremes of mood; and, in still others, it reduces the frequency of switching to angry alters. For Eleanor, lithium seemed to do absolutely nothing, and there was no hint of any change in her clinical state when I stopped it. I kept her on the antidepressant for about a year at her request, then stopped it, again without any hint of a change in her clinical state.

Eleanor entered therapy with memories of maternal neglect, and some sexual abuse by a male relative, but no trauma history severe enough to explain the existence of her twenty or so alter personalities. She journaled intensely, and did more work between sessions than I could keep up with, and she also worked hard in session. Gradually she was able to access, and bring out into the light of day, alter personalities who had hidden in internal darkness. Gradually, they revealed her trauma history, which consisted of paternal incest from an early age.

Over the course of four years of therapy, Eleanor recovered and dealt with what appeared to be all of her childhood trauma. Her personality system reached a point where it was working together much more cooperatively, with many old symptoms, phobias, post-traumatic reactions and other difficulties in remission, but she was not integrated by the time she decided to move to another province for a job opportunity. I referred her to another therapist I knew in that province, to continue her psychotherapy.

Eleanor had told me during my initial history taking that she was amnesic for a six-month period prior to her ECT. The amnesia was dense, and attributed by her to the ECT. When she first told me the story, I thought it peculiar, but didn't think much about it. I never speculated to myself that the amnesia might be attributable to other causes, be they dissociative in nature, or anything other than a complication of the ECT.

When I first started to get into the paternal-incest memories, I encountered evidence of the intensity of Eleanor's resistance to recovering them. During a session in which I used a prolonged verbal hypnotic induction in order to access several alters who were difficult to contact, a new child personality spontaneously emerged, and disclosed paternal fellatio and vaginal intercourse at age five or six. I had not been searching for paternal-incest memories, nor had I intended to contact this alter.

As I brought Eleanor out of trance, she suddenly declared, 'Those aren't my pictures! Those are Dr Ross's pictures!'

She was adamant that I had implanted these memories by suggestion, said that they were mine, and insisted I take them back. She was offended that I would ever think such a thing about her father, or try to get to think the same – despite the fact that I had never made any mention of the possibility of sexual abuse by her father.

It was several more months before Eleanor recovered these memories herself outside an induced trance state, and it took some time to piece them together. She eventually accepted them as her own memories of events that really happened. While this was going on, Eleanor realized why she was amnesic for the six months prior to receiving ECT.

During this six-month period many years earlier, Eleanor had begun to spontaneously recover her paternal-incest memories. She had never had any psychotherapy of any kind at that point in her life. The memories made her clinically depressed, which is why she was given ECT: in order to become non-depressed, it was necessary to block out the memory of the entire six months during which the incest memories had been returning. The ECT appeared to be an effective organic treatment for her depression, but actually it worked by providing a clinical myth to explain her amnesia. It was the myth that was the primary antidepressant, I think.

Is this how ECT works in a substantial subset of depressed patients? Perhaps depressions that are non-responsive to medication tend to occur more often in people with trauma histories, as hypothesized by the trauma model of psychopathology. Perhaps the short-term confusion and amnesia created by the ECT results in an organic amnesia for trauma, thus relieving the depression. Eleanor must have elaborated on her short-term organic amnesia by extending it backwards in time for six months.

As I thought about Eleanor's response to ECT, I mentally reviewed my research showing that people with MPD report as many positive symptoms of schizophrenia as people with schizophrenia, and my knowledge that many clinicians have difficulty differentiating psychotic symptoms from dissociative ones: it made sense to me that so-called psychotic depressions are often actually dissociative depressions in which the 'psychotic' features are voices of alters, ego states, and psychic fragments. Most clinicians call such depressions psychotic because they can't differentiate psychosis from dissociation. It would make sense, I thought, that apparently delusional levels of low self-esteem and self-blame, in melancholic depressions, might be linked to childhood sexual abuse as well.

Since psychotic and melancholic depressions are more often treated with ECT than are non-psychotic/non-melancholic depressions, perhaps psychiatry has been creating enemies for itself by treating trauma victims indiscriminately with ECT, without recognizing their underlying dissociative disorders. These patients would tend to be angry as a result of their abuse, prone to projection, and already disposed to join the antipsychiatry movement: these are possibilities Eleanor taught me to consider.

Another woman taught me how to think about the interaction between childhood sexual abuse and true bipolar disorder, which is not fundamentally a trauma disorder, but probably is, in its pure forms, a biomedical psychiatric disorder. I mention her to complete the logic taught to me by Eleanor.

This other woman had a true bipolar disorder which was

well controlled by lithium, except for exacerbations, which often responded to haloperidol. However, when manic, she was wildly hypersexual, a behaviour completely out of character for her. She also had a history of childhood sexual abuse, for which she was still partially amnesic. Hypnotic exploration of her childhood trauma, and consideration of her overall life situation, led me to the conclusion that this woman was a victim of ongoing paternal incest. Her father had probably been abusing her at night, when she was heavily sedated by bedtime clonazepam, as well as at other times.

Although treatment of this woman's childhood sexual trauma would not take away her bipolar mood disorder, it might well extinguish the sexual acting out during her manic phase, and in addition might render her more lithium-responsive. It is possible that the sexual-abuse memories were an anti-lithium engine in her psyche, so to speak. Following this reasoning, one should always enquire carefully for, and suspect, childhood sexual abuse whenever there is severe sexual acting out, even if the behaviour seems to be attributable to mania, psychosis, drug intoxication, or some other factor.

ECT is also effective for mania, though it is not usually used because, in most cases, the mania can be controlled with anti-psychotic medication. The anti-manic effect of ECT might also be the result of an organic dissociation of trauma memories, and related sexual impulses. This hypothesis would apply, if to anyone, only to the traumatized subset of patients with manic-depressive illness.

Eleanor taught me to consider the possibility that many psychiatric medications might work by reinforcing dissociation, and suppressing symptoms, or by dismantling dissociation and allowing normal dissociated thought and feeling to return. I explore these ideas further in chapters 16, 25, and 26.

16

Temporal-Lobe Epilepsy and Schizophrenia

I received a written request from a colleague one day that I admit a patient on an elective basis for a diagnostic assessment and treatment planning. The other psychiatrist specifically chose me to do the work-up because of my expertise in dissociative disorders. Her patient was a young woman who was being treated simultaneously for temporal-lobe epilepsy and schizophrenia. I admitted her a few weeks later.

Rochelle was a single, unemployed, twenty-four-year-old woman on welfare. She was short, stocky, and of less-than-average intelligence: she was very socially isolated, and had never had a sexual relationship with a man in her adult life. Her medications included three different antipsychotic medications, two anticonvulsant medications, a sleeping pill, and an anticholinergic medication to counter the side-effects of the antipsychotic medications. Despite these medications, Rochelle experienced many symptoms most of the time: she heard voices in her head telling her to kill herself, had high levels of anxiety, couldn't sleep because of nightmares, often had periods of missing time lasting a few minutes or hours, had been sexually abused by a babysitter before age ten, and often felt unreal or as if in a dream.

She occasionally had an olfactory hallucination of the smell of lemons, which was thought to be a symptom of seizure activity, as were her periods of missing time. When I reviewed her extensive past charts, I found assessments by four different neurologists and a neurology fellow. The neurology fellow did the most thorough assessment, and came to the conclusion that Rochelle did not have a seizure disorder. The neurologists all independently raised the possibility of pseudo-seizures, and several of her EEGs were normal, while one showed probable artefact and no definite abnormality. Altogether, she had four or five EEGs on her chart, and several normal CT scans. There was no documentation of any change in her symptoms as a result of taking the anticonvulsant medications: her anti-convulsant blood levels had been drawn many times, and were often subtherapeutic.

The diagnosis of schizophrenia was also not supported in the documentation. Her chronic auditory hallucinations and de-personalization experiences were taken to be symptoms of schizophrenia, and her blank spells symptoms of epilepsy. The more parsimonious explanation that both were attributable to a single disorder, MPD, had never been considered.

The MPD was quite straightforward to diagnose. Rochelle was amnesic for periods of self-abuse with burning cigarettes while on the ward, and her voices could readily be engaged in rational, indirect conversation. She described a wide variety of different dissociative, post-traumatic, and psychosomatic symp-toms, and it was clear that her behaviour during blank spells of several hours' duration was organized, purposeful, and did not appear out of the ordinary to outside observers – a pattern which excluded epilepsy as a cause of her missing time.

Rochelle never exhibited any disorganized or psychotic thinking, and there was no description of schizophrenia-like thought processes in her old charts. She had been hearing voices since childhood, and did not exhibit the pattern of an onset of psychotic symptoms followed by deterioration in psychosocial function, which is part of the usual diagnostic picture of schizophrenia. If she had schizophrenia, it would have to have been a childhood-onset form with continuously present auditory hallucinations, no episodes of psychotic think-ing, and no distinct deterioration in function subsequent to an exacerbation of the illness: in fact, her function had simply

never been good. Rochelle did not have the emotional emptiness of schizophrenia; instead, she experienced post-traumatic
hyperarousal much of the time.

When the concept of MPD was explained to her, Rochelle
accepted it as making sense; however, she refused to consider
any uncovering psychotherapy, which was the right decision
for her to make. If she even talked about the sexual-abuse
memories, the voices would get extremely angry and she would
have a blank spell; coming out of the blank spell, she would
find fresh cigarette burns on her arms. This behaviour pattern
has never been reported in the schizophrenia literature, to my
knowledge, but is characteristic of MPD. As well, even the
gentlest explanation of her MPD caused increased anxiety,
nightmares, and fearfulness. Rochelle just didn't have enough
social supports, psychological strength, life skills, intelligence,
or inner determination to participate in intensive MPD psychotherapy. How did I proceed, given her psychological handicaps?

I tapered and then discontinued one anticonvulsant, then the
next, with no change in her symptoms. I reduced the three
antipsychotic medications to one, and the dose of anticholinergic medication, and discontinued the sleeping pill. I then
gradually increased the dosage of the one remaining antipsychotic medication, trifluoperazine, to 120 milligrams a day,
which is a very high dose.

On this treatment regime, Rochelle was less anxious, had
fewer nightmares, slept better, had fewer blank spells, stopped
abusing herself, and reported that the voices were quieter, less
frequent, and less angry: the symptoms that responded to trifluoperazine were those of her dissociative disorder. She was
discharged to out-patient follow-up with a diagnosis of MPD, a
written and spoken explanation of why she was not a candidate
for psychotherapy, and a recommendation that she be treated
with high doses of maintenance antipsychotic medication
indefinitely. I hoped, but was not confident, that she would
never develop tardive dyskinesia, a feared side-effect of antipsychotic medications, involving involuntary muscle movements.

It appears that the antipsychotic medications can be helpful
for some MPD patients who are not candidates for psycho-

therapy. I used to think that these medications have only a non-specific sedating effect in MPD, that they act to dampen down the personality system in a non-specific fashion. In many MPD patients, antipsychotics have no effect, possibly because the dosage is inadequate, while in others they have a disorganizing effect.

Rochelle made me consider the possibility that antipsychotic medications are actually antidissociatives. If they act in MPD by non-specific sedation, then trifluoperazine ought not to have much effect, since it is not very sedating: Rochelle did not show any sedative side-effects following her morning dose. Perhaps, I thought, the medication was acting by walling off the dissociated alters and their memories more completely, thus reducing the post-traumatic nightmare intrusions, blank spells, voices, and anxiety.

There appear to be several pathways to auditory hallucinations, one of which is a childhood-trauma pathway. Some pathways, perhaps, are more antipsychotic-responsive than others, the usual pattern being that MPD voices do not improve on antipsychotic medications, while schizophrenic ones do. Perhaps Rochelle's voices arose from a slightly different neuropsychological mechanism from those of most people with MPD, and therefore responded better to medication.

The widespread idea that MPD does not respond to antipsychotic medication has no scientific basis. It may be an artefact of selection bias, inadequate dosage, and insufficient trials of different classes of antipsychotics. The selection bias is attributable to the fact that the dissociative-disorders field sees treatment failures from elsewhere in psychiatry, but not the treatment successes. Patients like Rochelle, with previously undiagnosed MPD, are referred to psychiatrists like me, and usually appear not to be helped by antipsychotic medication, although this result is, in many cases, linked to inadequate dosages. Undiagnosed MPD patients who respond well to lower doses of antipsychotic medication, by contrast, will not be seen by MPD experts, because they are treatment successes within orthodox psychiatry.

The percentage of MPD patients who do well with intensive

psychotherapy, and the percentage who do best on high-dosage antipsychotics with supportive psychotherapy, are unknown. I would estimate that the group Rochelle is in is 25 per cent or fewer of the total pool of undiagnosed MPD patients currently chronically enmeshed in the mental health system; however, in the absence of research data, this is merely a guess.

A likely possibility is that there are many homeless people with undiagnosed MPD in North America who have been misdiagnosed as suffering from medication–non-responsive schizophrenia by psychiatrists who have not seriously considered MPD. How many of these people have drifted down to homelessness because of inaccurate diagnosis, incorrect treatment, and inadequate insurance is unknown, but I imagine that the number is substantial.

Research to date on schizophrenia is open to criticism because of the failure to differentiate MPD from schizophrenia, and the unwitting inclusion of undiagnosed MPD patients in studies of schizophrenia. There are many people like Rochelle going through life with an incorrect diagnosis of schizophrenia, and some could do well in psychotherapy. Perhaps even those who cannot participate in active uncovering psychotherapy might benefit from supportive care that took their childhood trauma into account.

A final consideration is the possibility that Rochelle had both MPD and schizophrenia at the same time. Although I don't think this was so in her case, I have seen other patients who did appear to have both conditions at once, or an intermediate disorder which combined elements of both. The response of such patients to medication and psychotherapy, and the number of people affected by such mental health problems, is unknown: I have included Rochelle's case history to highlight the problem of the relationship between MPD and schizophrenia, and the likelihood that many people with misdiagnoses of schizophrenia could do better if their dissociative disorder was recognized.

17

A Little Girl Inside

A therapist based at a community agency asked me to sit in on a session. Her nineteen-year-old client Loni had been telling her about a little girl inside for the past several months. (Loni had started to see the referring therapist when her previous therapist had moved to Montreal.) The therapist had been invoking the inner-child metaphor, and had been normalizing her client's statements, making remarks to the effect that everyone has a child inside, that we all have a child aspect to our personalities, and that it is good to be in touch with your inner child. Loni had continued to insist that this was different, and said that the little girl wanted to come out to talk. The therapist had never seen a case of MPD before.

Loni was attractive, wholesome, relaxed, and casually dressed. Her blonde hair and hazel eyes highlighted striking cheekbones. As I talked with her, she explained, as she had to her therapist, that there was a little girl inside who wanted to come out and talk. She could feel the little girl, knew she was twelve years old, and heard her voice inside. Loni liked the little girl and wanted to get to know her.

Loni also experienced blank spells frequently, and had begun to recover trauma memories about a year and a half earlier, which is what had brought her into therapy. While in a shopping mall, she saw an old boyfriend, and suddenly had a flashback of him raping her, an event for which she had been completely amnesic. Several other memories of sexually aggressive behaviour by boyfriends also came back at about the same time. Although she had been working hard in therapy, it appeared that she wasn't making as much progress as expected: her post-traumatic symptoms were not resolving. After discussing the concept of a little girl inside, without mentioning anything about MPD, I suggested to Loni that she close her eyes, relax, and allow the little girl to come and talk, which happened quite easily. Loni's manner changed dramatically as Julie opened her eyes. Her feet assumed a pigeon-toed position, her lips pouted a bit, and her manner became childish: Julie was ten. She spoke in a manner characteristic of some child alters, which is hard to describe: the diction changed slightly, with a slight modification of 'r' sounds into 'w,' almost a slight lisp, and a kind of cute-little-girl quality.

Julie's eyes and facial expression were much more animated, childlike, spontaneous, and charming than Loni's. The host personality, Loni, was somewhat restricted in her emotion, and was more composed and adult. Julie was charming and engaging. One's natural response was to soothe and protect her, whereas Loni evoked a more neutral reaction.

Julie explained that there were two others as well as her, and said she wasn't supposed to say too much about them. They were Donna, aged about fifteen, and Shirley, aged sixteen. Shirley was angry, and Donna was quiet and shy. Julie said that Donna would not come to talk to us, and warned us to watch out for Shirley because of her anger. Julie explained that she knew all about Loni and what she did, and was also aware of everything Donna and Shirley did when they were in control of the body. Loni, though, did not know anything about the other two alters, and had only a slight awareness of Julie's existence: Julie had been actively trying to get Loni's attention for the past few months, but thought that Loni would be scared to get to know her too fast.

I did not pursue any trauma memories in the first session, and in the second set the goal of making contact with Shirley. I called Julie out, talked with her briefly, then asked to speak to Shirley. As soon as Shirley opened her eyes, she stood up, looked very angry and tense, swore at me, and left. In the next session, Loni said she was disturbed about finding herself back at home, unaware of how she had got from my office back to her home.

Several times over the previous year, Loni had woken up, holding razor blades above her wrist, or with pills laid out on the table for an overdose. We assumed that it must be Shirley who was doing this, which proved to be the case. Within a few more sessions, the therapist and I, acting as co-therapists, had gotten to know Julie quite well, and Shirley a little bit. Julie began to reveal memories of paternal incest occurring from an apparently early age up until about a year previously. Shirley became more friendly and cooperative as we got to know her.

We made friends with Shirley by treating her with respect, making a point of wanting to talk to her and having her input, legitimizing her anger as a normal response to being abused, and asking her to help us with planning the therapy. Donna was the most difficult to get to know because of her shyness, and because she could stay in executive control for only a minute or two before slipping away. When Donna was out, we dealt with neutral, non-threatening material in an attempt to desensitize her to being in executive control. We were not sure of Donna's function, since she did not seem to have much life history of her own.

The personality system was organized in two layers, with Loni by herself in the first layer, and the other three co-conscious of each other in the second layer. There were no other internal voices, and Donna, Julie, and Shirley denied ever having any blank spells.

By trial and error, we discovered that the second layer had a switching sequence which could never be modified. If we wanted to talk to Donna, we first had to talk to Julie: it was not possible to call out Donna, except from Julie. Similarly, if we were talking with Donna, and wanted to call out anyone else, it was necessary first to go back to Julie. If we tried to call out Shirley or Loni, nothing would happen. We were never able to determine a functional reason for this switching sequence, but it was immutable.

Julie did intense abreactive work on her memories, many of which were highly disturbing. She remembered one occasion when her father came into her bedroom dressed in women's clothing, stuffed live spiders into her vagina, then had intercourse with her. The abuse appeared to have continued up until about one year earlier, it turned out, because she had memories of her father coming to her apartment and pounding on her door, being let in, and apparently having sex with her. Julie said she could not remember what happened after he entered the apartment. Why the abuse had stopped, other than the fact that Julie had been in therapy, we didn't know.

The community agency at which the co-therapist was based had been receiving crisis calls from Julie during the period in which her father was still coming over. Julie would phone up, hysterical, and say that her father was there, and she had to let him in. The phone workers would try to convince her not to open the door, but she would always hang up, and later report that her father had been there again. At one point, her prior therapist had hired a private detective, who had followed the father from work to her apartment and seen him enter it, despite the father's claim never to have been there by himself.

As we discussed the events inside the apartment after the father entered, it gradually became apparent that the four alters were amnesic for much of what happened. As well, they began to experience other blank spells lasting less than an hour. We therefore knew that there was a third layer, and asked to speak to whoever knew what happened during the blank spells.

This request resulted in our meeting Kelley, a nineteen-year-old alter, who confirmed that she had been there all along, but had started to come out only recently. She said that she didn't do anything in particular while out, but was just enjoying the chance to be in executive control. Kelley was like Loni, in that she was the only person on her layer. She was aware of everything the four alters on the two layers below her did, and they had no awareness of her.

As we moved into this phase of the therapy, Loni abandoned the role of host personality, and went inside for nine months.

She became psychotic, and when called out would hold her head, hallucinate, rock, and be unable to carry on a conversation. By default, Kelley took over as the host personality for almost a year. Before Loni had left, she had gotten to know Julie a bit, and was beginning to be co-conscious with her. Loni had watched several of Julie's abreactions, and had felt the feelings that went along with them. It became clear that we had been pacing the therapy too fast for Loni to handle, but back in 1986 the field was not as aware of pacing issues as it has become in the 1990s.

There turned out to be several more layers above Kelley, each of which we entered in sequence. We would identify, get to know, and work with the alters in one layer, thinking that there were no further layers. Once a substantial amount of work had been done in a given layer, the alters would begin to report dissociative experiences, including blank spells; hearing unidentified voices; having thoughts, feelings, and actions put into them; being controlled by someone unknown; and finding strange writing in the journal, or finding objects inexplicably present or missing.

We would ask to speak to someone we hadn't yet met, and gradually we would get into the next layer. By the time we got into the fourth or fifth layer, the original four alters we met had been integrated, and at one point, when thirty or so known alters had all joined together to become one, we thought Loni was fully integrated.

The trauma we uncovered during this period up to the first apparent complete integration consisted of paternal incest, more sexual assaults, witnessing a murder, and physical and emotional abuse by her mother. There were no other children in the family, so we never had a chance to interview siblings for possible confirmation of the abuse.

One of the alters told us about what appeared to be a contract rape by her father. She was at a hamburger stand one weeknight, at about 11:00 p.m., and was walking through the dark parking lot to her car. A big, bearded man who looked like a biker came up to her, pulled a knife on her, forced her into his van, raped her, and said that her father had paid him to do this. He gave her father's first and last names.

Another time, she was in an unsavoury part of town late at night when her father cruised by in his car, apparently looking to pick up a prostitute. He spotted Loni across the street. She ran away down a side street, but he pursued her by car and then on foot, caught her in an alley, pulled a gun on her, and raped her.

Loni described what seemed to be sudden switching prior to the sexual abuse. Her father, normally a polite and gentle man who did not drink, and was never abusive to wife or daughter in his usual self, would suddenly become intensely angry, would talk dirty to her, and would sometimes pound her head on the floor prior to sexually assaulting her. She said he looked different, that his eyes changed, and that she was sure it was an alter personality who abused her.

The father appeared to be genuinely amnesic for the abuse, saddened and perplexed by his daughter's accusations of incest, and convinced that her memories must be distorted versions of assaults by someone else. The mother thought Loni was chemically imbalanced, angry and vengeful for no reason, or just 'sick in the head.'

As we got deeper into the layers of the personality system, more and more bizarre memories came forth, including sexual abuse by her mother. She recalled being sent home from school with vaginal bleeding on several occasions while in elementary school, with a note from the school nurse. At these times she was further abused by her mother. She also recalled several incidents in which her father sexually abused her in front of her mother, and said that her mother went into a trance state, tears flowed down her cheeks, and she got up and went upstairs. After the abuse was over, both parents and daughter either came out of trance or switched to their host personalities, and everyone carried on as if nothing had happened.

The memories came out in a sequence most of the time, with a body memory first, increasing intensity of the body memory, appearance of the involved alter, abreaction behind an amnesia barrier, then gradual sharing of the memory with the rest of the personality system. One child alter in the fourth or fifth layer always felt that her skin was on fire, and couldn't bear to be touched during session: this alter eventually recovered a memory of having intercourse with her father on the beach after a day of suntanning and swimming, during which she had gotten a severe sunburn.

Among the approximately fifty known alters was a rich array of different kinds of alter personalities, including one whose job was to run away and hide when the father's perpetrator alter personality was looking for her. This alter once hid in the therapist's building while we were having a session there, and was very hard to find. There was a mute alter who only wrote, a number of observers, many different persecutors, mystical alters, and many children.

One personality displayed a different kind of amnesia from the usual pattern. She had blank spells for periods of time while she was still living at home, when she would get up at night and wander through the house. At first I assumed that this meant another alter personality came out after the first one had woken up, but with exploration of this possibility, and on the advice of other alters, I finally concluded that no other personality held the memories of what had been happening. I therefore decided to hypnotize the alter who had woken up at night, to try to find out what had been going on. In trance, it became apparent that this personality had gotten up in a waking state, then gone into a trance state, without switching to another personality. In the trance state, she had gone to the kitchen, gotten a knife, and walked into her parents' bedroom with the intention of stabbing them to death. For an unknown reason, though, she had always gone back to the kitchen, put the knife away, gone back to bed, and gone to sleep without first emerging from trance. She therefore remembered only getting out of bed, and nothing else.

It was eery watching this alter personality in trance talk about being in her parents' bedroom, with a butcher knife poised above them. I wondered how many other episodes of family violence without any apparent explanation are carried out by alter personalities or in trance states, based on abuse for which the perpetrator is amnesic.

Loni appeared to be fully integrated at one point, was doing much better functionally, was not clinically depressed, and was not reporting any dissociative symptoms. After a few weeks, though, she started to report strange messages on her answering machine, periods of depersonalization, and evidence that she had been getting up and going out during the night: she found her shoes and clothes in a different position, or damp, dirty, or rumpled, and seemed to be extremely tired for the amount of sleep she had gotten.

Shortly, she begun to hear a voice talking to her inside her head, and we knew for sure she was not integrated. I therefore asked to talk to someone else inside who remembered what was happening during the periods of missing time, and found myself talking with a representative of yet another layer, for which Loni was amnesic.

We had not been able to understand why, over the previous three years, Loni had been moving more slowly in therapy than she should have, given how hard she worked, the quality of the treatment alliance, her intelligence, and the relative ease with which the new layers opened up, once discovered.

One of the alters in the new layer disclosed that the paternal incest was ongoing. We learned that this layer contained an elaborate system for dealing with the father's visits. There were ten or twelve alters in the layer, divided into a good side and a bad side. Each side had a leader who was aware of the activities of all the alters in the layer on both sides, though less high-ranking alters on each side were amnesic for the activities of some of the others.

When the father knocked on the door, the leader of the bad side automatically took executive control, rendering Loni amnesic. This alter then directed a switch to another alter, who had sex with the father. Following completion of the sex, the father would interrogate Loni about what she was revealing in psychotherapy. To deal with this, the leader of the good side would cause a switch to a child alter whose memories of disclosures in therapy she would temporarily pull out. The child would then report that nothing had been disclosed in therapy, without the father realizing that a switch had occurred.

The leaders of the good and bad side struggled back and forth to control this scenario, with a status quo reached as described. The bad-side leader would make Loni experience a kind of *la belle indifférence* for any evidence of recent intercourse, rumpled sheets, or missing time. Usually her father was only there twenty minutes or so, so there was not much missing time to account for.

Other alters in this layer began to describe incomplete memories of what sounded like ritual abuse by the mother. Incomplete pictures of people outdoors in hooded cloaks, possibly Loni being partially buried, and her mother being present were recovered. There seemed to be candles involved, and possibly some blood. Since Loni could not recover while the abuse was still going on, we helped arranged for her to move to Montreal, where she started working with her former therapist again. She stayed in a women's shelter which would allow her to live there for up to a year, was well connected to her therapist, and had formed the beginnings of a support group.

In less than six months, Loni began to talk to her therapist, and in occasional phone calls to me, about how much she missed her parents, how she wanted to have a relationship with them before her father died, and how she could keep herself safe if she moved back to Winnipeg. The layer of alters that had disclosed the ongoing incest had not completed its work, the ritual-abuse memories were still fragmentary, and she was actually in no condition to return, which I told her.

Over the next month or two, Loni decided that she never had MPD, that the memories were simply fantasies, and that her parents were safe. She decided to move home, and live with her maternal aunt, who kept close ties with her parents. I told her that I thought she did have MPD, that she had been a victim of paternal incest until the time she had moved to Montreal, and that I could not work with her if she returned to Winnipeg in a state of denial.

I explained, both on the phone and in writing to her, that

there were only two possibilities, both of which lead to my not working with her anymore: first, she was right that she never had MPD and was never abused. In that case, the three years of therapy we did with her were seriously off track, unhelpful, and mistaken. She needed to start work afresh with a new therapist not contaminated by our errors.

Alternatively, the MPD and incest were real, in which case she could never get better while still being abused, and treatment was futile. I told her I could not participate in such an arrangement, believing, as I did, that she was still having intercourse with her father. She moved back to Winnipeg, and I have not talked with her for three years.

Loni was the person who taught me about ongoing trauma. I have since met a number of women, ranging in age from late teens to forties, who proved to be having ongoing incestuous intercourse with their fathers. The oldest-aged case I have heard of is a forty-six-year-old woman living in the same house as her father, and sleeping in the same bed.

Whenever there is insufficient treatment progress, given the amount of work the person is doing, I suspect ongoing trauma, as I also do whenever a person appears stuck in shame, guilt, hopelessness, self-blame, or depression without any adequate explanation. Other clues I have learned to be alert for include particularly dense amnesia, two-way amnesia between alters, and chaotic switching among four or five alters who share the role of host.

I once assessed a young woman in the Emergency Department whose alters knew nothing about one another, and whose days were broken into disconnected fragments, without any continuity of executive control. After five or six months of therapy, she disclosed ongoing paternal incest. Other forms of ongoing trauma that interfere with treatment include involvement in prostitution, extensive use of street drugs by alter personalities not known to the therapist, physically abusive marriages, and involvement in destructive, abusive relationships of all kinds. What to do in such cases is a difficult dilemma.

On the one hand, one should not abandon such patients just

because they are still being abused: this is obviously inhumane, and is not based on any adequate evidence that such people are untreatable. The opposing argument is that MPD psychotherapy is a scarce and valuable resource which should be dispensed in the most effective and efficient manner possible. It does not make sense to invest hundreds of hours of therapy time in people who are not able to extricate themselves from ongoing abuse.

The decision I made not to see Loni again was difficult, and I was tempted to try to contact her many times. I thought the alters in the background needed to hear clearly what my position was, and I assumed that there were yet more layers listening in the background. If she was also a victim of ongoing ritual abuse, this would compound the problem, and make treatment even more difficult.

We had worked very hard with Loni. She had taken many overdoses, presented many behaviourial and management problems, put us in many double binds, and entangled us in many uncomfortable situations. She had had countless work-ups for psychosomatic symptoms which were surely all body memories of ongoing incest, and had exhausted a variety of different community resources, friends, and supports.

In part the decision not to see her was based on exhaustion, exasperation, and projective identification. Projective identification occurs when the patient projects her feelings onto the therapist, then unconsciously engineers the situation so that the therapist actually feels the patient's projected feelings. Additionally, the therapist acts out the feelings back on the patient. In this instance, perhaps, Loni projected her feelings of badness and hopelessness onto me, and I rationalized my rejection of her with arguments to myself about case management. The rejection, perhaps, was my way of getting rid of the bad feelings Loni had projected onto me. I don't know.

If I did act out her projective identification by refusing to see Loni again, it didn't work very well for me: I feel sad when I think of Loni in her apartment, knowing that one of her inner children is still having intercourse with her father, probably on a weekly basis.

18

A Foster Child

My purpose here is not to describe Monica's treatment or her
personality system. Rather, it is to recount the abuse she
received during her childhood, and the treatment she received
from psychiatrists in the late 1950s and 1960s. I reviewed
many pages of microfiched state hospital records, correspon-
dence from lawyers and social-service agencies, and Charter
Hospital records prior to writing this chapter, and intend to
emphasize that victims of severe childhood trauma, whether or
not they have MPD, need treatment that takes the trauma into
account. They may be helped by properly prescribed medication; however, often in the past, they have received psychiatric
treatment which has been far, far from helpful.

I met Monica during a brief admission to Charter Hospital
and have been consulting to her therapist since her discharge.
Monica has been in intensive treatment for MPD in northern
Texas for two years, and has never been 'a problem' in the
sense of behavioural difficulties, acting out, or making trouble.
Yet she is the most truly suicidal multiple-personality patient
I have met.

Part of Monica's therapy involves resolving her grief over the
decades during which she repressed her pain and abuse memories with medication and alcohol. She considers these to be
lost years, not in the sense of amnesia, but because she was not
able to live happily. When her care was first taken over by a
psychiatrist with knowledge of MPD two years ago, Monica was
on eight or ten different medications. Right now she is on

three: the antidepressant fluoxetine, which was started on the somewhat poor chance that it might help; lorazepam, to help her sleep; and small doses of an anti-inflammatory drug prescribed by a neurologist at a pain clinic.

The therapeutic work with Monica has involved only a little direct contact with alter personalities. Most of the time we talk indirectly to the voices, and Monica reports on what they are saying inside her head. The voices have specific names, and control the rate at which she recovers her memories of child abuse and the trauma she experienced on psychiatric wards. The voices had taken some executive control of her body prior to the therapy, but not much.

Diagnostically, Monica is currently on the borderline between full MPD and partial forms of it in which the personality states do not take control of the body. In her childhood, though, the personality states took control to be the victims of sexual, physical, and emotional abuse. Like many psychiatric disorders, MPD may tend to settle down a bit in the forties, fifties, and later in the life cycle, in the sense that there is less switching of personalities, and therefore fewer blank spells, and less dispute and conflict between the personalities.

The degree of activity of the alter personalities differs from one person to the next, and ebbs and flows with different tasks and crises throughout the life cycle. We only know a little bit about the natural history of MPD, since we lack long-term follow-up on any sizeable number of cases.

It was clear when she entered MPD treatment that, despite her older age, Monica needed treatment focused on her childhood trauma. She was in a lot of pain, and was not benefiting from her large number of different medications. Her risk of eventually completing suicide was high. The treatment began with a sodium-amytal interview designed to help her recover dissociated feelings about her past. Once the door was opened, memories and feelings began to come back, she started to hear voices again, as she had in the past, and she experienced a few blank spells. Some psychiatrists would view this as evidence that the sodium-amytal interview made her worse.

They would be right. Often a person must get worse in order

to get better. The getting worse is not hard to understand, and is caused by the turmoil and pain that accompany the recovery of abuse memories, which is bound to be difficult and upsetting. The therapist's job is to try to see to it that the pace is neither too fast nor too slow, which can be difficult. A slow pace results in the therapy being excessively lengthy, with both patient and therapist becoming discouraged; a fast pace can overwhelm both patient and therapist, and can result in going too slow, because the patient puts on the brakes by 'acting out' and tries to slow down the therapy in an indirect, self-defeating manner. Sometimes the patient's behaviour is considered to be the problem in such situations, when it is really the therapist's technique that is at fault.

We have had the inverse of this problem in a muted form with Monica. She has been discouraged and despairing much of the time, because she feels she is not making progress and wants to speed up. She doesn't believe us when we tell her she has done a tremendous amount of work recovering and dealing with memories, and learning to be more assertive. What progress she will admit to, she credits to the voices, saying that she couldn't have done any of it on her own. She doesn't accept that the voices are part of her.

Monica is one of the few MPD patients I have worked with who have been frankly delusional. She has proposed many bizarre and impossible 'explanations' of who the voices are, and at times I have wondered if the therapy we were doing was at all helpful. She has told her psychiatrist that he injected the voices into her during the sodium-amytal interview, that they are controlled by a machine housed in a nearby building, and that he communicates psychically with the voices to control her mind. Some psychiatrists would diagnose her as suffering from schizophrenia, and would say it was malpractice not to prescribe antipsychotic medication when she is delusional, hearing voices, and suicidal.

Monica has certainly displayed three of the four As of schizophrenia, said by Bleuler to be the core of the illness. These are disturbances in associations, such as Monica's delusional logic;

autism, which is a self-absorbed quality with failure to connect with others, which Monica has not displayed during therapy; ambivalence, or difficulty making decisions; and affective blunting, which means a burned-out, empty quality to one's emotions. These features are thought to be attributable to whatever the biological defect is in schizophrenia.

As Monica progresses in therapy, her affective blunting is diminishing, as is her ambivalence. She still offers delusional explanations of the voices, but otherwise her thought processes are perfectly rational. She only appeared to have schizophrenic blunting of affect because she had dissociated the pain, anger, and fear caused by her childhood trauma. She only appeared to have schizophrenic ambivalence because of her passivity and fearfulness, which are, in part, the result of her having been conditioned into the victim role. I suspect that therapists who have claimed to be able to treat schizophrenia with psycho-therapy may actually have been dealing with undiagnosed cases of MPD.

It is not always easy to tell the difference between MPD and schizophrenia. It is important to do so, though, because a person with MPD may benefit dramatically from psychotherapy that deals with the childhood abuse.

Monica was born out of wedlock to an adolescent mother during the Second World War. For the first four and a half years of her life, she lived in an orphanage. Early on, she was described as small for her age, with a large head and thin extremities. There is a good chance that she would be described today by a paediatrician as suffering from failure to thrive. She played mostly by herself, and did not join in with the other children much: this sounds like Bleuler's criterion of autism for schizophrenia.

Monica's first foster placement was for nine months. According to the social worker's notes, the foster mother thought Monica was 'dull and stupid,' and she appeared to be depressed and lacking energy. Monica was returned to the orphanage when the foster mother became pregnant.

According to the memories Monica has recovered, she was

sexually abused by the foster father in this first home, beginning before her fifth birthday. She was not allowed to go to church because of her bedwetting, and at this time would be home alone with her foster father. He would call her into his bedroom, force her to fellate him, then force her to lick the remaining semen off his penis. To ensure that Monica would not tell, he would strangle her with a belt, and threaten to beat her on the bare buttocks with a belt. If Monica appeared upset when the others returned from church, he would explain that he had had to discipline her for her bedwetting.

These memories were held by little Monica, age four, who gave them back during therapy. In one of her foster homes, the parents killed and cooked Monica's pet rabbit, and made her eat it.

The next two months of her childhood were spent in the orphanage again, except for a three-week hospitalization, required, according to the notes, 'because her appetite varied.' Then Monica went to her second foster home, where she stayed for a year. She turned six at this home. According to the social-work notes, this placement ended because of conflict between Monica and the foster mother over her bedwetting, and the foster mother's lack of understanding of her problems.

According to the voices and the memory they gave back, Monica was sexually assaulted by a male friend of the family while in this home. He came over to babysit while the foster parents went out. He took Monica upstairs, undressed her from the waist down, pulled his pants off, lay down beside her on the bed, put Monica on top of him, and penetrated her. After climaxing, he went to the washroom to get a towel, came back, and told Monica to stay on the bed until he told her to get up. He then inserted several fingers in her vagina, took them out, and smelled them.

At this point the teenaged natural daughter came home. The man told her what he had done, and threatened her into silence. Monica heard this and began to cry. The man took her upstairs again, and this time ejaculated on her face and stomach, while the foster sister watched. He made her lick his penis

9

following orgasm. He then warned Monica not to tell anyone, told her to go clean herself up, and went downstairs. According to the memory, he came back a third time, and made her fellate him, but Monica bit his penis as he was coming to orgasm. He slapped her, got angry, and left.

The foster daughter told Monica not to tell her parents. She helped Monica clean up, then phoned the Child Protection Services, told them what had happened, and asked them not to tell her parents. According to Monica's memory, Child Protective Services came and got her, and took here back to the orphanage.

The third foster placement lasted for a year and a half, from just after Monica's seventh birthday until she was nine. There were four other girls in the home, with whom Monica got along well. The foster mother described Monica as stubborn and defiant, and once hit her with a wet bedsheet: Monica was still wetting her bed. The reason for this placement breaking down is not given in the records.

At this third home, Monica was hit whenever she wet the bed, and sometimes was made to sleep in the bed a second night, without the sheets having been changed. She was used as a domestic slave for cleaning the floors and washing. She was strapped once a week by the foster father for wetting the bed and not playing with her foster sister. She was punished by being made to stand in her room for hours, and she always got a strapping if she wet her pants. She was made fun of, and called names by the foster parents.

Both parents together would punish Monica by making her take off her clothes and stand naked for prolonged periods, and they made fun of her body: the foster father would insert his fingers in her vagina, and then laugh. Because Monica would not consent to fellate the foster father, he raped her vaginally nine times. When Monica told the school principal about the abuse she was receiving at home, the foster parents asked him to strap her so she would not lie anymore, which he did.

According to the social-work notes, the fourth foster family decided not to legally adopt Monica because of a 'rumour' that she was once sexually assaulted. The origins of this rumour are not given in the notes. The fourth foster placement lasted for seven and a half years, up until Monica was sixteen years old.

The fourth foster mother is described in the social worker's notes as being an overprotective, hypocritical woman who pretended she was concerned for Monica's welfare when talking to a professional, but who, at home, screamed and yelled at her all the time and took advantage of her willingness to work. The foster mother also ran her down a lot, and compared her unfavourably with her own daughter.

At this fourth home, the sexual abuser was the foster grandfather, whom she had to watch for several hours every day because he was ill. The grandfather repeatedly sexually abused her, primarily with fondling, fellatio, and manual masturbation of Monica. He told her not to tell anyone, and told her that if she didn't sexually service him he would die. Shortly after she first refused to perform any more sexual acts, he died of a heart attack, a death for which she blamed herself for more than thirty years.

When the grandfather told the foster father what had been going on, according to a memory which is not entirely clear, the foster father forced her to fellate him in front of the other children, to show them what happens to bad girls like that. Monica isn't sure about the details or accuracy of this memory, but is sure that she performed oral sex on him once. She isn't sure if the other children were present, and isn't sure what the grandfather told the father.

The fifth foster home lasted until Monica turned eighteen, and she then stayed on as a boarder for a time after that. This was the best home she had, and she was not abused there. Case-summary notes from 1965 refer to sexual abuse by a foster father at age five involving attempted intercourse, but not to any specific events. Notes describing a brief marriage in her twenties say that she was 'subject to the most despicable forms of mental cruelty from her husband.' He was abusive sexually and emotionally, as well as unfaithful.

Monica was first admitted to a psychiatric ward at age

eighteen, at which time she received a diagnosis of schizophrenia. According to the hospital records, she was discussed at a diagnostic conference, and given a diagnosis of schizophrenia 'for statistical purposes,' but this cryptic explanation is not elaborated on. At any rate, she carried this diagnosis for the next eight years, until the notes come to an end.

Up until the age of twenty-six, Monica was in and out of hospital, and was followed as an out-patient in-between. Until she was in her mid-twenties, the places she lived in were referred to as foster homes, and she was described as having sibling-rivalry problems with the children of the foster parents.

According to the notes, the fourth foster mother phoned Monica in hospital several years after she left that home, and blamed her for causing a recent miscarriage. The evidence thought by doctors to indicate that she suffered from schizophrenia included hearing voices; being afraid of people; wanting to run away; and wanting to blow up her fourth foster mother, which was thought to be a paranoid delusion. She was described as being preoccupied with alleged sexual assaults that she received as a child, and cruel treatment at her foster homes.

The abusive, controlling behaviour by the fourth foster mother is well described in the first admission history. The first ward she was admitted to, before she was transferred to another hospital, is repeatedly referred to in the notes, in a matter-of-fact manner, as 'Psycho.'

In a period of about a month, prior to transfer to the hospital where she received the rest of her treatment, Monica was given thirty-six insulin-coma therapy treatments and seven electro-convulsive therapy (ECT) treatments. Insulin-coma therapy, an archaic treatment which is no longer used, involves giving the patient injections of insulin to make his or her blood sugar drop so low that a coma results. This was quite a dangerous procedure, and could result in death. She was on 100 milligrams per day of chlorpromazine, an antipsychotic medication, at the time of transfer. There is a gap in the notes, until thirty-three months later, when she was being discharged.

The notes describe a course of fifty insulin-coma treatments, given over fifty-five days, and forty-five ECT treatments, given over a period of three weeks, during this long admission. This practice of giving huge numbers of shock treatments, called *regressive ECT*, has been abandoned. It was expected that, at the end of a course of regressive ECT, the patient could be lying in a foetal position and incontinent.

The current recommendation of the American Psychiatric Association Task Force on ECT is that a course of ECT consist of a minimum of four, and a maximum of eight, individual treatments. These treatments involve what is called *modified ECT*: the patient is anaesthetized by an anaesthetist, then administered muscle-paralysing drugs that wear off very quickly, and then given the electro-convulsive treatment to induce a seizure lasting about one minute. It is the seizure that has the antidepressant effect. A single treatment, from being put to sleep to waking up, takes only about twenty minutes, and the patient remembers nothing, except being put to sleep. The muscle paralysis prevents an injury from the muscle contractions that occur during the seizure.

Monica had what is called *unmodified ECT*: she had no anaesthesia, no muscle relaxants, and was given the ECT wide awake. She remembers being strapped down, having a rubber bit stuck in her mouth, having the electrodes attached, and the switch being thrown. She estimates that she received 200 ECT treatments at three different hospitals in less than a decade. We were able to verify 127 from full records at one hospital and partial records from a second.

Modern ECT is a humane, safe, and effective treatment for selected patients with very severe depressions. It can cause an amazing, full, and rapid recovery from profound depression. I don't hesitate to recommend it when I think it is warranted, although antidepressant medications have largely replaced it as the favoured mode of treatment. The ECT Monica received was not modern.

At discharge, Monica's medications included 50 milligrams per day of trifluoperazine, another antipsychotic, which is a

high dose. She also received 10 milligrams per day of procyclidine, a drug given to counteract the side-effects of antipsychotic medication. This fairly high dose of procyclidine could
cause side-effects of its own, including dry mouth, constipation, and urinary retention.

The next year, the notes describe trouble with a boyfriend
which reactivated undescribed sexual fears and a compulsion
to masturbate. This compulsion to masturbate did not resolve
for more than thirty years, until she recovered the memories of
being masturbated by her foster grandfather. At this time, she
was on 50 milligrams per day of trifluoperazine, 20 milligrams
per day of procyclidine, and now 125 milligrams per day of the
antidepressant amitriptyline. All three of these drugs have
anticholinergic effects, including dry mouth, constipation, and
urinary retention, as well as rapid heart rate. If the anticholinergic effects are severe, they cause a delirium, in which
the person can be disoriented, agitated, and hallucinating.

A few months later, the dosages were 40 milligrams of trifluoperazine, 20 milligrams of procyclidine, and 75 milligrams
of amitriptyline. Then, three days later, her medications were
800 milligrams per day of chlorpromazine, quite a high dose,
and 100 milligrams of a different antidepressant, imipramine.
She was given a course of ECT, during which the imipramine
was increased to 150 milligrams per day.

The next month, 3 grains per day of a barbiturate were added
at bedtime. The month after this, her sleeping medication had
been changed to a different non-barbiturate medication. Three
months later, now two and a half years after her first discharge,
she was on 600 milligrams per day of chlorpromazine, 150
milligrams per day of imipramine, and 15 milligrams per day
of trifluoperazine, but no procyclidine. There is no medically
rational reason to prescribe this combination of two different
antipsychotic medications. A month later, the trifluoperazine
had been stopped, and 15 milligrams per day of procyclidine
had been added back on. The trifluoperazine was then restarted. Over the next few months, her dosages of trifluoperazine and chlorpromazine went up and down, the former vary-

ing between 15 and 30 milligrams per day, and the latter between 450 to 600 milligrams per day.

Because she was retaining fluid and gaining weight from the chlorpromazine, a diuretic was added. By the end of that year, her chlorpromazine had been stopped, and she was taking 45 milligrams per day of trifluoperazine, plus the imipramine. This only lasted a week, and she was back on 400 milligrams per day of chlorpromazine, with no change in the trifluoperazine or imipramine. The barbiturate also reappeared at this point. A week later, she was given another course of ECT.

During the course of ECT, she started vomiting, so dimenhydrinate was added. She was also given thiamine for a while for no discernible reason. By the end of this course of ECT, three years after her first discharge, now twenty-four years old, she was on 45 milligrams per day of trifluoperazine, 500 milligrams per day of chlorpromazine, and was back on amitriptyline at a dosage of 150 milligrams per day, but no procyclidine. A month later, the dosages were 60 milligrams of trifluoperazine, 320 milligrams of chlorpromazine, and 100 milligrams of amitriptyline.

The next month, the dosages were 75 milligrams per day of trifluoperazine, 500 milligrams of chlorpromazine, and 150 milligrams of amitriptyline. A week after this, the amitriptyline had been reduced to 100 milligrams, and the chlorpromazine increased to 650 milligrams. Within another month, a third previously unprescribed sleeping pill had been added.

Yet another month went by, and the trifluoperazine was now up to 90 milligrams, and the amitriptyline back up to 150 milligrams, with no change in the chlorpromazine. A week later, the trifluoprazine was increased further to 100 milligrams. After another three weeks, the amitriptyline was reduced to 100 milligrams, with no change in the other two medications.

Another two weeks went by, and the chlorpromazine was reduced to 470 milligrams, with no change in the other two, while the sleeping pill was changed back to one prescribed previously. Then, after another three weeks, the chlorprom-

azine was put back up to 650 milligrams, and the trifluoperazine reduced to 45 milligrams. The diuretic was restarted.

By the middle of the following month, the trifluoperazine
was at 50 milligrams, the chlorpromazine still at 650 milligrams, the amitriptyline had been stopped, and she was on 10
milligrams per day of a third antidepressant, tranylcypromine.
The dosage of this drug was increased to 30 milligrams per day
by the middle of the next month. Two months later, she was
on 100 milligrams of trifluoperazine, 400 milligrams of
chlorpromazine, and 150 milligrams of imipramine, and the
tranylcypromine had been stopped. A week later, the chlorpromazine was reduced to 250 milligrams.

Another two weeks went by, and a fourth sleeping pill, never
previously prescribed, was added to the sleeping pill she was
already on. This new sleeping pill was also a barbiturate. Within another three weeks, the trifluoperazine had been stopped,
and she was on 700 milligrams of chlorpromazine.

A month later took us into the new year, now four years
from her first discharge. The chlorpromazine was now at 800
milligrams. The antidepressant was then stopped, and three
months later there is a note saying that she was being prescribed methylphenidate (Ritalin) to counteract the sedation
caused by the chlorpromazine. She was also on a sleeping pill.

Prescribing an amphetamine to counteract the sedation
caused by an antipsychotic drug, while also giving a sleeping
pill, is unheard of: for one thing, amphetamines make psychosis worse, and can cause psychosis in a person with no psychiatric problems. As well, trifluoperazine is far less sedating than
chlorpromazine, and could have been prescribed instead. To
give an amphetamine and a sleeping pill at the same time is
also highly questionable. Three weeks later, the sleeping pill
had been changed back to the second barbiturate, and she was
described in the notes as extremely drowsy.

The next month, she was on 600 milligrams of chlorpromazine, the barbiturate, and a fourth antidepressant called trimipramine, at a dosage of 100 milligrams. Then there is a gap in
the notes for three months, at which point she is on 900 milli-

grams of chlorpromazine, no antidepressant, a fifth sleeping pill, and back on 15 milligrams of procyclidine. After another month, the tranylcypromine was restarted at 10 milligrams per day, and increased to 30 milligrams the next week. The chlorpromazine was increased to 1,000 milligrams.

She carried on with this combination for two months, taking her into another year, and now five years out from her first discharge. At this point, her chlorpromazine was increased to 1,100 milligrams. After another two months, she was on 1,000 milligrams of chlorpromazine, and the antidepressant was now trimipramine, at a dosage of 150 milligrams per day. The sleeping pill was changed back to the first barbiturate. A week later, the sleeping pill was changed back to the first non-barbiturate sleeping pill. A month later, the chlorpromazine was back up to 1,100 milligrams.

A week after the increase in the chlorpromazine, the sleeping pill was stopped, and the second barbiturate was restarted, but chlordiazepoxide was added, in a dose of 50 milligrams at bedtime. This drug belongs to the diazepam (Valium) group, and should not be prescribed together with a barbiturate. These three drugs together could cause serious oversedation, motor impairment, cognitive impairment, and respiratory depression.

There is a one-line mention in the records at this date that her landlord tried to get into bed with her.

A week later the chlordiazepoxide was stopped, and 20 milligrams of diazepam was added at bedtime, with the barbiturate continued. Four days later, the diazepam was changed to 10 milligrams three times a day. The next month, the procyclidine showed up again, this time in a dosage of 5 milligrams at bedtime. Since the procyclidine is given to counteract the side-effects of the chlorpromazine, it makes no sense to give 5 milligrams at bedtime, since the counteractive effects of the procyclidine will be present only while the patient is asleep.

By early in the next month, Monica was receiving 800 milligrams of chlorpromazine, 200 milligrams of trimipramine, and 300 milligrams of diazepam per day. By the middle of that month, the procyclidine was increased to 5 milligrams twice a day, and the following month to 10 milligrams twice a day. By the end of this month, the trimipramine was up to 300 milligrams, a high dose, and the chlorpromazine was down to 600 milligrams. The doctors could not understand why she was dizzy, although dizziness from low blood pressure is a common side-effect of both trimipramine and chlorpromazine. In two more weeks, her diazepam was reduced to 20 milligrams.

The next month, the trimipramine was stopped, and she was back on 150 milligrams of imipramine, with the diazepam back up to 30 milligrams. Then, the next month, there is a note that chlordiazepoxide was stopped, although there was no note that it had been restarted, and trifluoperazine was restarted at 30 milligrams per day. A week later, the trifluoperazine was down to 20 milligrams. The next week, it was put up to 40 milligrams. Three days after this, she was started on a third barbiturate. The reason for starting the third barbiturate, phenobarbital, was that, on the telephone, she described a period of loss of consciousness which 'may be epileptic nature,' according to the grammatically incorrect note. In another two weeks, early in the next new year, her chlorpromazine was at 800 milligrams per day, and her procyclidine at 15 milligrams per day, with no change in her trifluoperazine or phenobarbital. The chlorpromazine was increased because she had headaches, for which a painkiller was also added.

Less than another week had gone by when her chlorpromazine was increased to 900 milligrams, the trifluoperazine stopped, and desipramine, another antidepressant, was added, at 100 milligrams per day. Desipramine is a metabolite of imipramine, which means that the body breaks imipramine down into desipramine. Both are active antidepressants. One of the old non-barbiturate sleeping pills was represcribed as well. After another month, the desipramine was up to 150 milligrams.

Three months later the anti-epileptic medication Dilantin was added for no discernible reason other than headaches. Two days later, she was described as having had several blackouts, thought to be possibly attributable to the chlorpromazine, so the chlorpromazine was reduced to 800 milligrams, and a dosage of 10 milligrams per day of trifluoperazine was added.

There are very few notes for the next two and a half months, then she is on 600 milligrams of chlorpromazine and 150 milligrams of yet another antipsychotic medication, methotrimeprazine, and her antidepressant has been switched back to amitriptyline, at 100 milligrams. She is on another new sleeping pill as well.

The next month Monica, again only on the phone, described a spell of rigidity and twitching, so the doctor wrote, in parentheses, in his notes 'G.M. seizure?,' meaning he was wondering if it was a grand-mal seizure. He therefore reduced her methotrimeprazine, and added phenobarbital. The antipsychotic and antidepressant medications she had been on could all cause seizures, but these side-effects were most likely the kind of muscle side-effects procyclidine is supposed to counteract, and not seizure activity. In any case, the symptoms could not possibly have been those of a grand-mal seizure, and, had they been, more than a phone assessment was required before an anticonvulsant could even be considered.

Two weeks later, her medications consisted of 400 milligrams of chlorpromazine, 150 milligrams of methotrimeprazine, 150 milligrams of amitriptyline, the sleeping pill, and now, amazingly, a tablet of placebo, as required. Six days later, the amitriptyline was increased to 200 milligrams. Two days after this, the chlorpromazine was at 300 milligrams, and the methotrimeprazine at 200 milligrams. In another two weeks, the methotrimeprazine was dropped to 100 milligrams, and a week later the chlorpromazine dropped to 200 milligrams.

Two weeks later, the methotrimeprazine was back up to 150 milligrams, and a week after this the chlorpromazine was put up to 300 milligrams. This regimen was maintained into the next new year, seven years after her first discharge. Then, in the first month of that year, the chlorpromazine was changed to 100 milligrams one day, alternating with 200 milligrams the next, and the amitriptylene was increased to 200 milligrams.

Two months later, the chlorpromazine was at 200 milligrams

every day, and a further 200 milligrams every second night, while the amitriptyline was down to 100 milligrams. A week after this, the amitriptyline had been increased to 150 milligrams. This is where the records end, as Monica moved to another city to work. Monica's account of her treatment in this other city includes large numbers of ECTs, numerous medications, and an explanation to her boyfriend by her doctor that he should insist on fellatio to help her overcome her problem with it.

At one point during this period, when Monica was on a barbiturate, two different Valium-type drugs, and high doses of codeine, she was described as staggering and having pinpoint pupils. The opinion of the physician writing in the chart was that the staggering and weak legs were due to hysteria (although she was on enough opiates to cause pinpoint pupils), and large doses of sedatives. She was also noted as having urinary retention at one point, with no idea as to the cause, although she was on large doses of several different medications, each of which alone could cause this problem.

Having reviewed all this material, I thought that the doctors probably did not know about her sexual-abuse history, or thought it to be delusional. I was very surprised to find notes in the chart from her first year in hospital describing a sodium-amytal interview done when she was eighteen years old, for the purpose of uncovering traumatic experiences. The notes describe the sexual abuse by the foster grandfather, his death, her blaming herself, and the abuse in the first foster home at age four, and linked her compulsive masturbation to the sexual abuse.

Monica had mentioned that there was a young doctor at this hospital who was very kind to her, and talked with her. She said he left because of his distaste for the way she was being treated. Granted, that may be an idealized or distorted memory, but this doctor's name disappears from the notes within the next year. Within a month of the sodium-amytal interview, Monica was started on her course of forty-five ECT treatments, given over about a month. The notes say that she was so confused after this that she had hardly any memory left regarding the remote and recent past.

The trauma was uncovered, not dealt with, then suppressed with massive amounts of ECT and medication. This was a successful, though unintended strategy, since the ECT and medications were presumably directed at her symptoms, not at deliberate suppression of her abuse memories. The memories were not permanently lost. We were able, retrospectively, to identify the specific alter personality responsible for the auditory hallucinations prior to her first admission in 1959, what was being said, and why: Little Monica was telling her to run away.

Although we did not find independent confirmation of all her abuse memories, some were described by physicians with the same details we were hearing from her almost thirty years later. The dates of her placement in each of the foster homes, as she told them to us from her own memory, were accurate. Her estimate of the number of ECT and insulin-coma treatments she had was accurate. The suicide of a co-patient she cared for, and which she told us about, was described in the records. We did not find any inaccuracies.

We did find a mention in the notes of sexual advances by a staff member, which she rebuffed, and which were not disciplined. We did not find mention of two important items. She said that she was told by her doctor that she had had a cardiac arrest following an ECT treatment, and that he was cancelling all treatments for a while. There was no mention of this, but there was an unexplained break of a week in her course of forty-five ECT treatments, although she had several per day throughout the rest of the course.

Nor did we find an account of her being raped by an orderly. He was assigned to take her out for a walk, and forced intercourse on her in some bushes, then threatened her with further rapes and dismissal of her claims of assault as delusions if she told anyone. Monica thinks the orderly hoped she would be amnesic for the rape as a result of the ECT. One thing Monica never mentioned to us was her doctor discussing the possibility of a lobotomy with her, but this is documented in the notes.

We are carrying on with Monica's therapy. The treatment she received in the state hospital (not in Texas) was barbaric and incompetent. I have described the massive, irrationally prescribed medications at tedious length in order to convey the magnitude of the malpractice. I have to wonder how many other undiagnosed MPD patients have filled the asylums over the centuries, and been victims of institutional abuses, ranging from being held in chains, to neglect and irrational polypharmacy, to sexual assault and rape. During her therapy, Monica uncovered a memory she believed to be clear and accurate: other memories were confused and uncertain, but this trauma never was anything other than sharp and definite, once she recalled it.

One night, Monica was lying awake in the infirmary of the state hospital, when one of the psychiatrists and a male co-patient quietly entered the room. They did not know she was awake, and proceeded to smother an old woman sleeping in a bed across the room. The next day, the male co-patient committed suicide by jumping from a water tower.

A year or so before meeting Monica, I read in a newspaper about a psychiatrist in Australia who sexually abused countless patients in a government mental hospital over many years, gave them countless courses of ECT, and was thought to have driven many to suicide, and to have killed many. This psychiatrist even had patients brought to his home from the hospital by taxi for sex. All these events were factual, and testified to by many people.

I also thought of the movie starring Jessica Lange in which Frances Farmer, a minor Hollywood starlet, was sexually abused in mental hospitals in the 1950s, and I wondered whether she also had undiagnosed MPD. Working with Monica, and later supervising her therapy, I wondered whether the ECT, drugs, and insulin comas had permanently damaged her brain. She had tremendous difficulty getting her memories clarified, and I wondered whether some of them were organically destroyed. If so, this would be psychiatry's most sinister method of repudiating the seduction theory.

Monica and several other patients I have met with similar, though less extreme, histories of institutional and medical abuse led me to suspect that the anti-ECT movement is fuelled in part by massive overprescribing of ECT to trauma victims. I believe that the apparent therapeutic effects of ECT may, in many cases, have actually been an organic dissociation of trauma memories. This effect, like the antidepressant effect of ECT, would have been temporary, and may have created a backlash against psychiatry. I suspect that some of the most angry individuals in the antipsychiatry movement are people with undiagnosed MPD who have been mistreated with huge doses of incorrect medications, ECT, and institutional sexual abuse.

In Canada, I occasionally received newsletters written by people who described themselves as ex-inmates of the psychiatric system. I used to think these people were delusional and hysterical, until I began to hear histories like Monica's. Monica might have received less abuse, and have survived with less organic memory impairment if she had been an ex-inmate of the criminal justice system, I think, rather than the psychiatric system. Although psychiatry has become much more humane over the last forty years, many of these old abuses persist in muted form: for instance, a variety of studies indicate that, in anonymous responses to mail-out surveys, 5 to 10 per cent of physicians, psychologists, and social workers admit to having had sex with their patients or clients, and I have seen numerous instances of grossly incompetent polypharmacy in active hospital charts in Winnipeg.

A final thought: I wonder how many trauma victims have been given lobotomies over the years.

19

Anne Sexton

Anne Sexton, a Pulitzer Prize–winning poet, was born in 1928 and committed suicide in 1974. I was only vaguely aware of her in late 1991 when her former psychiatrist, Dr Martin Orne, became the subject of an ethical controversy in the American Psychiatric Association because he had released audiotapes of therapy sessions to Sexton's biographer. He had done this with the family's permission, but the Ethics Committee of the American Psychiatric Association was concerned that his doing so might, nevertheless, be a violation of patient confidentiality. Apparently there was little or no content in the tapes that Sexton had not already made public through her poetry.

I decided to read Sexton's biography when I read a review of it in the December 1991 issue of the *American Journal of Psychiatry* written by Dr Donald K. Goodwin. Goodwin writes: 'Over the next 18 years she had many diagnoses. She had suicidal depressions and mania, heard voices (at least once), went into trances, had amnesia and phobias, was hypersexual, neglected her children and sexually abused one of them, and had battered wife syndrome – all at the same time. She overdosed repeatedly and was in and out of nearly every psychiatric hospital in the Boston area during the eight years that Orne saw her and the 10 years that followed. Her Axis I diagnosis was probably bipolar disorder. Axis II? Anybody's guess. There probably should be a separate category for poets.'

I realized, reading this paragraph, that Anne Sexton probably had undiagnosed MPD. Martin Orne is a leading figure in the hypnosis literature, editor of the *International Journal of Clinical and Experimental Hypnosis*, wrote papers prior to Sexton's death demonstrating that memories recovered during hypnosis can be true or false, and has always been interested in the potential of hypnosis to contaminate forensic cases. He was the first person to publish a paper of mine on MPD, which appeared in a special issue of his journal devoted to the disorder in 1984. I remember being very impressed by the intelligence and dedication of Orne's editing of my paper. I also recall being struck by his preoccupation with iatrogenesis in MPD: he was very concerned to emphasize this issue and ensure that I addressed it in my paper.

Much of the special issue was devoted to the Kenneth Bianci 'Hillside Strangler' case, in which Orne had been an expert witness. Orne testified that Bianci was faking MPD, and his persuasive testimony is reviewed in detail in a 1984 paper: Kenneth Bianci's insanity defence based on MPD failed, and he was found guilty. In 1988, Orne participated in a debate at the American Psychiatric Association Annual Meeting in which he took the position that MPD is rare, and that most cases diagnosed in the 1980s are iatrogenic artefacts created when a suggestible hysterical patient is asked leading questions by a naïve diagnostician.

One's position is that true MPD is rare and that false-positive iatrogenic diagnoses are harmful, cause regression, and should be discouraged by not feeding into the patient's role-playing. He is preoccupied with the idea that a diagnosis of MPD results in the patient not being held accountable for his or her behaviour.

If Anne Sexton had undiagnosed MPD, I realized, and committed suicide because of the failure to diagnose and treat her condition properly, and if Martin Orne was at some level aware of this, then his public position on MPD could be primarily defensive in nature and not truly an intellectual or scientific stance. I decided to read the biography specifically to see if I could find enough information to support a diagnosis of MPD. I expected to find, at best, scattered circumstantial evidence to support a diagnosis of MPD and was therefore unsure whether anything publishable would come of my reading. I established two competing hypotheses before starting the biography: the first was Orne's – namely, that it is important and therapeutic to discourage any tendency towards MPD in hysterics like Anne Sexton, who don't really have the condition. The second hypothesis was that Anne Sexton had true MPD and might have had a dramatically superior outcome if her alter personalities were brought into the therapy and her trauma uncovered and worked through.

I soon found circumstantial evidence supporting my clinicial intuition. On the first page of the Foreword, Dr Orne writes (p. xiii): 'It is difficult to communicate fully how pervasive Anne's profound lack of self-worth was and how totally unable she was to think of *any* positive abilities or qualities within herself. When I pressed her to think hard about what she might be able to do, she finally revealed that there was only one thing that she might possibly be capable of doing well – to be a good prostitute and to help men feel sexually powerful.'

This statement raises the possibility of childhood sexual abuse. Both the feeling of being a prostitute and the lack of self-worth are typical of victims of severe chronic childhood trauma. On the next page, we see that Anne Sexton presented a clinical picture inconsistent with the working diagnosis, another feature common in patients with undiagnosed MPD. Orne writes (p. xiv): 'Originally, when Anne sought help following the birth of her second child, she had been diagnosed as having postpartum depression. When I first saw her in therapy in the hospital in August 1956, a year after the birth, her thoughts and behaviors were not really consistent with the presumptive diagnosis. As I began to get to know Anne, I realized that she was showing ideation that one might expect in a patient with a thought disorder.'

Later (p. 65), the different diagnoses Sexton received, again typical of undiagnosed MPD, are listed as ' "hysteric," "psychoneurotic," "borderline," and "alcoholic".' It is evident from other passages that the inability of psychiatrists to make a clinically meaningful diagnosis led to many complications. In her Preface, Diane Wood Middlebrook, the biographer, writes (p. xix): 'She conducted this career in the context of a mental disorder that eluded diagnosis or cure. Suicidal self-hatred led to repeated hospitalizations in mental institutions. She became addicted to alcohol and sleeping pills. By the time she committed suicide in 1974, misery had hollowed her out and drinking had obliterated her creativity.'

Martin Orne treated Anne Sexton for eight years, from 1956 to 1964, while he was in Boston, and transferred her to another therapist when he moved to Philadelphia, where he is currently at the Institute of the Pennsylvania Hospital. The reason Orne began audiotaping Anne Sexton's sessions was that she was unable to remember them. He had Anne listen to the tapes to try to recover memory of what happened during treatment. Orne's diagnosis is made in the Foreword (p. xv): 'As we continued to work together, it became increasingly evident that in addition to her tendency to absorb symptoms and mannerisms from those who impressed her, Anne's core problem was that she suffered from a severe difficulty of memory. While to some extent each of us is selective in what we remember, Anne's selectivity was extreme in the sense that she literally remembered almost nothing of relevance from one session to the next. In short, for this and other reasons, it was clear that she had a condition that traditionally was known as hysteria.'

This description by Martin Orne establishes that Anne had a complex, chronic dissociative disorder, since she experienced recurrent episodes of psychologically caused amnesia. This clinical information alone would warrant an aggressive diagnostic workup for MPD at any contemporary dissociative-disorders clinic. Orne describes other dissociative symptoms later in the Foreword (p. xvii): 'There is one aspect of Anne's life that has not been clarified, that is, her tendency to become uncommunicative in a self-induced trance, which could last minutes, hours, or, in a few rare circumstances, even days. Typically, the trance episode could easily be ended by a therapist familiar with the symptom. But in therapy and out, the problem persisted: when Anne was extremely angry, she was given to entering a trance and becoming unresponsive. Treatment helped to decrease these events, but they were never eliminated. Anne also had a remarkable fascination with death, and it seemed likely that she used some of these trance episodes to play out the role of dying, which perhaps helped her not to suicide.'

Recurrent episodes of both trance and amnesia establish that Anne had either dissociative disorder not otherwise specified (DDNOS) or MPD. Research I have done with the Dissociative Disorders Interview Schedule and the Dissociative Experiences Scale involves comparing 166 cases of clinically diagnosed MPD with 57 cases of clinically diagnosed DDNOS: the finding is that DDNOS is a milder variant of MPD related to less severe but still significant childhood trauma. By the end of Orne's Foreword, it is clear that Anne Sexton was at least three-quarters of the way out the dissociative spectrum, to MPD.

Orne's hypothesis is that Anne Sexton role-played dying in order to avoid actually killing herself. An alternative hypothesis is that the trance was an autohypnotic protective withdrawal designed to shut down murderous rage, rage that was directed towards her children, and finally towards herself in completed suicide. We will see extensive evidence in favour of the second hypothesis below.

It is common for adult women in treatment for MPD to describe evidence of MPD in one or both parents, which can include clear descriptions of switching and names of parental alter personalities. I kept an eye out for such descriptions of Anne's parents and found the following about her father (p. 14): 'Forgiveness came very hard to Anne. She retained distressing memories of her father's drinking binges, partly because in childhood she didn't recognize them. "He would just suddenly become very mean, as if he hated the world," she later told her psychiatrist. "He would sit and look at you as though you had committed some terrible crime. He hated everyone! Mostly I remember the expression on his face." It seemed that he singled her out for verbal abuse when he was drinking, complaining that her acne disgusted him and that he could not eat at the same table with her. She felt invaded by his expressions of revulsion,, and it seemed that no one tried to shield her from these attacks.'

This is a typical description of switching in an alcoholic father with undiagnosed MPD, but it is not conclusive for the diagnosis. Amnesia and abrupt changes of behaviour are usually written off as produced by the alcohol in men with serious alcohol-abuse problems, when often the alcohol is actually triggering the emergence of abusive alter personalities. In such men, a careful psychiatric history will reveal periods of recurrent amnesia going back into childhood, 'alcohol blackouts' when the person has not been drinking, and abrupt emergence of violent behaviour during periods of sobriety, accompanied by a history of serious abuse in childhood, auditory hallucinations starting before the alcohol consumption, and other classical features of MPD. One can suspect, but not conclude, that Anne's father had MPD. Could it be that she felt 'invaded' by incestuous rape, not just by verbal abuse, and that this was the 'terrible crime' her father expressed in his face and projected onto her when he looked at her? If true, this would be the typical blame-the-victim psychology of an incestuous paedophile. These were my thoughts as I read the paragraph about Anne's father, not expecting to find more conclusive evidence of paternal incest. The passage establishes serious emotional abuse of Anne by her father.

What about Anne Sexton's mother? She was also an abuser, as documented in discussion of psychosomatic symptoms in Anne arising directly from the abuse (pp. 14–15):

Arthur Gray Staples [Anne's maternal grandfather] died in April 1940, and during the following summer Anne was hospitalized at the Lahey Clinic for severe constipation.

Anne later recalled this as a very traumatic period in her life, remembering her mother routinely inspecting her bowel movements and threatening her with a colostomy if she didn't co-operate with efforts to regulate her elimination.

Anne's mother also abused her sexually (p. 59):

Sexton was to raise the question of whether she was 'normal,' by which she meant heterosexual, early in her psychiatric treatment, and later to explore it in the context of sexual intimacy with women. Behind that question were other memories that troubled her self-esteem, focused on genital inspections by her mother. From the earliest period of toilet training, she had to report to her mother daily and show her the stool before flushing it away. This was a common child-rearing practice at the time. But Sexton also recalled another humiliating experience, from about her fourth year: her mother laying her down on the bathroom floor, pulling her legs apart, and inspecting her vulva, 'looking at me and saying how we had to keep it clean and mustn't touch – there was something she looked at and it was growing, and I know – I don't remember, I know – I had a little cyst – they had to operate and take it off.' As Dr. Orne commented, 'In many ways, her mother [and not her father] was the dangerous relationship.'

The point is, the veracity of the incest narrative cannot be established historically, but that does not mean that it didn't, in a profound and lasting sense, 'happen.' It is clear from many sources that Sexton's physical boundaries were repeatedly trespassed by the adults in her family in ways that disturbed her emotional life from girlhood onward. As she put it, 'I have frozen that scene in time, made everyone stop moving. I thought I could stop all this from happening. That's what I want to believe – when I'm in that hard place – that's not what I believe now, just when I'm that child in trance. I can't grow up because then all these other things will happen. I want to turn around and start everything going backward.'

This is not conclusive evidence but is suggestive of the existence of a child alter personality stuck in the past at the time of the trauma, and constantly reliving the trauma internally. If such a child existed, it might have been contacted and healed in an active MPD psychotherapy. Is there any direct evidence of the existence of alter personalities in the biography?

The subsequent quotations, in my mind, conclusively establish the diagnosis of MPD. The first of them, though, is merely suggestive. The way in which I built up the diagnosis of MPD in reading Anne Sexton's biography is much the same as the way I build it up during a diagnostic assessment in the clinic: I look for suggestive evidence and indirect clues, then keep them in mind as I pursue the history, waiting to see how they link up with other details and whether they lead to a definite diagnosis.

With that intention, I read a brief description of Anne's nanny, Nana, who was a maternal great aunt, during a period when Nana was in an apparent delirium (p. 16). I thought the passage might be evidence of Nana's being aware of the existence of alter personalities in Anne: 'Anne, visiting her in her room, would often find her distracted and uncomprehending: "You're not Anne!" Nana would cry out. Anne remembered Nana calling her "horrible and disgusting" and once attacking her with a nail file. One night, before Anne's horrified eyes, Nana was carried off to a mental hospital. Electroshock therapy seemed to improve her condition, and she returned home. "She wasn't like someone mad, she was suffering," Anne remembered.'

As I made note of this passage as a clue to MPD in Anne, I thought to myself that I was stretching things. Nevertheless, I considered the possibility that Nana's 'delirium' was really a dissociative state, and that she and Anne had seen something about each other that the doctors had missed. Could Nana, too, have had MPD? It is stated several times in the biography that Nana indulged in extended back rubs, hugging, caressing, and other sexualized behaviour with Anne: could there have been more? Could Anne Sexton have been sexually abused by her father, her mother, *and* her great aunt? If this was truly a multi-generational incest family, such abuse would be possible, and it would be possible that many members of the family had dissociative disorders.

On page 16, there is a further description of Nana's possible perception of Anne's MPD and an unequivocal description of an internal auditory hallucination. I suspect that this was the voice of a persecutory alter personality who eventually forced Anne to complete suicide. The passage also describes the extreme self-blame characteristic of incest survivors. Additionally, Anne's idealization of Nana suggests the possibility of terrible historical facts being covered up by the idealization: 'After Anne Sexton's own breakdown, she worried about ending up in a mental institution like Nana. More important, she believed that she had personally caused her great-aunt's breakdown, and that Nana, who condemned her as "not Anne" but a "horrible and disgusting" impostor, had sentenced her to break down as well. Nana's rage took root in Sexton as a frightening symptom, which she described as a "tiny voice" in her head "shouting from far away," telling her she was awful, often taunting her to kill herself. "[I] should never have left Nana. She'd never have gotten sick – then I'd always be just me."'

One of the indirect clues to MPD is the passivity experiences described by the German psychiatrist Kurt Schneider but mistakenly thought by him to be symptoms specific for schizophrenia. These experiences are also called 'made' actions, thoughts, and feelings and involve the experience that one's actions, feelings, or thoughts are not one's own; that one is not the agent of one's own behaviour but is, instead, controlled by some outside power or force. In MPD, these experiences result from the intrusion of unrecognized alter personalities into one's actions, thoughts, or feelings. Such experiences are suggestive of, but not conclusive for, the diagnosis of MPD. A description similar to Schneiderian passivity, but lacking the explicit identification of an outside force driving the behaviour, is given in Anne's own words as she talks about her husband, Kayo (pp. 26–7): '"When he's gone I want to be with someone, I want lights and music and talk. When I say running I don't mean running from something, but something I express by action – people, people, talk, talk, wanting to stay up all night, no way to stop it. I don't really *want* to have an affair with anyone, but I have to; it's the quality of action. I first had this feeling, I suppose, when I was dating, after Kayo went into the service.

Pound, pound, pound heart: makes me feel crazy, out of control."'

My hypothesis about Anne Sexton having MPD was strengthened when I read a description of her (p. 30). This is a diagnostic clue overlooked by Dr Orne, the *American Journal of Psychiatry* reviewer who made a diagnosis of manic-depressive illness, and the biographer: 'Her closest neighbor, Sandy Robart, recalled that "Anne always dropped ten years or more in her mother's presence. She was overwhelmed – she was awed. I think it was probably an attempt to please. I can see her standing at the phone in the kitchen, talking to her mother, and feeling that Anne had turned into a little girl."'

This is a naturalistic observation of a switch to a child personality outside therapy by someone who never considered the possibility of MPD and is evidence of switching of executive control outside therapy. It will seem to the sceptical reader that I am concluding too much from too little at this point, and seeing MPD everywhere, but the conclusive evidence to follow will confirm my contention.

Anne had many psychosomatic symptoms besides constipation, including 'intense pains in her stomach, for which her internist found no physiological basis. She became prone to attacks of anxiety that left her panting and sweating,' (pp. 32). She also experienced Schneiderian rage attacks (p. 32–3): 'Increasingly, Sexton became prone to episodes of blinding rage in which she would seize [her daughter] Linda and begin choking or slapping her. In later life she recalled with great shame a day she found Linda stuffing her excrement into a toy truck and as punishment picked her up and threw her across the room. She felt she could not control these outbursts, and she began to be afraid she would kill her children.'

Dr Orne's thoughts on the case are introduced again at this point in the biography (p. 39):

Dr. Orne recalled that when he began treating Sexton, 'She was very, very sick, but like many interesting patients didn't fit textbook criteria. I did the diagnostic work on her when she was at

*the hospital, which indicated that she was hysteric in the classic
sense: like a chameleon, she could adopt any symptom. She
experienced profound dissociation, and she had lesions of memory. Some therapists were convinced that Anne was schizophrenic.
I don't doubt that hospitalized in a ward of schizophrenics, she
would exhibit their symptoms; that is why I discharged her as
soon as possible from Westwood Lodge, where there were schizophrenic patients in treatment. But I never saw evidence in her of
loose associations or formal thought disorders, or other major
symptoms of schizophrenia. She certainly had a depressive illness
for many years, which was never really resolved. One wonders
whether the new antidepressant drugs might not have successfully
treated the more serious aspects of her depression.'*

There are several things to comment on in this passage. First,
the statement that Anne never exhibited symptoms of schizophrenia contradicts Dr Orne's statement in the Foreword that,
at times, she had a thought disorder, and also contradicts the
evidence of auditory hallucinations and Schneiderian passivity
experiences in the biography. If these symptoms were dismissed as chameleon-like hysteria (assuming they were ever
observed by Dr Orne), why is it that the 'depression' is thought
to be genuine? And why did other therapists think Anne Sexton was schizophrenic if she never exhibited Schneiderian
symptoms?

Anne Sexton's symptom profile from the biography, including the diagnostic confusion with schizophrenia, is classical for
MPD, and fits the description in MPD textbooks perfectly. If the
newer antidepressants might have treated the 'more serious
aspects of her depression,' this would presumably include her
suicide: an implication of this position is that Dr Orne could
not be faulted for his patient's suicide because it was biologically driven and the necessary biological treatments would not
come on the market for more than twenty years.

The biographer echoes this viewpoint (p. 37): 'At the outset
of Sexton's treatment, Dr. Brunner-Orne had noted the possibility that her difficulties derived from a postpartum depression;

later notes, however, convey doubts that she had a "true" organically based depression. Yet anecdotal evidence of break-downs on both sides of her family suggests a genetic predisposi-tion to a biologically based illness, a supposition reinforced by Sexton's extreme physiological symptoms: wildly alternating moods, anorexia, insomnia, waves of suicidal and other impulses, rages, rapid heartbeat. It is possible that biochemical imbalances throughout her life intensified the underlying psy-chological vulnerabilities that were the primary focus of her psychotherapy.'

This hypothesis about mental illness is omnipresent in con-temporary psychiatry. According to this biological hypothesis, no one is to blame for Anne Sexton's suicide except her bad genes. The other people in her life, including her mother, father, great aunt, and doctors, are not at fault because biologi-cal psychiatry had not yet advanced to the point at which serotonergic antidepressants were available; therefore, her bio-logically based illness was beyond cure. In this reductionist model, Anne Sexton's suicide was as biologically based as cancer.

The biomedical of mental illness may have facilitated wealthy families in institutionalizing their relatives in genteel, expensive, psychoanalytically oriented mental hospitals, where the 'schizophrenic' family members could wander the grounds and receive 'humane' but ineffective psychoanalysis. How many of these 'schizophrenics' had undiagnosed MPD and were hidden away from public view by multi-generational incest families?

Who is Dr Brunner-Orne, you might have asked? Dr Brunner-Orne is Martin Orne's mother. He first saw Anne Sexton while he was covering for his mother while she was away on holiday. Anne was originally referred to Dr Brunner-Orne because she had treated his father for alcoholism. Dr Brunner-Orne's notes are quoted (p. 26) as stating that Anne had 'difficulty control-ling her desire for romance and adventure,' suggesting that Dr Brunner-Orne also missed the post-traumatic nature of Anne Sexton's acting out.

Feeling that the case for a diagnosis of MPD was still inconclusive at this point, I read the following (pp. 54–6):

Throughout the period of treatment annotated by Dr. Orne, Sexton referred casually and knowledgeably to concepts such as transference, resistance, defense, regression, acting out – all in the course of providing the doctor with 'memories' that sound suspiciously like updated versions of Freud and Breuer's Studies on Hysteria. *It seems likely that by 1958 Sexton had read the case history of the first hysteric in psychoanalytic literature and had found another namesake in the famous patient Freud and Breuer called Anna O. Moreover, Orne and Sexton were both taking notes on her case, he in longhand, she in poetry. As she was to tell him rather grandly later on, 'Therapy is a minor art, Dr. Orne!'*

For whatever reason, a particularly dramatic development in her own case was the emergence during the summer and fall of 1957 of a flamboyantly naughty role she liked to play, called Elizabeth, and of a memory or fantasy, narrated in trance, about an incestuous experience with her father.

Early in Sexton's therapy, the Elizabeth persona began making appearances while Sexton was in trance by scrawling messages in childlike handwriting across pages torn from a lined notebook. Sexton told Dr. Orne how she had chosen the name. Leaving his office after an episode of automatic writing, she had become very despairing. She had walked for a long time, thinking about suicide and trying to forget herself, and she had begun to be afraid that someone would notice her and ask her name. 'Looked (for some reason) at the back of my watch [inherited from Elizabeth Harvey, her father's mother] and the initials E.H. were on it. So I thought, "I must be E.H." [...] To [my] truthful knowledge I had never been "Elizabeth" before.'

By September, she was typing letters which she left unsigned, though 'Elizabeth' appeared in the return address on the envelopes. Somewhat comically, the writer claimed that she had to type her introductory letter in the dark so Anne wouldn't read it. 'Help me somehow,' Elizabeth urges Dr. Orne. 'There must be something you can do about this except sit there like a blinking toad.' Anne would be more cooperative 'if she were less afraid of what you thought. [...] I'm the one who'll talk.' Elizabeth explains that formerly, Anne 'thought of me as a brother that died – she used to think about him all the time – there wasn't really any brother – but she liked to pretend about him – I'm not so different from her but I would tell you what she doesn't dare think – She acts her life away. [...] I am part of her sometimes but she is not part of me. [...] Nana knew I was not Anne.'

Elizabeth wanted Dr. Orne to put Anne under hypnosis during therapy, so that she, Elizabeth, could speak openly: 'If you give her time to get dissociated enough she will be willing ... I know a lot,' she promised. When Dr. Orne wouldn't agree to hypnotize his patient, both Anne and Elizabeth began appealing for a session under sodium pentothal. Together 'they' laboriously typed a letter, one line superimposed on another: 'Only sometimes do I lie,' says one; 'it's me that wants pentothal,' says another.

At several points in her therapy, Sexton made an association, while in trance, between the name Elizabeth and 'a little bitch,' the angry words her father once used when he was drunk and spanked her for some naughtiness. She also associated this phrase with a night, recalled several times in trance at widely spaced intervals, when her father came into her bedroom and fondled her sexually.

In this passage, the child alter personality, Elizabeth, who holds paternal-incest memories, is asking to come into therapy and disclose the trauma, and the adult host personality is co-conscious and agreeing to the request. If this is correct, then the proper response would be to work actively with Elizabeth in therapy. How do the biographer and Dr Orne justify suppressing Elizabeth as a regressive role-play?

On page 57, the biographer devotes several paragraphs to doubting the reality of the sexual abuse, pointing out that Anne was reading about incest at the time she was making the disclosures, and adducing the family's denial as evidence in

favour of the memories not being real. What about Dr Orne?
On pages 60–1, we read:

*Her 'Elizabeth' characteristics attracted approval, even though it
was approval she didn't wholly respect; and she had now been
able to associate these with the poetry class.*

*But Sexton's desire to give these characteristics a name and a
personality signalled what Dr. Orne regarded as a dangerous tendency. Discussing Elizabeth later, he commented that after a brief
initial interest in this manifestation, he observed that Sexton was
perilously close to developing multiple personality disorder, so he
disengaged himself from acknowledging Elizabeth as a person distinct from Anne. 'It was helpful to let her play out the fantasy of
Elizabeth, to develop aspects of herself that had been held in
check. Let me emphasize that this was a fantasy: Anne did not
have multiple personality disorder, though she could have been
encouraged in that direction,' he said. 'Once my interest dropped,
so did hers, and no doctor ever saw Elizabeth again.' As therapy
went on, Dr. Orne stressed the positive sides that Sexton
expressed through this persona: her charismatic leadership, her
sense of fun, her capacity for pleasure, her self-confidence.
' "Elizabeth" expresses a side of your childhood which showed
some assets you never really owned,' Dr. Orne told her. 'The
"magic" you, "Elizabeth," is the one who involves people. But you
don't view it as you.' The focus of therapy as it pertained to Elizabeth was an effort to help Sexton recognize and tolerate the feelings she wanted to split off and act out.*

Dr Orne's hypothesis is that 'Elizabeth' was a fantasy role-
play that had to be suppressed before it got out of control.
'Elizabeth' was a playful way of expressing aspects of Anne's
character she wanted to disown and act out. It was good therapy, according to Dr Orne, not to feed into this escape from
reality.

My understanding of the case is that Elizabeth was not a role
for expressing pleasant abilities and feelings but an alter per-

sonality who held abuse memories. The focus of Martin Orne's therapy was to suppress the information about the trauma and the feelings that went along with it, and his diagnosis was an example of reverse iatrogenesis: he suppressed Anne Sexton's MPD and her alter personalities by demand characteristics, therapist attitude, and direct instruction. The therapy reinforced pathological dissociation and at the same time invalidated the seriousness and efficacy of the patient's dissociative defence. Elizabeth was told she was unreal and that the doctor didn't want to talk to her anymore. It is remarkable how confident biographer and psychiatrist are about the correctness of their hypothesis, given the fact that Anne Sexton killed herself.

Why did Dr Orne decide to suppress the 'Elizabeth' role while encouraging the poet role? How did he decide that the poet persona was more real or healthy than the child one? The answer to this might seem self-evident – namely, that 'Poet' was a functional adult role which brought meaning to Anne Sexton's life and a respected position in the adult world.

Unfortunately, this is not the psychological reality of Anne Sexton's life. The poet persona was, in fact, an artefact of therapy: the poet alter personality was deliberately fostered and encouraged by Martin Orne at the expense of the other alter personalities in the system, including Mrs A.M. Sexton, the mother and wife; Elizabeth; the angry voice that instructed suicide; the promiscuous personality; and any other personalities not described in the biography. Anne Sexton the poet was stimulated by the therapy to a level of malignant hypertrophy, resulting in exacerbation of the neglect and abuse of Anne's children, extensive frustration and suffering for her husband described in the biography, failure of her marriage, alcoholism, and eventual suicide.

The evidence in support of this contention begins with this passage (p. 61):

Writing put her into a state similar to a trance, making her dangerously inattentive to her children, she was aware. Being in an institution full-time, she thought, might ease the burden of guilt

*she felt about ignoring her family. 'Only time I am there is when
I am thinking about poetry or writing – shuffling between methods
of escape – liquor, pills, writing – I don't have anything else.'*

*Just as the act of writing took Sexton out of herself, into what
she felt was another identity, so the finished poem conveyed
meanings she had no consciousness of intending.*

The last sentence could apply to any writer, but in Anne
Sexton's case the phenomenon was the result of switching
between alter personalities who were partially or fully amnesic
for each other. The biographer's understanding of Anne Sexton
is that she transmuted her ability to concoct pseudo-memories
into art, developing a true and meaningful identity as a poet.
Actually Anne was socialized in her therapy to believe that her
trauma memories were not real and not worthy of serious
sustained psychotherapeutic exploration.

Two passages (pp. 62–3) convey the basic principles of the
therapy, the poetry career, and the biography:

*For the next month, spurred by distress over Dr. Orne's plans and
the increasing extravagance of what she now called 'truth crimes'
– 'lies' that she had been dealing with as 'memories' in trance –
Sexton typed about fifteen single-spaced pages of this personal
record. 'I do not understand why I must do these things – it
makes me lose sight of any true me,': this was her main theme. 'I
suspect that I have no self so I produce a different one for different people. I don't believe me, and I seem forced to constantly
establish long fake and various personalities.' She doubted even
the sincerity of her two suicide attempts; these were, she suggested, attention-getting acts. But her worst 'truth crime' was the
invention of Elizabeth. 'I made her up – I think I did. [...] Any
element of truth about her is just a certain freedom of expression,
a lack of sexual (I guess) repression. I could say "she feels" but
not, o never me.' Sexton also admitted having faked the 'total
amnesia' about Elizabeth she had been professing to Dr. Orne. 'I
would feel better, less guilty, if I thought Elizabeth were true – I
would rather have a double personality than be a total lie,'...*

Yet all that was 'sick' or 'hysterical' about her behavior in day-to-day life could be turned into something valuable through the act of writing poetry. Poetry too required a trancelike state for its disclosures. 'Only in that funny trance can I believe myself, or feel my feeling,' Sexton observed. If in therapy trance led to lying, at her typewriter it led to art. She could draw a simple equation: in trances she was a channel of lies; at her typewriter she was a channel of poetry. 'Think I am a poet? false – someone else writes – I am a person selling poetry.'

Anne Sexton's literary world failed her as well. The poets, editors, critics, and others in that milieu lacked the serious literary-critical standards, the serious ability to *read*, that should have made it evident – obvious, in fact – that the poetry is morbid, unhealthy, and extremely limited in range, rhythm, emotional depth, and energy. Anne Sexton's work is the poetry of a single alter personality and of an organism heading to suicide: it taps only a tiny subregion of the whole human being's memory, experience, thought, and feeling. The world might be more enriched if it had a volume of Elizabeth's writing to read.

The fact that Anne Sexton was only an alter personality, and that she represented an escape from the serious work of life and therapy, is supported by the following paragraph (p. 65):

This was a decisive change of identity, and she had firmly achieved it by the end of 1957, when she discontinued the practice of submitting her poems for publication under the name Mrs. A.M. Sexton and began signing them 'Anne Sexton.' Later she would comment, regarding her first book. 'By God, I don't think I'm the one who writes the poems! The don't center in my house – I can't write about Kayo, nothing – I was very careful about the picture on my book: didn't want it to look suburban, wanted just to be a face, a person whose life you couldn't define.' Renaming herself was a stage in her symbolic reconstitution: she annulled the 'Mrs.' that indicated her dependent relationship to a husband and stepped forth in a euphonious triad of syllables all her own.

Anne Sexton's renaming herself was not a stage in a symbolic reconstitution, it was a stage in a progression towards suicide. The malignant overtaking of Anne Sexton's lifespace by one alter personality, reinforced by her psychiatrist and her literary friends, was protested by her husband, who is made to look possessive and petulant in the biography. Elizabeth probably concluded that Dr Orne didn't want to talk to her because she was a bad girl, a confirmation of her guilt and self-hatred which would have been compounded by her doctor's leaving her to move to Philadelphia. Besides the costs borne by Anne Sexton herself, there was a heavy price paid by the family, as described below (p. 73):

On a typical day, as she described it, she would 'take half an hour to clean the house,' then rush to the typewriter, not moving until Linda came home from nursery school at lunchtime. 'Linda eats, then I put on a record or put her in front of television and go back to my desk. At moments I feel so guilty I read her a story ... I'm always willing to cuddle, but I won't bother to prepare food: there I sit.' Sexton realized she was being neglectful, but the pressure angered her too. 'If I didn't have [Linda] there to reflect my depression it wouldn't be so bad,' she told her psychiatrist. 'Any demand is too much when I'm like this. I want her to go away, and she knows it.' Nothing she was learning about herself in therapy seemed to help her function as a mother, and she struggled with shocking feelings of rage toward Linda. 'I've loved Joy, never loved Linda ... Something comes between me and Linda. I hate her, and slap her in the face – never for anything naughty; I just seem to be constantly harming her ... Wish I didn't have a mother-in-law at my every move. They act as if I were crazy or something when I get angry.' Sexton felt as though she were leading two lives, one in treatment and one in the midst of her family.

The therapy was reinforcing undiagnosed MPD rather than assisting Anne towards integration. Given the fact that, in the absence of effective treatment, incest tends to keep being transmitted from generation to generation in multi-generational incest families, one realizes that Anne Seston's children were at risk for sexual, emotional and physical abuse, and neglect. The following passage about Anne's daughter Linda is particularly poignant, given that Linda is now, in identification with her mother, a published novelist (pp. 324–5):

As Linda neared puberty, she had begun to dislike her mother's intrusiveness more than ever. For several years she had been pretending to be asleep when her mother got into bed with her and clung to her. But one night, when Linda was around fifteen, Anne had insisted that she come to the big bed and spend the night. Kayo was away on a trip, and Anne didn't want to be alone. They watched television for a while; then Linda fell asleep. In the middle of the night she woke, feeling that she couldn't breathe. It was dark, but she realized that her mother was lying astride her, rubbing against her and kissing her on the mouth. 'I felt suffocated. I remember pulling out of bed and throwing up. Mother followed me into the bathroom, and soothed my head.'

With that final quotation, the argument in favour of Anne Sexton having MPD is difficult to refute.

It has not been my purpose in this chapter to single out Martin Orne for attack, or to speculate about his reasons for making the audiotapes of his sessions with Anne Sexton public. Martin Orne has had the courage to state his opinions in public and to make his therapy available for public scrutiny. As it was not an expected standard of psychiatric practice to be able to diagnose MPD in the 1950s and 1960s, Martin Orne cannot be charged with diagnostic incompetence or failure to practise to reasonable standards. In fact, he is much more receptive to the diagnosis of MPD than many psychiatrists.

We should try to learn from Martin Orne's mistakes so that they can be avoided in the future.

I suspect that many potentially treatable people with undiagnosed MPD have committed suicide. For instance, although I have no evidence to support such a diagnosis, Sylvia Plath, a poet Anne Sexton knew, also wrote morbidly about sex and death, and might have had a dissociative disorder. Sylvia Plath committed suicide, as did Virginia Woolf, a victim of childhood sexual abuse whose writings could be reviewed for evidence of a dissociative disorder.

The main point of this chapter is to present a compelling argument for the iatrogenic complications of failing to diagnose MPD. Anna O also had MPD. Her diagnosis can be supported convincingly by quotation from Breuer and Freud's case history in *Studies on Hysteria*, as I did in my book *Multiple Personality Disorder: Diagnosis, Clinical Features, and Treatment.* Anna O, whose real name was Bertha Pappenheim, decompensated when forced to nurse her dying father, who may have sexually abused her; however, there is no mention of childhood sexual abuse in the case history. Anna O achieved a healthier adjustment than Anne Sexton. She became a social worker and ran a home for teenage prostitutes and unwed mothers, most of whom were probably sexual-abuse victims. Anna O was able to undo in her professional life some of the long-term consequences of the paternal incest she probably experienced in her own childhood. Bertha Pappenheim's diagnosis of MPD is certain, but her incest history is speculative; for Anne Sexton, both are certain.

Part Two

Case-Studies Related to Multiple Personality Disorder

20

A Man Who Wandered

Pure cases of psychogenic fugue are relatively rare, so rare, in fact, that I have encountered more of them in newspapers and on television than in my clinical practice. Psychogenic fugue involves sudden travel away from one's usual place of work and residence to another location, combined with amnesia for one's previous life. In fugue, there is also either identity confusion, assumption of a partial new identity, or even creation of a full new identity. In civilian populations, fugue often seems to occur as an escape from general life stresses rather than as a reaction to a specific intense trauma, and it does not seem to be related to child abuse in the way MPD is, although people with MPD often experience fugues as part of their disorder.

Cases of fugue were reported in the nineteenth century, the most famous of which was that of Ansel Bourne, a man who left his hometown and lived under another identity for a period of years, during which time he was amnesic for his prior life. An undiagnosed MPD patient may be described as having a 'fugue episode' or a 'dissociative reaction' by clinicians who do not consider MPD a likely possibility, but since MPD is actually more common than fugue, one has to wonder how many cases of fugue reported in the media are actually undiagnosed cases of MPD.

Ernie had already recovered from his fugue when I saw him in consultation upon his return to Dallas. He was referred to me by a colleague in Houston who had attempted to treat him in hospital. Ernie was in his mid-fifties, and was definitely a Texan, with his cowboys boots, jeans, and good-ol'-boy mannerisms. I liked him immediately.

Things had been going more or less normally in Ernie's life until he left to go to the bank one morning, about six weeks earlier. His wife did not see him again for five weeks. Ernie came to the attention of medical authorities when he was found dishevelled, disoriented, and recently beaten up in a public washroom, and was taken to an emergency department, where he was admitted as a John Doe. He didn't know who he was, or anything about his past life, and didn't know how he had gotten beat up, or ended up in the washroom.

Ernie was thoroughly checked over for stroke, dementia, and other possible organic causes of his problem, then admitted to the psychiatric ward, where he stayed for three weeks before finally being identified. During this period, he was treated with hypnosis in an attempt to recover his memories, and gradually started to remember his past life. The only problem was that the life he was remembering was entirely fabricated, or confabulated, in medical terminology.

The hospital notes describe how John D was starting to remember things, and how his past was starting to get pieced together. He had grown up in El Paso, but was very vague about the details of his life. Little real progress was made for three weeks, until, by chance, a temporary nurse assigned to the psychiatry ward for evening shift recognized John D as a man who had lived in her Dallas neighbourhood fifteen years earlier.

As soon as she saw him, the nurse exclaimed, 'Ernie! Hi!'

Ernie reacted initially with confusion, but when the nurse sat down with him, and reviewed details of his life she knew, such as his wife's name and his prior address, the memories of his actual life started to come back quite quickly. When his wife was located, and contacted by telephone, she spoke directly with him, and the amnesia then cleared rapidly.

Following the typical pattern for fugue, Ernie's amnesia for his real life lifted simultaneously with the onset of amnesia for the period of the fugue. Now he could remember nothing from the time of leaving to go to the bank up until the time of the conversation with the nurse. Since nothing important seemed to have happened during the fugue, the three-week amnesia did not require treatment in and of itself.

I asked Ernie if he had been under any stress prior to the fugue, and he described not-too-severe financial problems, and considerable tension in his relationship with his in-laws. He felt that they were interfering, controlling, and hostile to him. His level of stress did not seem to be particularly high, or even higher than average for contemporary urban existence. He had taken a few hundred dollars out of the bank at the onset of the fugue, but had not used any charge cards prior to being assaulted and having his wallet stolen in Houston.

The purpose of the fugue was not really clear, other than to get away temporarily from some general stress. His wife accepted him back readily and was not concerned about his leaving again in the near future. After providing him some general education about psychogenic fugue, I decided to get some information about Ernie's childhood, to see if childhood events shed any light on his psychology. My questioning led to an unexpected conclusion.

It turned out that Ernie had arrived in Dallas in the early 1960s, but was amnesic for his life from late adolescence until arriving in Dallas. He had somewhat foggy recollections of his childhood in Tyler, Texas, but was able to give me considerable detail. For instance, he gave me the full names, birthdates, and dates of death of both parents, and described the prolonged nursing of his mother he had had to do prior to her death in his mid-teens. There was about a ten-year amnesic period, from shortly after the death of his mother until his arrival in Dallas.

He also told me another curious fact: Ernie could not get a social security number because he could not establish his identity. There was no record of the birth of an Ernie X in Tyler, nor were there records of the births or deaths of either of his parents. A contact in Tyler verified the absence of this documentation for me, so I knew it was not just another memory distortion: there really was no record of the parents Ernie remembered growing up with in Tyler.

During the period of his fugue, Ernie identified himself first as Joe, then elaborated on this to create an identity of Joe Williams from El Paso. Once out of the fugue, he identified his father as Edward X: it turned out that the mayor of El Paso during the period Ernie would have been a child was named Edward Williams (I have changed all the names to protect Ernie's identity). Somehow he was piecing together bits of information that, if properly sorted out, might lead to his true identity.

Ernie had had his fingerprints run through the FBI computer to see if he could be identified that way, without any luck. I began to suspect that Ernie was not Ernie, and that 'Ernie' was a fugue identity created in the early 1960s. When he went to Houston in a fugue and became Joe Williams for three weeks, he had experienced an acute fugue superimposed on a chronic fugue, something I had never heard of before.

Ernie described numerous concussions he received as a child, including an accident in which he was going down a steep hill on his bike at high speed when he ran into a brick wall, and went into the brick head-first over of his handlebars. Since this childhood could have been entirely confabulated, I had no way of guessing whether his memory and identity problems might have had something to do with repeated concussions, possible brain contusions, and organic brain damage.

Then Ernie revealed another perplexing detail: he said that he had searched unsuccessfully through all the major city telephone books in the United States, attempting to find someone with the same last name.

With a wry look, Ernie bent over towards me and whispered, 'Doc, do you know what X means?' I suddenly realized that Ernie's last name was an obscure slang term for vagina. It appeared that, in the early 1960s, this man had entered a fugue state and renamed himself Ernie Vagina! He had been in this fugue continuously for thirty years, until he superimposed a second fugue on top of the primary fugue. As soon as I realized this, I understood that there was no way of knowing whether Ernie Vagina was the first, second, third, or fourth fugue identity this man had created.

Ernie did not want to dig into his past any further, and declined treatment or follow-up. I saw him twice, and do not expect to see him again. He was talking about moving back to Tyler to get away from his Dallasite in-laws, and his wife was agreeable to this. His wife, who sat in on the sessions, said that she had always known him as Ernie X, and that this name and identity were good enough for her. She, too, was content to leave the past alone, which could contain previous wives, children, and debts.

I wondered about the relationship between this form of fugue and MPD, and where the original identity and its memory traces were. I assumed that Ernie was, in effect, an alter personality who had been created in young adulthood, and that the prior host personality still existed in some kind of internal suspended animation and could potentially be reawakened with sodium amytal, hypnosis, or psychotherapy. I wondered what early trauma motivated this man to become Ernie Vagina, but I decided to leave well enough alone. Perhaps if he ever disappears permanently, I will hear from his wife.

21

A Bump on the Head

I got involved with John in 1986 when I was consulted by his
in-patient psychiatrist. The reason for the consultation was a
request for hypnosis: John thought that the answer to his problems was buried somewhere in his mind, out of his reach, and
that it could be found if he was put in a trance state. The psychiatrist thought John was just looking for a 'magical' solution
to his problems, and wanted me to confirm this opinion and
not use hypnosis at all. The point of the consult was for the
'expert' to tell John that hypnosis was not the answer.

John told an interesting story. He was twenty-nine years old,
single, unemployed, very isolated socially, and going nowhere
in life. He had been admitted for suicidal impulses, but had not
done anything to harm himself, although he had taken two
overdoses five and seven years earlier. He had had no previous
contact with psychiatry, had never been in any form of therapy,
had never been abused as a child, did not have a drug or alcohol problem, and had never been in trouble with the law.

John said that he was fine until two years previously, when
he was in a car accident. He was not wearing a seatbelt, and hit
his head on the windshield. He arrived at the hospital in con-
vulsions, was in a coma for three days, and could not remember anything from just before the accident until three weeks
later. A CT scan of his head and an electroencephalogram done
not long before I met him were both normal. Extensive psychological testing revealed a normal level of intelligence, and no

signs of brain damage, or organic impairment resulting from
the head injury.

John claimed that something happened to him while he was
in coma that changed his life: he became chronically suicidal,
and could not shake this feeling. His parents, though, denied
that there was any observable change in his personality or
behaviour. What was it that happened? This is the question
John wanted me to answer using hypnosis. It was clear that he
was explaining long-standing problems as having been caused
by the accident.

Three different psychiatrists, including me, his in-patient
psychiatrist, and the psychiatrist who had been seeing him in
the out-patient department prior to admission, agreed on the
diagnosis: mixed personality disorder. Depending on who you
ask, or your point of view, this is not really a diagnosis. It is
really, I think, a piece of shorthand psychiatrists use to communicate with each other. Mixed personality disorder means
that the person has serious general problems in life that do not
fit any particular pattern. When that is the only diagnosis, it
implies that medications are unlikely to help.

In addition, there was a possibility of dysthymic disorder, a
chronic, mild-to-moderate depression that never reaches the
level of a full clinical depression. It is very hard, if not impossible, to tell if the dysthymia is separate from or a facet of the
mixed personality disorder. The main point about dysthymia
is that the depression, even though not full-blown, may
respond to antidepressant medication. When this happens,
some of the problems thought to be resulting from the 'personality disorder' may also improve significantly. When there is no
dysthymic disorder present, though, medication does not seem
to help. These rules of thumb are not firmly established, and
require more research, though there are studies to support
them.

As I was reviewing John's chart, I was surprised to find several sentences in the nursing notes which contained information not mentioned anywhere else in the records. According to
the nurse, John had described an entity named 'Slim,' who he

talked to inside his head, and who sometimes influenced his actions and his life. Slim was not commented on again in several weeks' worth of later notes. I was surprised by this because auditory hallucinations, if that's what John was having, would have changed his diagnosis to something else. What that something else might be, I was intrigued to try to find out.

When I met with John on the ward, he said that he was keen to try hypnosis right away, so I booked a second session for the next day, having completed my review of his history. He proved to be a good hypnotic subject, although he did not go into a deep trance with post-hypnotic amnesia. He did become much more relaxed and, as he sat in a reclining chair with his eyes closed, his face began to become much more expressive and full of emotion. This occurred in the context of what is called 'guided imagery,' a process by which the therapist walks the patient through an internal landscape or set of images.

John described a vivid internal landscape that he was able to move around in. He was out in the countryside somewhere, on a road with his motorcycle, when he came to a big wall in a field. He felt that there was something on the other side of the wall which he had to find out about, but he didn't know how to get over the wall. I asked him how high it was, and he said it was too high to see over, or climb over. I asked him to see if the wall came to an end anywhere, but he said it stretched off far into the distance in both directions.

The problem was how to get over the wall. I assumed that a dissociated aspect of John was on the other side of the wall, and I wanted to help him get in touch with it. I asked him to imagine that the wall was getting smaller and smaller, shrinking down to a size that he could easily climb over. Although he found it difficult to concentrate and believe that the wall could shrink down, after a few minutes it did, whereupon he climbed over it, and found himself in another part of the field.

As soon as John was over the wall, he began to cry, tears rolling down both cheeks, both eyes still closed. He had never been able to cry before. It was strong, full crying with much facial expressiveness and sobbing. He said that he was sad and in pain about how his life was going in general, and about the effect of the accident on him. As the crying spell came to a natural conclusion, John said he felt better, and was glad he had been able to experience the pain and tears, which he had not been able to feel previously.

After more conversation, I brought John out of his light hypnotic trance, and reviewed the session with him. He had full recall of being on the other side of the wall, and said it felt like connecting with another part of himself. Several times during the session, he had started to chuckle, and I asked him about this too, since the chuckling did not seem to be connected to the conversation. He said that it was Slim chuckling. He had felt Slim around somewhere, could tell he was close, but never actually saw him in the internal landscape.

I made an agreement with John to try to talk directly with Slim in the next session, then asked more about this poorly defined character. John said that Slim seemed to be middle aged, and that he had somehow entered his head during the period of coma. He was angry at Slim for a variety of poltergeist activities and 'tricks' he played on John. John was convinced that Slim repeatedly intervened in his life at a psychic level to cause trouble.

For instance, Slim often made tools, electrical appliances, and motors not work temporarily. He would sometimes make John drop wrenches while he was working on his car or bike, could make engines run backwards, and had made a toaster not work for a while. Slim's motivation for doing these things seemed to be twofold: he was mischievous by nature, but he also had a malevolent, interfering, destructive aspect. Slim was deliberately trying to make things hard for John, and prevent him from being successful in life. A number of times Slim had caused John to be clumsy or interfered with his ability to work, resulting in his losing jobs.

John didn't know where Slim came from, but felt he was clearly not a part of himself. Slim was like a guardian spirit, except that he was more troublemaker than guardian. With this information, I asked to talk to Slim during the next session, while John was again in a light trance, and reclining in the chair.

Just as John's face had changed dramatically when he started crying, so there was a definite change when Slim was talking. John was always serious in manner, without much spontaneous movement or facial expression, but when Slim was present, the face was wrinkled with grins, there was a lot of chuckling, and, if his eyes were open, there would have been an impish twinkle in them. Slim didn't like being pestered, though.

Slim thought that John's unhappiness and suicidal thoughts were funny. He wasn't the least bit concerned about an actual completed suicide, and didn't think that John would ever go that far. He wasn't interested in talking to me, and wouldn't divulge much information. In fact, he slid out of executive control repeatedly, and I had to call him back a number of times. To do so I would call out, 'Slim, Slim, are you there? I'm asking to talk to Slim. It's me, Dr Ross, calling for Slim. Slim, are you there?'

I sometimes had to repeat this quite a few times before the chuckling would start again, and I knew that Slim was present. When I asked Slim if he was involved in making John suicidal, he denied it, and when I asked him if there was anyone else there besides him and John, he denied that too, but seemed to be made very uncomfortable by the question. He answered scornfully, as if it the question was preposterous.

When John came out of trance, he again remembered everything clearly. He was amazed that I had been able to talk with Slim directly, but didn't think that Slim would likely come out to talk again. He was hopeful, though, that this way of working might help him with his problems. I agreed to see John again with the psychiatrist who would be following him after discharge, which occurred in a few more days.

Working with John in the Out-patient Department, it proved to be very difficult to get in touch with Slim. Using hypnosis and repeated calling of Slim, the most I could get was an occasional transient chuckle. John felt that Slim was not cooperating, that this was typical of his attitude, and asked if I had any

other ways of making Slim talk. I said that I couldn't force him
to talk, but that sodium amytal might help.

Over the next few months we did a number of sodium-
amytal interviews, which did help in making contact with
Slim. In one session, John was walking through an internal
landscape, looking for Slim, when he caught sight of him, and
was able to give a description of his physical appearance. Slim
was about four feet tall, middle aged, round-faced, and was bald
on top. At one point, as John was approaching him, Slim transformed himself into a statue, and stood cold and immobile,
while John pleaded with him to warm up and talk. John got
angry when Slim wouldn't do so.

During direct conversation with Slim, I got a different portrait. Slim described himself as probably being about twenty
years old. He said he didn't know where he came from, but he
expressed delight and pleasure about tormenting John, and
'messing things up' for him. He bragged about his psychic
powers. In one session, he admitted that he didn't want John
to kill himself, because if this happened Slim would also die.
He was very concerned that we were going to try to trick him,
or gain power over him, and he saw us as being on John's side.
By 'us,' I mean John's out-patient psychiatrist and myself. Slim
was a bit like John, in that he tended to cover up his fears and
insecurities with boasting, grandiosity, and bravado.

At this point another problem occurred. It was clear that
John was enjoying the high he was getting from the sodium
amytal. It was impossible to contact Slim directly without
sodium amytal, and John said he couldn't get better if we
couldn't work with Slim; therefore, if we didn't use sodium
amytal, we would be condemning him to further unhappiness.
After four or five sodium-amytal interviews over two or three
months, I simply had to tell John that that was all the barbiturate interviews I could do. I told him that his psychiatrist
would be continuing to try to make contact with Slim, but that
this might be a slow process. Slim might need a lot of time
before he could trust John's psychiatrist.

During this period John, decided that there must be another

part of himself that the suicidal feelings came from. He felt that the desire to die was imposed on him by another part of himself, and that if this imposition stopped, he would not feel like dying. He came to this conclusion because Slim did not seem to be causing the feelings directly, although he did things to frustrate John.

Much of the therapy provided by John's out-patient psychiatrist over the next two years focused on helping him to take ownership for his feelings, and see how they were connected to his difficulties in getting on track in life. Working directly with Slim did not prove to be helpful. It was never possible to establish a working relationship with Slim, or to get him to agree to a goal of integrating with John. The technical difficulty of contacting Slim made it hard to work with him, since it required repeated calling of his name, and he would stay present only for short periods. Just calling Slim's name over and over could waste a large part of a therapy session.

According to John's perception, this way of proceeding doomed the therapy: he couldn't get better if Slim wouldn't cooperate. He therefore devalued the out-patient psychiatrist as technically ineffective, and lamented the fact he could never get real help. Over the two years, he did make some progress, although there was no dramatic improvement. By the time the therapy came to an end, John was no longer plagued by constant suicidal feelings, he had taken a one-year course in a trade, and he felt better about himself. But he was still very isolated socially, didn't have any clear direction in life, and was not happy.

Like Slim, John used what are called *narcissistic defences.* To compensate for feeling like a failure, he concocted grandiose ideas about being an inventor of genius. Some of these convictions bordered on being delusional. He thought that he had invented an extremely efficient car engine that would put the oil companies out of business, for instance. By the end of the two years, John relied less on such tactics for boosting his self-esteem. Although Slim had not gone away, he did not actively interfere in John's life much anymore.

It was clear that Slim was a device John used to explain his failures and problems in life. The strategy of the therapy was, in part, to work with Slim directly, but since this wasn't possible, the plan became to support John in his efforts to perform more satisfactorily at whatever he chose to do. If he experienced success, John wouldn't need Slim as an explanation for his failures, because there wouldn't be so many failures. Slim could simply fade out, and both John and Slim could save face by not having to give up the myth of Slim the internal poltergeist.

This is the way things proceeded. A wide variety of different problems and difficulties in John's life were dealt with in the therapy, without definite resolution of any of them. The outpatient psychiatrist, who is a good psychotherapist, explored John's relationship with his parents and siblings, his sexual experiences, his lack of friends, and many different insecurities, and supported him in his efforts to live in a more satisfying fashion. The lack of clearcut progress was no reflection on the psychiatrist's skill, and I certainly wouldn't have expected to do any better myself. John took antidepressant medication during most of the two years, and this seemed to help improve his mood and reduce his suicidal thinking, though it was impossible to separate the effects of the medication from the effects of the psychotherapy.

John's case illustrates the difficulty of treating dissociative disorder not otherwise specified, compared with treating full MPD. 'Dissociative disorder not otherwise specified' is the diagnostic term for dissociative disorders that do not fit one of the classical patterns, and it includes partial and incomplete forms of MPD.

Therapy with someone who has full MPD, assuming that the patient can commit to the treatment, and do all the painful work, has structure, direction, and a plan. There are many specific tasks to do, and one can see progress being made, step by step, in a logical progression towards integration. In comparison, many psychotherapies seem to involve a good deal of aimless conversation: many therapies seem vague and directionless, and seem to go on indefinitely, without any clear goal.

As I said, John's therapy was a bit like this, not because the psychiatrist lacked skill, but because John's internal world didn't have the complex, detailed structure of MPD. Additionally, what structure did exist, was not workable. Slim just wouldn't come into the therapy. Nevertheless, I felt I learned something from working with Slim. Try as I might, I could not amplify Slim into a full MPD alter personality, though this is what sceptics say happens in all MPD cases, which are all artificially created illusions. By not cooperating in therapy, Slim taught me that I cannot create alter personalities very easily, even when I try to bring dissociated internal states out into full executive control of the body.

Also, John left me wondering about what did happen to him psychologically during this period of coma. Slim was built on a foundation of rationalization and denial, but maybe there was some neuropsychological truth to John's story. Maybe something really did happened as a result of the blow to John's head, resulting in the creation of Slim. We know that head injuries can result in subtle personality changes that persist for a long time. Why not subtle dissociations? I have no answer, but I hope that someone will do serious research on the dissociation caused by physical head trauma. If organic dissociation occurs with head injuries, and we can understand it, perhaps that will help us to work more effectively with people who have used psychogenic dissociation to cope with emotional trauma.

Perhaps there are other Slims on neurology and neurosurgery wards, and in rehabilitation hospitals, who could enter into conversation with their physicians.

22

Something Out of *The Exorcist*

When I first met Erica Simmons in the Emergency Department, she was an attractive, married woman in her early twenties, with two young boys, and diagnoses of schizoaffective disorder and borderline personality disorder. She was taking a tricyclic antidepressant and a phenothiazine antipsychotic medication, was actively suicidal, and wanted to be in hospital. When I offered her out-patient therapy three times a week on an ongoing basis, she was willing to go home, which she did.

In the therapy of this particular 'borderline,' Erica Simmons, I created a strategy for defining and neutralizing her pathological interpersonal behaviour patterns, which I called *cognitive loop analysis*. The logical structures of her self-defeating behaviours were diagrammed on paper, named, and discussed with her directly. Early in the course of her therapy, it became evident that her primary diagnosis was dissociative disorder not otherwise specified. I never did uncover the underlying trauma, partly because I treated her early in my residency, but nevertheless the treatment was highly successful, because it was based on a countertransference that differed radically from the usual hostile one towards borderlines.

When I changed psychotherapy supervisors several months after meeting Mrs Simmons, my new supervisor refused to supervise me on the case because, according to him, she was too sick, not suitable for psychotherapy, at too high risk for hospitalization, and not the kind of light neurotic case he wanted to supervise. When I told him that this would leave me unable to continue a treatment to which I had made a commitment and on which I had received prior supervision, he told me that was my problem, and to 'terminate' her.

The bringing to an end of a course of psychotherapy is called 'termination' in psychiatry, a phrase loaded with countertransference hostility. Rather than terminating Mrs Simmons, I arranged for another supervisor and treated Erica in the manner I describe below, while presenting a bland, normalized version of the therapy to my new, less hostile supervisor. My new supervisor would have told me to stop what I was doing also if I had described what was actually going on.

The core logical structures of 'borderline personality' exhibited by Erica were the *borderline paralytic loop* and the *borderline entrapment loop*. These are examples of a general class of psychic structures I call cognitive loops. The loops are inherent in all human encounters, but appear in pathological form in psychiatric patients. They function at once intrapsychically and interpersonally.

Analysis of the borderline loops is a form of transference analysis, since the loops are re-created in the doctor-patient interaction. This form of transference work led to rapid sustained improvement in function, personal relationships, and general adjustment. The rules of the Simmons's marital interactions gave Erica's dissociative symptomatology a function, and were explicitly defined and contrasted with the rules of the therapy. The marital rules were, in turn, formulated by me as a subset of Erica's extended-family rules. These rules will be presented below. Mostly, I treated the cognitive loops rather than working on the dissociative symptoms directly.

Mrs Simmons's presenting complaint in the Emergency Department was a complex set of disturbances of mood and perception. During the first pregnancy, three years earlier, she experienced a sudden outburst of anger during which she destroyed many things in her apartment. While in this angry state, she pursued a group of ill-defined 'presences,' which were 'sensed' and 'felt' in her apartment, but not directly observed visually. Since that time, she had had many similar outbursts, and the presences, which had come to be called 'her people,' had become a nearly constant feature in her life.

The people became most real when Mrs Simmons went down into her basement, which she did frequently when in a 'negative' mood, during which time she was fed up with everything, hated everything, and felt like she would like to leave the real world for good. Often by swarming around her, and exerting poorly defined control and power over her, the people could make it extremely difficult for Mrs Simmons to come upstairs.

The other disturbances of perception were also florid. On many occasions she had seen faces in the shadows involuntarily, but she could make such faces disappear by concentrating. Additionally, if she stared at someone too long, either the person would change into someone else, or the person's face would become distorted in a horrible way. Then Mrs Simmons found it difficult to look away.

The first such facial transformation occurred when Mr and Mrs Simmons were in Montreal on the second night of their honeymoon. In the middle of the night, the groom's face turned into that of his new father-in-law. In the middle of that night, the newlywed couple telephoned to the maternal parents-in-law in Winnipeg, and then decided to change their reservations to return to Winnipeg by jet in a few hours. However, Erica soon calmed down, and they finished their honeymoon as planned. This incident was the only sign of 'sickness' Erica could recall prior to her first pregnancy. Since she had become pregnant with her first child, Erica's husband had changed into either her father or her old boyfriend on many occasions, and once he spoke in the old boyfriend's voice. There had never been any olfactory hallucinations.

The mood disturbance began in the first pregnancy, and like the perceptual difficulties, waned between pregnancies, and became more prominent in the months prior to her admission. Erica spoke of having no feelings at all, of being empty inside, and of only 'going through the motions,' but, in contrast, she also complained of rapidly cycling moods.

Besides feelings of depersonalization and derealization, she had experienced both *déjà vu*, and *jamais vu*. Especially when in bad moods, she was preoccupied with thoughts of 'death and gore,' and fantasies of her children dying violently or of crib death. Sometimes she would check on them in their cribs, and if their hands were cold, not be sure if they were dead. She would then be unsure whether to call an ambulance, or to pick them up and hug them one last time before 'someone came to take them away.'

Erica also spoke of another, angry side of herself, which she referred to as 'she.' This 'she' could at times control Erica's thoughts, feelings, and actions; however, 'she' could not be more clearly defined. There was no history of alcohol or street-drug abuse, and there had been no surgery or major medical illness.

Erica's mother had told her that she had had a normal childhood, without any specific major trauma. Her developmental milestones were normal; she made friends easily, and performed satisfactorily at school. She was bottle fed, as were the other children. From the early weeks of life, though, she had always refused affection and hugging. Also, she was frequently found sleepwalking up till the age of fourteen. Until the age of sixteen, she voiced a desire to sleep with her father.

Mr Simmons had three sisters, ranging in age from thirty-four to forty-five, and his father had been a heavy-drinking alcoholic throughout Mr Simmons's life. The couple became engaged after a brief courtship, and married after a brief engagement.

When the marriage did not go well, Erica got pregnant in order to improve things. When that did not work, she got pregnant a second time, to see if the second child would make the marriage more satisfying. Her major complaints in the marriage were the absence of any real communication, the fact that her husband watched at least thirty hours a week of television, the phoniness of his friends, the sterility of suburban materialism, and their patterns of interaction, which were mapped out in psychotherapy.

The physical examination in the Emergency Department was

normal. Consultations with an endocrinologist and a neurologist during her prior psychiatric hospital admission did not yield anything other than a diagnosis of functional psychiatric disorder. All investigations, including thyroid studies and an EEG, were normal.

Erica's DSM-III diagnoses were Atypical Dissociative Disorder, called Dissociative Disorder Not Otherwise Specified in DSM-IV, and Borderline Personality Disorder, for which the following criteria were present: identity disturbance, affective instability, intolerance of being alone, devaluation/idealization, dissociative symptoms, angry outbursts, and chronic feelings of boredom and emptiness. An organic brain syndrome, resulting from either metabolic or focal temporal-lobe pathology, had been considered during her admission, as had an affective disorder – bipolar, cyclothymic, or psychotic depressed. She also had a psychosexual disorder consisting of inhibited desire and arousal.

Most important in the differential diagnosis was the possibility of a schizophrenic prodrome, or an atypical psychosis, both of which might imply a poor prognosis. For completeness, schizotypal personality disorder and schizoaffective disorder were included in my differential diagnosis; however, I ruled them out during the course of the therapy.

During her prior psychiatric admission, Erica had been started on an antidepressant. The clinical data supporting treatment with an antidepressant were feelings of hopelessness, tearfulness, impaired concentration, suicidal impulses, and marked self-depreciation. Although she was clearly unhappy, her mood had not been one of continuous and heavy depression. Though her mood disturbance had been cyclothymic by her own report, the depressive phase predominated.

I interviewed Erica for about one and a half hours. We discussed a number of issues, including her medication and how the interview had gone. She said that my presence posed a problem to her. She said that she could not allow people to come too close, because then she would begin to care about them. If she cared about them, which would inevitably happen, she said, if they cared about her, then it would hurt too much when they went away. During a prior Emergency Department consultation, she had told another resident a similar story: if she came too close during the interview, it would be too difficult to go away.

As we continued to talk that Thursday afternoon, I was struck by the absence of the schizophrenic 'pane of glass,' the so-called praecox feeling. Erica was full of dysphoric feeling, and was intensely concerned about the dynamics of our developing relationship. There was nothing flat or empty about her, and I dropped schizophrenia from serious consideration. Using the term in the broad and general sense, my countertransference was a mixture of the erotic and the paternal.

Within several more sessions, Erica no longer cried at home, her mood was no longer depressed, she joked and laughed on occasion, her eye contact was extensive and varied in quality, and she was no longer suicidal. Now she had something to live for: me. The people, though still barely perceptible, were no longer threatening to her, and were unable to disturb or control her. A central theme of our conversation was trust. Erica had not developed a secure basic trust prior to her psychotherapy. But she could now trust me, she said. We agreed that trust is a reciprocal relationship, not a private possession, and that her trust in me depended on my allowing her control and responsibility.

By the next Monday, Erica had maintained a symptomatic remission for nearly ninety-six hours. The next day, after discussion with her, I discontinued her antidepressant medication, which she never required again in nine years of follow-up.

With remission of the severe dissociative and depressive symptomatology achieved, we moved into a different phase of the therapy. I began to discuss her symptoms in terms of coping strategies, and introduced the concept of *ego glue*. Ego glue, I said, is a substance which holds the ego together. Erica had a shortage of this material, and consequently her ego tended to fall into pieces and dissociate: parts of it broke off and became 'the people,' other parts broke off when she went into trances, still another part got separated off and existed as a nebulous but malevolent 'she' in the unconscious. One task of therapy was to develop a secure, dependable source of ego glue, I said.

I did not realize that the concept of a deficiency of ego glue as a cause of dissociative symptoms had already been stated in the nineteenth century by Pierre Janet, not having read him at that point. He invented the concept, but did not use the term.

Erica chose a husband who grew up in a female-dominated family with an alcoholic father. He did not have the strength to disengage his wife out from his mother-in-law's influence. Whenever Erica got too 'sick,' her mother would come over for long hours to handle things. The family myth was that the unhappy, unindividuated young housewife was sick. She had a blood disorder, a hormone imbalance, 'moods,' postpartum and biochemically based depression, or at any rate a 'mental illness' of some kind. This myth had never been challenged until psychotherapy. Erica accepted these perceptions of mine in the form I have just described. We soon agreed that it was not the wife who was sick: it was the marriage that was sick, and the wife was showing the symptoms. The medical-model myth of her symptoms insulated all family members from responsibility for, and consciousness of, their own roles in the family drama. I laid out her options as follows: to stay sick; to get better and leave her marriage essentially unchanged, but to be able to cope with it; to get better and get a legal separation; to kill herself. She stated her resolve to opt for one of the two healthy paths.

As we discussed Erica's marital life more fully, I defined the following eight rules of her marital interactions:

1 / If you say I'm sick, then you don't really understand that I'm not sick. That makes me more sick.
2 / Wife is sick.
3 / Husband is ineffectual.
4 / If husband does what wife wants, he is weak.
5 / If husband does what he wants, he will feel guilty, which proves he is weak.

6 / If husband were strong, wife would not be sick.

7 / Husband is strong = independent; understands wife not sick; is sexually satisfying, genuine, capable of communication.

8 / If wife gets too sick, mother will be called in, which

a / proves wife is sick;

b / proves husband is ineffectual;

c / proves mother thinks wife is sick and unable to leave home;

d / proves husband is in same role as in family of origin, therefore has not left home, therefore has not removed patient from mother's sphere of influence, which proves husband is ineffectual;

e / proves patient has not left home, which keeps mother strong, and stronger than husband.

These eight marital rules governed the moves and counter-moves in the family system. They are represented diagrammatically in figure 3. We talked at considerable length about the family, before I first met Mr Simmons, and Erica had given me an extensive description of his interpersonal strategies.

Erica found her spouse particularly irritating and unfulfilling because he always 'understood.' His all-too-predictable response, which she described with sarcasm, bitterness, exasperation, anger, and mockery, was 'I understand.' But he never really understood; that was merely his bland, placating, stereotyped way of discontinuing the conversation. He would indicate in a phrase that he understood, and then bury himself in the newspaper again or resume accumulating his thirty hours a week of TV viewing. Erica said that her husband was a shell, and that she never got anything out of him except meaningless niceness. She denied any positive sexual desire for him. As we reviewed the rules of the marital interactions during the therapy, she adopted the attitude that her marriage was basically dead, that she couldn't force her husband to change, and that he was unlikely to change on his own. However, she resolved to change her own rules for personal relationships, and no longer to be made sick by the marriage.

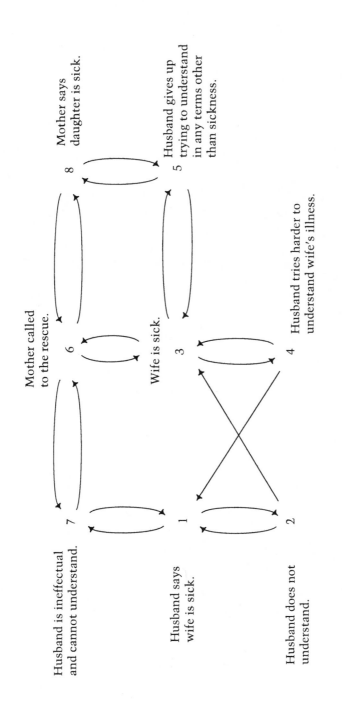

Figure 3
Rules of the Family Game

Since I could not change the rules of the marriage, I thought my next move would be to define the rules of the therapy, and discuss how the two differed. The rules of the therapy were:

1 / If you say I'm sick, then you don't really understand that I'm not sick. That makes me more sick.
2 / Wife is not sick.
3 / Therapist is effective.
4 / Therapist passes responsibility to wife, acts as co-explorer, evades bind of doing/not doing what patient wants. Or, patient must do what she wants.
5 / Therapist is strong = independent; understands wife not sick; is genuine, capable of communication.

Of these rules, the second could be adopted by the husband. That, I said to him, would be the first step in his changing the rules of his marriage.

An issue that soon came up in therapy with Erica individually was 'What do you want your husband to do when you go into a trance at home?' His previous responses had been fearful and powerless, in Erica's estimation. It became clear that Erica exhibited core signs of borderline personality disorder in her manipulation of her husband by psychiatric symptoms, and in her distorted, split perception of him. Vigilant for of all Erica's interpersonal moves, I needed to ensure that I did not fall prey to such borderline control.

When Erica's psychiatric symptoms became particularly florid, and on many other occasions as well, she placed her husband in what I call the *borderline paralytic loop*. The logic of the paralysis is as follows:

1 / I am desperate and unhappy.
2 / You must do something (you cannot do nothing).
3 / Everything you do is no good.

The loop is depicted in figure 4. As shown in the figure, each term in the loop feeds back positively on each of the others,

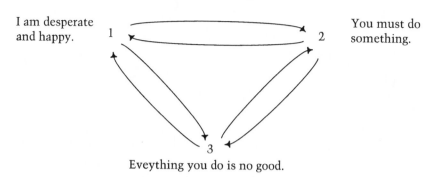

I am desperate and happy. 1

You must do something. 2

Eveything you do is no good. 3

Figure 4
Borderline Paralytic Loop

producing an intolerable situation for the bound other. There are two possible responses to being placed in such a loop: paralysis and projective-identification rage. The husband dissociated his rage, and responded with paralysed intellectual blandness.

When Erica became particularly 'sick,' her husband could not ignore the situation, and had to do something. Yet his repertoire of responses was extremely limited: he could phone his parents-in-law, ignore Erica, tell her to 'snap out of it,' or tell her to 'smarten up.' All these responses were rejected by Erica as proof of her husband's inadequacy.

Erica placed me in a borderline paralytic loop. This occurred several weeks after I first met her, when she phoned me at about midnight to tell me she was considering going down in the basement to let the people take over forever. The people had never been so real and powerful.

Initially, I played into the paralysing imperative by suggesting things she might do. These, all of which were rejected, included going to bed, going to the Emergency Department, going for a short walk, and going down in the basement to let things run their course. Going to the Emergency Department was rejected because no one there would understand, and because she might become violent while her husband was driving, causing an accident.

My anxiety began to mount as our brief conversation continued: the logical outcome of a sexually charged house call, with all its implications for future sexual escalation, was all too apparent. I evaded the bind in two ways: first, by being conscious that I was in a borderline paralytic loop, and second by rejecting the second imperative. I did nothing, not because I didn't care or was too lazy, but because a cardinal rule of the therapy was that responsibility lay with the patient. Erica elected to go down to the basement, and passed the phone to her husband. I recall the relief I felt when his commonsense-reality voice penetrated my auditory cortex, and I understood why she needed such a husband: here was secure footing.

The outcome of this episode was survival by Erica. She made no further phone calls. The phone call was examined at great length during the next session, and the logic of the paralytic loop was defined for her, without the technical term being introduced. Erica has accepted the principle that, although she didn't consciously get sick for that purpose, her sickness did place people close to her in difficult positions.

When I next talked with Erica's husband, he described going down into the basement and finding his wife in an extremely strange state. He said it was 'like something out of *The Exorcist.*' She was angry, alien, and talking in grunts and growls. She did not appear to recognize him, and sat on the floor in that state for hours before she finally snapped out of it. She then went to bed and has been amnesic for the episode ever since.

The second core logical loop of borderline personality disorder which Erica demonstrated I call the *borderline entrapment loop*. The logic of this loop is as follows:

1 / You must be infinitely available and perfectly loving.
2 / If you come too close I will reject you.
3 / If you allow yourself to be rejected I will punish you.
4 / Once I have punished you, I will demand that you be infinitely available and perfectly loving.

As shown in figure 5, the entrapment loop is a self-perpetu-

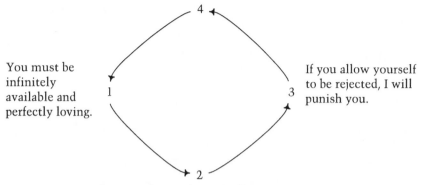

Figure 5
Border Entrapment Loop

ating circle from which escape is impossible, unless new rules are introduced. The possible responses of the bound other are endless oscillation between the imposed poles of rejection and attraction, and abandonment.

Erica simultaneously placed me in both a paralytic and an entrapment loop one afternoon during an out-patient psychotherapy session. She was 'psychotic,' suicidal, and homicidal, and said that the people were going inside her elder daughter (she could see them there), and that if she could kill her daughter while they were in there, she might get rid of the people forever.

Erica imposed an entrapment loop on me in the following terms: if you send me home, I will kill my daughter; if you admit me, I will kill myself; you must do something about this. I simply refused to take ownership of the problem or its solution, and she went home.

The first rule of the borderline entrapment loop is broken by the standard procedure of setting fixed and rigid limits on the interaction – no extra sessions or emergency phone calls. The third rule is broken by maintaining a standard clinical distance, and by not responding to punishment. Consciousness of the general form of the entrapment loop, and the particular terms of the loop in this therapeutic interaction at this moment, allowed therapy to continue in a positive vein. The loop and its logic were discussed extensively at the next session, and again Erica accepted my contention that she was testing me.

I also reviewed the fact that Erica had to learn to rely on herself in order to maintain her supply of ego glue. The sadomasochistic rejection-attachment-punishment cycle was derived at least in part from her pathological relationship with her mother, I said. Erica was acting out in the transference the paralytic and entrapment loops of her childhood, which I formulated in terms of a narcissistic mother who would not let her daughter separate and individuate. She accepted these formulations, which I presented in non-technical terms, and since entering therapy had made significant changes in her relationship with her mother. She was more independent in many ways.

We never explored Erica's early childhood in any detail at this point in the therapy, because the childhood origins of the loops were of no intrinsic interest to me. The narcissistic mother sufficed as a hypothesis which focused attention on Erica's current problems of living.

Subsequent to the midnight phone call, another aspect of Erica's psychopathology came to the fore, that is, her chronic emptiness and boredom, features of her borderline personality. Two months after first meeting Erica, I took a month's vacation, which activated her sense of abandonment and resulted in a borderline abandonment depression. She became diagnostically depressed, without dissociative features. I saw her on my first day back from vacation, a Thursday, and she slashed one wrist superficially that night after seeing me and the other one Sunday night, having waited a month to do so.

After slashing the second time, Erica phoned a male neighbour, a former psychiatric in-patient, from her bedroom, and asked him to come over to her house to tell Mr Simmons, who was watching television in the living-room, that she had slashed again. He did so, and took Erica to the hospital while her husband stayed home. Cognitive loop analysis had not yet cured Erica's borderline interpersonal transactions!

The admission was brief. After discharge, I defined the situation for Erica as follows: I was in a bind. I could continue therapy, never go on vacation, and thereby prevent wrist slashing. Under such conditions, however, I could never do therapy, because the treatment alliance would be broken, and I would have been coerced into therapy by the threat of further slashing. My solution was to see her once a month for half an hour, which was to stop therapy, and refuse to be coerced. At the same time, paradoxically, therapy continued. Responsibility was passed back to Erica, and I refused to play by her rules.

Thus, Erica was still in therapy, but I could take a month's vacation without her acting out her anger on her wrists, since she wouldn't miss a session, and wouldn't experience abandonment. She never slashed again.

Erica's dissociative disorder responded rapidly to a structured cognitive style of therapy which also allowed her to explore her dissociative symptoms. Twenty-eight months after being admitted to hospital for schizoaffective disorder, at the end of her active psychotherapy, she no longer entered dissociative trances, had radically matured her relationship with her mother, had made many positive alterations in her married life, had undergone a tubal ligation without florid difficulties and after lengthy discussion with her husband, and no longer experienced the intense dysphoric affect, painful emptiness, or desperation that characterized her earlier transference.

At times in the therapy, the dissociative symptoms led me to consider a diagnosis of MPD, and Erica offered several theories of exorcism and possession to account for her usually nebulous 'she.' However, 'she' never materialized in sufficiently concrete form to make MPD a serious consideration.

The borderline entrapment and paralytic loops were useful in Erica's treatment. At the very least, even if they had no specific therapeutic impact, awareness of the entrapment and paralytic loops made the work easier for me. It is all too easy to fall victim to borderline binds, and knowledge of their logical form, with accompanying rules for how to evade the binds, was useful for both participants in the therapy.

Erica's case illustrates several points, and raises several questions. First, her dissociative disorder was treated to long-term stable remission without any physical or sexual abuse being uncovered, and the symptoms stayed in remission for eight years of follow-up. If Erica had been a victim of paternal incest, it must have been 'she' who held the memories, but successful treatment did not require direct contact with the dissociated part-self. Can one conclude that direct work with the dissociated states may not be necessary in many complex dissociative disorders, including some cases of MPD? I don't know, but this is a real question in the field.

I did make use of several dissociative-hypnotic interventions, though the emphasis was on cognitive and systems analysis. For instance, Erica was being so bothered by the people in her basement at one point that it was difficult for her to get her laundry done. Carrying an imaginary staff I gave her, she could easily make it to the washer and drier, since the energy field of the staff kept the people at bay. Not only may it be possible to treat complex dissociative disorders without contacting the part-selves directly, but it may not even be necessary to use techniques derived from the classical psychotherapy of MPD.

In this case, successful treatment of the Axis I dissociative symptomatology resulted from a focus on the Axis II borderline psychopathology. Much of the work was typical psychodynamic borderline therapy – setting limits, interpreting the transference, and so on – while, at the same time, much of it was like strategic family therapy. The key difference between my work and the usual 'management' of borderlines was the nature of the countertransference, which was primarily paternal-protective and erotic, without the sadistic element that dominates orthodox psychiatry's response to borderlines. Also, the erotic element was not acted out.

Erica's therapy might appear to support the statement, often made by MPD sceptics, that MPD patients should be treated like borderlines. Actually, I think, the truth is the other way around: borderlines should be treated like MPD patients, in terms of countertransference. My approach to Erica was not based on the trauma model of psychopathology, since I had not thought of it yet, but it contained the elements that led to my understanding MPD and its implications for general psychopathology. I arrived at the trauma model from a starting-point of the correct *attitude* towards Erica, an attitude I had to maintain in conflict with my supervisors, most of whom are as hostile to borderlines in 1992 as they were when I met Erica in 1982.

It is virtually certain that, without effective psychotherapy early in her contact with the mental health system, Erica would have become a chronic mental patient with a diagnosis of schizoaffective disorder, schizophrenia, or bipolar disorder. She would have spent many months in hospital by her mid-twenties, and would have been prescribed lithium, numerous different antidepressants and antipsychotics, carbamazepine, several different benzodiazepines, and probably ECT. Instead, after beginning therapy, she had one brief admission over ten years, functioned well psychosocially, entered a much healthier second marriage, and was able to work.

Unfortunately, Erica contacted me by telephone just prior to my departure to Texas, and appeared to be in an early relapse of her dissociative symptoms for the first time in ten years. I wish her well, but I don't know that she *is* well.

23

Indecent Exposure

I was consulted by an agency outside the hospital concerning a young man in his early twenties who had been caught and convicted on five counts of indecent exposure over the previous five years, at regular intervals of about one offence per year. The most recent offence had occurred a month earlier, and he had served time in prison for one of the offences. The reason I was consulted was that he was completely amnesic for all the indecent exposures, although he did not deny his guilt, and his amnesia had never been mentioned in any of the criminal proceedings.

Jim's parents had died in an accident when he was a boy, and he had been raised by relatives. He had never been abused physically, sexually, or emotionally, and had no other criminal record. He had always been self-supporting, and did not have a problem with drugs or alcohol. He had had a full physical assessment, including a normal electroencephalogram and CT scan. I saw him, together with the doctor who referred him, in a medical examining room.

Jim was a good-looking, pleasant young man who was very cooperative, and appeared to be answering honestly. He seemed like a 'regular guy.' He confirmed that he had never been abused himself, and said he had never been abusive towards women. He had never been involved in vandalism, theft, other deviant sexual practices, or any other forms of antisocial behaviour. He said that his sexual adjustment and relationships with women were good, and that he was exclusively heterosexual. He had never been involved with any therapists or psychiatrists prior to seeking help for his amnesia.

Except for the amnesia, there were no other dissociative symptoms and no hints of a possible multiple personality disorder. Besides the amnesia for the indecent exposures, he had had only a few other blank spells, of short duration. During these, he was alone in his apartment. Nothing out of the ordinary appeared to have happened during these blackouts, prior to which he felt tired and after which he sometimes fell into a deep sleep.

After taking his history, I discussed with him the idea of using hypnosis to recover the memories of the indecent exposures. Jim said that he wanted to remember so that he could understand why he did it, and then learn how not to commit further offences. I forewarned him that he might feel upset and bad about remembering, but that this would be a natural and unavoidable aspect of learning how not to reoffend. He accepted this readily.

Jim was amnesic not just for the criminal acts themselves, but for a period of time leading up to them; therefore, he was not aware of the mental state that led up to the crimes. He entered a hypnotic trance easily, and said right away that he could recall all the details of the offences. When I asked him if I was now talking to a different and separate Jim from the one I had talked to previously, or simply the same Jim in a hypnotic trance, he said without hesitation that he was the same person, just hypnotized.

Jim provided the details of the different exposures without difficulty. Prior to the most recent incident, he was walking to a friend's house, feeling frustrated with life in general, when he suddenly got the idea of exposing himself. He said, 'I felt like it was the only way I could vent my frustrations.' He went to the top floor of a parkade, where he saw a woman in her fifties get into her car. He described her physical appearance in detail. The window of the car was down. He approached to within a few feet of the car, lifted up his shorts, and exposed his erect penis.

The woman shouted, 'Get away, get away!' and started hitting him with her seatbelt. He wasn't sure, but he thought he grabbed her breast before he ran away, was chased by a group of men, and caught. The blank spell had begun as he was entering the parkade on the second floor from an adjacent store, and ended as he was being caught.

The previous offences were similar in pattern except that there was no physical contact between Jim and the victims. I don't know if this meant that the severity of the offences was starting to escalate. Each time he was feeling frustrated prior to exposing himself, and each time the exposure acted as a tension release. In trance, he said that, prior to each offence, he was, 'angry, frustrated, like I need to do it to release tension.'

Jim said of the victims, 'It's not that I feel anything for them, they're an avenue to use, no feelings for them at all, I guess. I don't want to hurt them, it's just like an object to use.' He provided details of the victims' clothing, the locations, and other information which could have been checked against police records if there was any need.

Still in trance, Jim agreed that it would be best to remember everything when he came out of hypnosis. I told him that he and I would meet with a woman who was going to be his therapist the next week, to recover the memories in the waking state. Jim agreed to this plan, and I suggested that he come out of trance with the amnesia intact.

Jim woke up, and could not remember any of the conversation under hypnosis. I explained to him that the memories were there, and that he had described the offences in detail. I said that I would hypnotize him a second time, with his therapist present, the next week, and that the memories would then come back. I reviewed again that this might be emotionally difficult for him, and he understood that.

The next week, Jim again entered trance easily, and again agreed while under hypnosis to remember everything when he woke up. When he came out of trance, he did, in fact, have a full and complete memory of the hypnosis sessions, and all the indecent exposures. He said he felt 'disappointed, upset, ashamed.' He agreed that he needed to work with his therapist in a short-term therapy to devise alternative ways of discharging his tension and dealing with his frustrations.

Part of the goal of the therapy would be to help him become more vigilant for the emotional signs of an impending blank spell and indecent exposure. He needed to be more aware of what led up to his criminal behaviour, so that the could put alternative strategies into effect before committing crimes. After discussing these matters with Jim and the therapist, I said goodbye to them, never to see Jim again.

During the proceedings for the most recent offence, the amnesia was again not mentioned. Jim never used the amnesia to claim diminished responsibility, and he never denied that his behaviour was criminal in nature. He seemed, as he had when I first met him, like a 'regular guy' who had, for some reason, developed a sexually deviant technique for releasing tension.

Of course, to do a full assessment I would want to speak with some of the women he had had relationships with, to learn how they perceived him. Perhaps his girlfriends felt that he related to them as objects rather than as human beings. But his account of his relationships seemed plausible, and he came across as a warm person. Why the indecent exposures, then? I didn't know. There didn't appear to be any particular reason why he had chosen this tension-relieving technique, out of the countless possibilities available to everyone.

I thought that his prognosis in terms of not reoffending was good. The purpose of the amnesia was clear: it was to prevent him from having to deal with the guilt and shame, while at the same time ensuring that his conscience did not interfere with his behaviour. There was not much likelihood that he would break out of the pattern if he could not remember the antecedents, and the exposures themselves, because he could not learn different strategies if he was amnesic.

Jim's was a simple and easily treated dissociative disorder. His diagnoses were psychogenic amnesia and exhibitionism. I would need five years of follow-up to be able to say whether the frequency of the crimes had decreased significantly, or stopped altogether.

I suspected, based on Jim's case, that dissociation is a component of many sexual crimes. It stands to reason that the more complex and serious the crimes, the more complex and severe the dissociation is likely to be. Serial rapists, sexual murderers, sadistic paedophiles, and other extreme sexual offenders may often have chronic, complicated dissociative disorders, including MPD. The only study examining this possibility, published by Eugene Bliss in the *Journal of Nervous and Mental Disease* in 1985, found high rates of MPD and dissociation among imprisoned sexual offenders.

The major reason that people do not want the sexual criminal's dissociative disorder recognized appears to be their perception that this might lead to diminished criminal responsibility, or even a successful insanity defence. Largely because of this fear, an avenue of understanding which might lead to successful treatment in some cases is not pursued. Even if 10 per cent of the future crimes to be committed by 10 per cent of violent sexual criminals could be prevented by diagnosis and treatment of dissociative disorders, that would save much trauma.

We should change the rules of the legal system so that a dissociative disorder cannot result in a reduced sentence. We should determine by careful study whether dissociative sexual offenders can be successfully treated when their childhood trauma and dissociative disorders are taken into account. It may be unrealistic to think that severe sexual offenders with MPD could benefit from specific therapy, but there must be many individuals like Jim who are not trying to evade responsibility for their actions, and who are seriously interested in treatment. We should find out if this is true.

24

Voyage to Didyma

Bill is an architect in his early thirties. He was referred to me by his wife shortly after I arrived in Dallas, and has never had any psychiatric problems. His wife asked me to see him because of dreams he had been having, and because of *déjà vu* experiences he had while they were on vacation in the Middle East. There seemed to be a connection between the dreams and the strange feelings Bill had while in Turkey. His wife thought that, with hypnosis, I might be able to uncover a connection between the two.

Bill had no psychiatric symptoms and no psychiatric diagnosis at the time I assessed him, and he had never had emotional or mental problems in the past. He was functioning well in his job as an architect, and the marriage was good. There were no problems with the two teenage children, the family was financially stable, and no one was medically ill. Bill had never taken street drugs, and was an occasional drinker.

Why did he want to see me? As Bill explained the reason for the consultation to me, I observed that he and his wife were at ease with each other, communicated openly, and felt warmly about each other. They both saw the dreams and the *déjà vu* as an interesting problem, and neither felt that Bill was unstable or emotionally disturbed.

Bill himself is a slightly overweight, middle-aged man with black hair, an angular face, and dark eyes. He is not clean-cut, nor is he poorly groomed. There is an air of slightly disorganized, slightly absent-minded disarray about his clothes, hair, and mannerisms – a touch of the absent-minded professor. There is something intangible about him that is not quite congruent with the precision and technical expertise one might expect from an architect: he seems a bit out of place in the modern world.

Bill wanted to see me for two reasons: he had been having recurrent dreams since childhood which he did not understand, and there were the *déjà vu* experiences in Turkey. The two were connected. Since he was a boy, Bill had been dreaming about what appeared to be ancient Greece. In the dreams he was a Greek boy about ten years old. The dreams were vivid and seemed real, and he remembered them clearly. Bill also had other dreams which were not recurrent, were not remembered clearly, and seemed to be the usual kind of dreaming everyone experiences.

In the dreams about Greece, Bill would walk around, play with friends, and seem to be living a normal life. The events were sequenced as in actual living, and the pace of the passage of time seemed normal. Nothing that defied the usual logic of waking reality ever occurred in the dreams. One of the recurrent activities in the dreams was playing with other boys near a temple: in his dream life, Bill had spent so much time playing near this temple that he had a clear image of it in his mind. Throughout his life, he had always felt that the dreams were more than just dreams, but he didn't know how or why.

Then Bill went on a vacation to the Middle East. One of the architectural sites he and his wife visited was the temple at Didyma, in modern Turkey. This is where the *déjà vu* began. Bill knew the landscape so well that he knew exactly what was going to be over the next hill, or around the next corner. He could picture details of buildings and landscape in his mind in advance of seeing them in the world. The temple was the one from his dreams, down to minute details.

However, there was one curious inconsistency. A few of the details of the actual temple at Didyma were not 'correct,' and did not match the details of the dream temple exactly. Bill noticed this while on vacation. On return to Texas, he read up on the temple at Didyma, and learned that it had been damaged in an earthquake, and repaired by the Romans. It appeared that the dream temple was the original version, which predated the earthquake.

What Bill wanted me to do was to try to sort out what was going on. Was the *déjà vu* hallucinatory? Was his mind playing some kind of trick on him? Or was the dream a memory of an actual past life in the ancient world? How could one tell which of these possibilities was real, and were there other possibilities? Bill and his wife came to me, they said, because they knew I use hypnosis, and because they had heard that I might be open to exploring various possible explanations.

From the first session, there was no hint of psychotherapy in my work with Bill. I acted as a consultant on a spiritual/psychological problem, not as a therapist. His was a problem in the sense of a puzzle or a conundrum, not in the sense of an 'emotional problem': Bill was motivated to see me by curiosity, not by conflict or pain.

After getting a description of the dream landscape, and satisfying myself that Bill did not have a mental disorder, I proposed to try hypnosis to see if we could enter and explore the dream landscape. I wasn't quite sure how this would work, but was willing to try a few approaches. Bill agreed.

I asked him to recline on the couch in my office, relax, and close his eyes. Taking a few minutes, I used suggestions for relaxation, physical warmth, and concentration, to induce a hypnotic trance. Bill easily relaxed, and appeared to enter a trance state within a minute or two. I decided to use a suggestion for a process akin to astral projection: I told Bill that he would remain in a relaxed state, reclining on the couch with his eyes closed, and that, while he was relaxed, he would begin to travel, in his mind, through space until he arrived in the landscape of the dream.

After another few minutes, I asked him if he could see anything. Bill said that it was dark, and he felt like he was travelling somewhere. Then he began to see something. At first, the picture was dim and unclear, but it soon became more real and solid. Over another few minutes, Bill 'emerged' into the dream landscape. First, it became visually real, then he heard sounds, and finally he began to feel the air and smell things. This sequence was preserved in all subsequent sessions: Bill would project through a region of darkness, then the landscape would begin to appear visually, followed by sounds, then touch and smell.

I asked Bill where he was. He was standing on a hillside, looking down into a valley, and could see the temple from where he was. The air was warm and still, the sky clear, and the sun in a position that suggested early evening. He could hear crickets or some other insect, and was aware that there were other people around. I asked him to look around and describe the scene more clearly, unsure if he would be able to respond to such a request.

It turned out to be easy to get Bill to do things in the dream landscape. I simply asked him to look left, walk down the hill, or perform some other act, and he would carry it out. He did this, not as an automaton, but as an alert, cooperative, and friendly person. Bill said that there were three or four people on a roadway below, and that someone very familiar was standing and waiting beside him. I asked Bill to look at this person, describe him, and tell me who he was.

The man had short grey hair, and big, broad shoulders, and wore rough workman's clothing. He had a short tunic with no sleeves, and wore sandals with heavy leather soles. Bill said that he couldn't quite remember this person's name, but that he was a strong, gentle person with soft features. Bill's uncertainty about the identity of the man next to him illustrated a second feature of our travels through his dream landscape: often he would be vague about details, saying he couldn't remember.

This was paradoxical. While in trance, Bill identified himself as being a young boy; he easily described his surroundings, responded readily to my requests to do things in the landscape, and always heard my voice clearly. Why should he have trouble remembering his name, his family members' names, and other information about the dream world? The degree of vagueness varied from one piece of information to the next, and from session to session.

With more questioning, Bill identified the figure next to him as his father. I decided to ask him what he called his father in his language, to see if I could begin to get a language sample from him. This also involved trance logic: if he was a boy from the ancient world, he couldn't understand English in order to translate. He said that the word for father in his language is *pater*. I remembered enough Latin from school to recognize the origin of that term.

He told me that he had a father, mother, and two sisters. His own name he gave as Androkleus. His sisters were called Penelope and Louisa. His mother, or *mater*, was named Georgina. How was I to understand this? Fantasy? Accurate recall of an actual past life? Trance channelling with a boy from the past? How could I rule any of these possibilities in or out? Instead of eliminating any of these possible 'theories,' 'models,' or 'explanations' for what was going on, I wondered how I could investigate further before deciding. I thought that a more extensive language sample might be useful.

I therefore set out to collect as much of the dream language as I could. This proved to be difficult, because the translation process was very slow. Bill could give me translations only a few words at a time, with long delays and pauses, and was often unable to remember the words in his own language. This was odd because when I asked him to engage in conversations in the dream world, he did so easily, reporting them to me in English without difficulty, although the primary conversation was supposedly going on in the ancient language with simultaneous translation.

I reasoned that, if Bill was translating from English into an actual ancient language he couldn't have learned in the twentieth century, a linguist ought to be able to identify the language. Production of a real language not available in Canadian libraries or spoken anywhere in the world today would weigh in favour of a paranormal phenomenon. If the language was a fantasy language derived from a variety of contemporary languages, that would argue against the reality of the dream landscape.

Before I did this, I asked the boy if he knew who I was. He replied that I was 'someone familiar.' When I asked him where I was in relationship to him, he said that I seemed to be above and behind him. When I asked him to look there, he said that, in fact, he couldn't see me, and that he was only hearing my voice. He said that I wasn't physically present in his world. He was not disturbed by this, and seemed to take it as something quite natural.

I decided to 'explain' what was going on. I deliberately decided to proceed as if I was actually talking with a real boy from long ago, because I wanted to maximize the chances of getting an authentic sample of an ancient language. Since a sample of a real ancient language could not be explained away as the product of suggestion, I thought there was no risk in this. If the dream landscape was real, I wanted to find out as much about it as possible. If it was fantasy, I still wanted to find out as much about it as I could.

I explained that my voice was coming to him from another place far away. I explained that I was sitting in a room in a building far away from his town, talking to a man named Bill who was in a special magic sleep. The magic sleep had opened up a hole between Bill's mind and the boy's mind. I was talking to Bill, my voice was entering his mind, travelling through the hole, and entering the boy's mind. However, I explained, I do not speak the same language. Somehow the hole was also translating, so when the boy spoke in his language, Bill then repeated what he had said in my language.

The boy readily accepted this explanation, and commented that the priests in his town regularly talk with gods and people far away. I said that I wanted the boy to translate some words for me. I would say words in my language, and I wanted him to say the same word for me in his language. This didn't actually make any sense, because the boy was supposedly hearing in his language and answering in his language all the time. When I said 'house' he should have heard *don*, repeated *don* out loud, and never heard the English word. I should have said 'house,' and heard Bill say 'house' in English.

However, when I asked the boy to translate the word 'house,' Bill said *don*. If this was real, how could it be working? Who was doing the translating? It appeared that the translator device must be in the hole, not in Bill's or in Androkelus's mind. How did the device respond to my English words by changing its output from English to the other language, and then back again to English? I didn't know.

The boy's account of how it worked was that, while he was trying to translate, he seemed to become very familiar with my language and lose his sense of his own language, which he could only vaguely recall. It was as if the Androkleus identity shifted from being the speaker of an ancient language to being an English speaker with a poor command of the other language. Here is some of the vocabulary I got:

house	*don*	father	*pat*
mother	*mat*	sky	*ciel*
field	*pluch*	brother	*fratre*
sister	*shosta*	sun	*sol*
king	*kreg*	bread	*clep*
soup	*cous*	porridge	*felta*
festival	*satira*	sleep	*dorm*
night	*note*	precious stones	*xyle*
tunic	*fros*	decorative stones	*xale*
sandals	*gilia*		

I then asked him to translate some simple statements. He responded as follows:

The sun is in the sky.	*Sol ne ciel.*
The father is in the field.	*Patne ne pluch.*
My name is Androkleus.	*Mya Androkles.*
I love my mother	*Me lup mate.*

I am ten years old.	*Mya ha diech.*
I am going to sleep now.	*Me peliech nach.*
I am hungry.	*Me grom.*
The air is hot.	*Nas chalt.*

Already, I was aware of inconsistencies in the vocabulary. The word 'father' had been given to me as *pater, patre,* and *patne.* I then asked the boy to count from one to ten. He responded with '*min, sua, tre, chitier, pia, ghess, sem, och, non, desh.*' I asked him to say the alphabet and he gave me the following twenty-one letters: '*agh, ghe, be, ve, de, ye, ya, dze, hach, le emm, nya, oma, pe, er, dse, che, te, fe, oo, echa.*' This sounded to me like a garbled variant of the English alphabet, not like the actual alphabet of another language. I decided to see if the numbers and letters were consistent from session to session. Four months later, I asked the boy to count from one to ten and he responded with '*ein, twa, tre, chetre, piat, sesh, shem, och, nof, dech.*' Asked to say the alphabet, he could only get as far as '*a, be, ghe, de, ye, ya, oo, fa.*' Asked at this time to translate a number of simple statements, he supplied the following:

I am ten years old.	*Me dech.*
I love my mother.	*Me lup mate.*
The sun is in the sky.	*Sol ne ciel.*
The father is in the field.	*Patre ne lup.*
I am wearing sandals.	*Me guon.*
We should go.	*Uroch gliess.*
I am hungry.	*Me fach.*

In a session six weeks later, the numbers one to ten were given as '*ain, tua, tre, chitier, pia, shem, shesh, och, nova, dech*' and the alphabet as '*ah, be, ve, ghe, dye, ye, ya, fe, he, ee, ka, el, em, en, peh, eire, she, se ...* [the boy falters at this point] *she, sche, te, oo, fe, szhe.*'

It was clear that the language samples were nowhere near

consistent, and that this was not a real language. What could I conclude?

I believe that I was never in touch with an actual ancient language. Does this prove that everything about the dream world was a fantasy? No. For instance, there could have been a real hole to an actual ancient world, but interference could have resulted in poor translation. This is like the problem of proving that there is no causal relationship between a rain dance and subsequent rain: believers in rain dances regard all dances followed by rain as proof of causality, and dismiss all failures as the result of technical difficulties. Even if the association between dances and subsequent rain is shown to be no greater than chance, the faith of believers will not be shaken.

Similarly, devotees of trance channelling will believe that Bill was a channel for Androkleus, despite the translation problems. What evidence would really convince everyone one way or the other? I wondered. I decided to find out more about the world in which this boy lived. I asked him to name famous people in his time, describe recent important events, name his town and language, and name any other towns or countries he knew about. Androkleus was extremely vague about all these things. He said that there were soldiers from the west stationed in his town. These soldiers, he said, spoke a language called Latium and came from Attica, or a place farther west. He had heard of a city called Perge, which was a healing place.

He wasn't sure of the name of his own town, but thought it might be Coros. He had heard of someone he thought might be called Cresus who lived up north, owned a lot of land, and was interested in books. Because this line of enquiry was unproductive, I decided to prompt him and some names. When I asked him if he had heard of Plato, he said that Plato was someone from the west who wrote and thought, and lived a long time ago. He couldn't say who trained Plato. He was aware of plays being performed about old wars in Illium.

It was clear that I wasn't going to get a coherent description of famous people, historical events, or ancient geography from Androkleus. I thought that his description, if detailed enough, might lead to an estimate of the time at which he was supposed to be living. From studies he conducted after returning from his holiday in the Middle East, Bill had concluded that the date was probably in the range of 30 B.C. to A.D. 40. This estimate was based on the date of an earthquake which damaged the temple and the approximate date of later Roman repairs to it.

Androkleus had mentioned that there were priests in his town associated with the temple. I knew that he could walk around in the landscape at my request, ask people questions, and tell me their answers, so I decided to pay a visit to the priests. One session, after the landscape had become clear and definite, I asked him if he would go to the temple and try to speak to one of the priests. He agreed, and off he went. The sessions were almost always extremely slow-paced, and the walk to the temple area was no exception, taking a good twenty minutes twentieth-century time.

Androkleus was friends with one of the priests' assistants named Arthen, and went up to talk to him. Arthen was described as about twenty years old and wearing a white, loose, light robe with a loose white belt, and sandals. After some discussion with the assistant, an interview with one of the priests was scheduled. This occurred over two sessions separated by three weeks.

The priest's name was Charissos. His priest's garb was also white, but fuller than those of assistants. It was heavier, and tied with a cord at the waist. There was a hood on the back, which was worn down, and he had elegant, sandal-like crisscrossing footwear made out of leather. He was in his fifties. Charissos had studied in a school or sanctuary in the north, near Perge, and had heard of both Hippocrates and Aesculapius. He said that Hippocrates was a healer on one of the islands not far away, and that he had lived more than five generations previously, prior to the end of the kings.

I asked Charissos if he knew of a disorder in which there appeared to be more than one person in the same body. He was familiar with that illness because it was known to his teachers, but he had not seen a case himself. He said that MPD is usually treated with ritual mystery ceremonies, and that the goal of treatment is integration and creation of a sense of connection with the world.

Regarding possession, he said that some healers believed in it, but he wasn't convinced that such patients are actually possessed. Strong differences of opinion between healers were common. He said he had met a possessed person himself, but felt that the mind is very powerful, and can play tricks on itself. He said that the treatment of possession can involve the creation of counter-tricks combined with relaxation, talking, and chanting, and that it can be done individually or in groups. There is often more than one healer present at the rituals.

I then asked him how he understood the current conversation. Did he think I was an independent being communicating to him through Androkleus's mind, or that I was a trick the boy's mind was playing on itself? He wasn't sure. I asked him if he could think of any way that he could test the hypothesis that I was actually an independent being, but he couldn't.

Charissos agreed to talk again, and said that he would discuss our conversation with his colleagues in the interim, to get opinions on it. For me, the conversation had the tone and feel of a rational interchange with an independent adult human being. Before we stopped talking, I asked him if he had ever heard of moving objects with the mind. He said he had never witnessed it, but that he had spoken to people who claimed to have witnessed telekinesis elsewhere.

Concerning mental telepathy, he was also sceptical, saying that there were rumours about people inland to the east with such psychic powers. Charissos appeared to be a rational sceptic who favoured psychological and non-paranormal explanations of human experience. Concerning life after death, he said only that there were many stories and philosophies, but that he was uncertain himself. Charissos wasn't acting like a typical channelled entity claiming wisdom and paranormal powers. He would have fit in well in a modern university department of psychology.

Prior to the next meeting with Charissos, I spent some time talking with Arthen because the priest was tied up with other business. Arthen said that the healers make extensive use of plants, relaxation techniques, and sleep therapy. They often induce a trance-like, healing, sleepy state in their patients, using vapours and rituals. They consider the uterus to be involved in a variety of diseases, and also consult the stars on medical problems.

When I asked him about the types of disease treated at his institution, he said that 'sometimes people feel as if they're somebody else, they seem to be two people in one, and sometimes seem to be very unhappy or depressed for reasons that don't seem to be apparent,' and that 'someone might injure others for no apparent reason, have difficulty with seeing, or very severe headaches, and sometimes be abnormally tearful.' He said that people could suffer from 'a whole range of different problems.'

At this point, Charissos emerged from a building with three other men, said goodbye to them, and came over to Androkleus. He said that he had consulted with his colleagues, and that they advised taking things slowly, and seeing where they lead: a cautious and conservative approach not typical of the usual channelled gurus. I asked him a bit more about MPD. He said that the alters may or may not have different names, and that there are usually only two or three of them. He said that patients are often frightened at their own behaviour, experience amnesia, hear voices, undergo sudden changes in moods, and sometimes suddenly don't recognize others. This latter item he regarded as a key diagnostic criterion.

Concerning the etiology of MPD, Charissos was vague. He said that MPD might arise from part of life that had been suppressed or a change of families. His own practice, he said, was limited mainly to physical disorders, especially intracranial tumours. I then asked him about his colleagues' experience with voices and mental telepathy. He said that both were alleged to be common, but that the communication was usually with others in the same present, not with others in a different time. I had explained to him in the previous meeting that I was both far away and in the future.

Finally, I asked him about oracles. He said that there was an oracle at Delphi that was currently active, and that the oracle was a special priest or priestess resident at a temple. His own temple, he said, was the Great Temple of Apollo at Postrafus, also sometimes called Didyma. People usually asked oracles about their own fate. Rulers, though, might consult oracles on proposed courses of political or military action.

Before our conversation came to an end, I asked Charissos if he would be interested in attempting an experiment. If we really were two independent healers in different times and cultures, I said, then we were communicating through a hole in time and space that connected Bill's mind with that of Androkleus. If words could be transmitted through this hole, why not objects? Would he be interested in trying to transport a material object through the hole?

Charissos replied that he doubted that this could be done, that he didn't know how to go about trying, and that he would have to think about it before agreeing to anything. I was proposing a physics experiment. If I could get an object to dematerialize out of Bill's hand and appear in the dream world, and an object to dematerialize out of Androkleus's hand and appear in Bill's, that would prove that modern science does not understand a major portion of the mind and the physical universe.

One could enclose a radioactive sample with a half-life of, say, one thousand years in a special container, transport it through the hole, have Charissos bury it in a specific spot, excavate it in the twentieth century, and demonstrate the decay in radioactivity in the sample, which would have aged two thousand years. My Nobel Prize for this experiment is pending because Charissos is not interested in the collaboration, and the sessions with Bill have come to an end.

Bill also doubted that such teleportation of material objects was possible. In fact, he was slightly scornful of the idea, as if it was patently nonsense. This was interesting, because it showed that the dream world and Bill's psyche would not simply follow every suggestion I offered. I encountered as much scepticism from both Bill and Charissos as I would expect to get from most modern people, and far more than from channellers or channellees.

However, Arthen brought up MPD spontaneously without my having mentioned it in any of the sessions. Bill knew of my specialty interest in MPD from his wife, but he and I never discussed it. This couldn't be a coincidence. Bill's 'unconscious mind' must have inserted the information about MPD because he knew that I would be interested in it. This was clearly theatre designed for me.

What does it mean to say that Bill's 'unconscious mind' knew I specialize in MPD? If the unconscious is unconscious, how does it obtain such information, write a script containing it, and project the script into the conscious mind? This is a process about which we know almost nothing. How does the unconscious create such elaborate fantasies, which have internal structure, are connected to everyday reality, and in many ways appear to be perfectly rational? Bill's dream world wasn't simply nonsense. What was it?

Also, what was it for? Bill didn't have a mental illness, he wasn't getting any material gain from his fantasy, and there didn't appear to be any emotional or social benefit derived from it. He had been having the dreams since childhood. And why the *déjà vu* in the Middle East? Was this all the mind playing tricks on itself, as Arthen and Charissos seemed to believe? If so, wasn't it odd that the dream contained its own critics?

We had only one more session, during which we moved around in the landscape some more, and talked to one of Androkleus's sisters. Bill concluded that we had 'gone about as far as we could go' with the hypnosis. He said he found it interesting, but that he didn't think it provided any real answers. He came in with an interesting psychological problem, had an interesting time exploring it, and left with it unsolved but still intriguing. I have not seen him since.

Bill could easily become a wealthy channeller, if so inclined.

Charissos could be contacted on stage and, for a mere $400 per consultation (payable in the twentieth century), he could diagnose and suggest treatments, which Bill could then carry out for further substantial fees. There are many people in our society willing to pay large fees for such medicine. But he's not going to do that. He carries on with a normal life, a man with recurrent dreams and memories of a strange vacation.

What does Bill's dream world tell us about MPD? I'm not sure, but I think it provides a warning. The mind is capable of creating extremely complicated and detailed fantasies which may not have any factual foundation. These fantasies may occur in dreams, hypnotic trances, and the waking state, in the same individual. All three psychic states can be connected by a structure which appears to be rational, internally consistent, and plausible. There was nothing chaotic or 'dream-like' about Bill's dream world: events there were as logical and orderly as in our world.

Might some MPD personality systems similarly lack a foundation in reality? Might some of the abuse histories be fantasies? I learned from the case described in chapter 4 that apparently real events reported, mourned over, and 'dealt with' in psychotherapy can be illusions deliberately created by alter personalities. If alter personalities can do that, why not the general unconscious mind? This question can be asked, not just of MPD patients, but of everyone. How much of our perceived reality is a creation of our own minds?

For most people, such questions are abstract, theoretical, and of little real interest. Not for Bill. He doesn't know what is going on in his own mind and his own experience. Why has he had the recurrent dream? Why did he have *déjà vu* at Didyma, and why could I talk to Charissos when he was in a hypnotic trance? If he never did have a past life in Didyma, and was not actually channelling, what was going on, and why? These are questions neither Bill nor I can answer.

Bill's case raises the same question about the experiences of people who have been abducted by aliens, and subjected to physical examinations aboard spacecraft. Such detailed and elaborate experiences could be dissociative/hypnotic illusions. The question about UFO abductions is: why do different people's minds create fantasies containing such consistent details, when the individuals have no prior knowledge of these details? Is this the collective unconscious at work? Or are the memories accurate recollections of real experience?

You would think that if so many people are being abducted, we would have some tangible proof of the existence of UFOs publicly available by now. But UFOs are no more proven than Bill's past life in Didyma. I have learned from Bill that psychologically normal, well-functioning people can have elaborate, detailed paranormal experiences. Minds capable of creating such elaborate inner theatre seem to respond to chronic childhood trauma in a special way. They create an inner world of personalities among whom the memories, feelings, and conflicts are parcelled out.

I have never met a patient whose abuse memories struck me as all, or even mostly, fantasies. By and large, I believe that my patients have experienced the abuse they describe. Of course, like everyone's memories, those of abuse are subject to elaboration and distortion. But the basic story is real. Having explored Bill's dream world, though, I have to accept that a small number of MPD patients might have abuse memories that are mostly fantasies. I hesitate to say this, because mental health professionals have erred far too much on the side of dismissing incest memories as fantasy throughout the twentieth century. It is also an error to blindly believe that all trauma memories must be completely accurate.

In the end, I can't dismiss everything about the voyage to Didyma as meaningless unconscious fantasy. Somehow, it all seems to mean something. Even if the dreams are just dreams, why did Bill have the *déjà vu* experiences? I don't know. But I wonder about it.

25

The Stranger Within

One of the hazards of coming on staff at a mental health institution is that people try to refer their 'interesting' cases to you. Often the cases may be described as 'challenging.' Usually, this means that the referring person is trying to transfer his or her most stressful, disagreeable client to you. An excessive amount of flattery by the referring person is a good indicator that the referral is, as we say in medical circles, 'a dump.' Trainees, not surprisingly, are not told about this problem in the life of new graduates.

When I came on staff at St Boniface Hospital, I had to decline a number of such referrals in the first couple of months. As I work more and more with multiple personality disorder, I have learned that some psychiatrists who do not believe in MPD are happy to refer their most difficult cases, which they diagnose as 'borderlines,' to me, and don't care if I 'call them MPD,' as long as I am willing to take over responsibility for the case. This is an unethical paradox: such psychiatrists will not diagnose MPD themselves, on the grounds that it doesn't exist, but don't mind transferring difficult cases to MPD therapists. In my second month on staff, after completion of my training, a psychotherapist asked me to consider taking over one of her patients. The therapist was honest with me, at least. She said that the patient was 'the most personality-disordered person I have ever met.' When I reviewed the chart, I saw that there had been a number of different diagnoses. The patient had seen four or five other psychiatrists briefly, and was described in their notes as extremely hostile, negative, and unpleasant. She was said to be untreatable.

Some quotes describing her included: 'a very angry, depressed lady'; 'a most dramatic personality disorder'; 'extremely inappropriate'; she wanted to be controlled and told what to do to get a hold on her illness'; 'I suggested that the family doctor be kind and firm with her and, if she were not compliant, to get her into hospital and perhaps also do some impulsion with her as well as the medication'; 'possesses a rather primitive character structure'; 'I told her she was self-righteously angry'; 'I told her that in general she can and does exercise a lot of control over her life and maybe she would be better off finding her own answer'; 'the outstanding feature of her depression is her extremely low self-esteem based on an inferiority complex'; 'very, very nihilistic'; and 'has a grossly distorted view of what constitutes cleanliness and neatness.' These comments are from six different physicians, writing over a period of a year.

I decided to see her, partly because she seemed to have gotten incomplete previous assessments. Some of the psychiatrists' comments, such as the one about 'impulsion,' didn't even make sense. There is no such thing as impulsion. I found it hard to believe that anyone could be that hateful, or that a lecture and advice to smarten up could really be adequate. Not all the notes were negative, and several physicians were genuinely concerned about her, but none knew how to help. Here was a chance to really test my therapeutic skills!

The month before I first saw Susan, she had been assessed for behavioural therapy and found unsuitable. Among a long list of complicated problems, she had a washing compulsion which occupied much of her day. She was unsuitable for behavioural therapy because of her extreme negativity, and unsuitable for treatment with chlomipramine because of her seizure disorder. Chlomipramine is an antidepressant which is often very helpful in obsessive-compulsive disorder, but it tends to lower the seizure threshold, resulting in more frequent seizures (fluoxetine was not yet on the market). She had also been found unsuitable for group treatment in two different settings, because of her hostility and ambivalence.

A note written a month before I saw her described a 'psychomotor seizure' lasting five minutes, which did not impress the observing physician as a genuine seizure. As well, one of the psychiatrists consulted had said that he did not think the seizures were genuine. Before the seizure, she was 'smiling and animated,' but after it she was 'whiney, dependent, despondent for five minutes. Very childlike. States she "blacked out," unable to remember behaviour. Picked up conversation where she left off.' It wasn't till several years later that I realized that Susan had probably switched to another personality state during the unconvincing 'seizure.'

Susan proved to be the most hostile person I have ever met. I have never encountered such extreme negativity before or since. The first session prior to my going away on vacation for three weeks was a get-acquainted session, and I gave her a lot of homework to do. I had in mind a carefully planned cognitive-behavioural treatment for selected symptoms and problems. It never occurred to me that she might have a dissociative disorder.

The homework included filling out weekly the Beck Depression Inventory, which is a standard measure of the severity of depression; a daily diary of all her food intake; a record of all binges, purges, and self-induced vomiting; two standard measures of the severity of eating disorders; and a record of all her thoughts and feelings immediately before and after every binge episode. It was evident in the first session that she met criteria for a number of different psychiatric diagnoses, including bulimia, depression, obsessive-compulsive disorder, and a personality disorder.

I saw Susan again a month later. She had amazingly high scores on all the forms I had asked her to fill out. She was averaging fourteen binge episodes per week, was using laxatives to control her weight, was walking ten to fifteen miles per day to burn off weight, was clinically depressed, suffered from panic attacks, had obsessive-compulsive disorder with numerous cleaning rituals, and had a long list of problems that might be addressed in therapy.

Her problem list included: bulimia; perfectionism, with co-existing fear of failure; compulsive face washing; being unemployed; being single; a monotonous, empty life; chronic back pain; inefficient time management; unresolved conflicts over a pregnancy earlier in her life; and being driven by a host of obsessive rules she felt were ingrained in her by her father. The homework task I set her in the second session was to find part-time employment.

The rationale for her getting a part-time job was that it would give her something to do, that working was inherently good for her self-esteem, to help her be less socially isolated, to provide us actual experiences to work on and analyse from a cognitive-behavioural perspective, and to provide some income. Susan had never been on welfare, despite a period of unemployment. I thought that any experience of success would be helpful, although I knew that she had lost numerous previous jobs because of her negativity and obsessive perfectionism, which made her very critical of others and hard to get along with.

Even in the second session, I got some sense of the full force of Susan's negativity. She described herself as grossly ugly to the point of being repulsive. She described herself as dressed like a pig, and her complection as horrifying to others. In fact, she was always well groomed and dressed, and had a normal complection. It took me a while to realize that Susan also had a delusional disorder called dysmorphophobia. Dysmorphophobia is a syndrome in which the person has delusions of being grossly ugly and misshapen, and actually sees himself or herself as extremely ugly. The condition may be related to the body-image distortion people with anorexia nervosa experience: an anorexic may look in a mirror and see herself as fat, even though she weighs only seventy pounds.

Susan's Beck Depression scores ranged from 54 to 60, out of a possible 63. To enter into a drug study assessing a new anti-depressant, the cut-off score used is usually 20, which indicates clinical depression. I had never seen a score above 40 before.

Her Hamilton Depression Scale score was 36. The Hamilton is a scale filled out by the clinician, and scores above 20 similarly mean a clinical depression. There was no doubt that Susan met diagnostic criteria for a major depressive episode. However, the picture wasn't typical.

She slept all right, was not low on energy, had not lost weight, and was not sad. On the contrary, she was full of angry, hostile energy. The sessions were actually quite gruelling for me. She would attack, attack attack everything with negativity. All her previous employers were incompetent idiots who ganged up on her maliciously, the previous doctors only wanted to get rid of her, and I didn't care about anything except practising therapy on her. The world stank, life stank, nobody cared, and she wished she was dead. Susan said dozens of times over the years I knew her that she wished someone would kill her, and let her out of this lousy world. She asked me to shoot her many times.

When I declined to shoot her, she railed against God for putting her on this earth, only to torture her and not let her escape. She said that God would not let her kill herself: she was such a failure, she couldn't even be successful at suicide.

Susan said that she was so ugly that other people crossed the street rather than walk past her. She thought that she was so revolting in her physical appearance that people were literally nauseated by looking at her. Yet she actually looked fine. I was amazed to learn that, up until a year previously, she had washed her face with urine on a daily basis, to try to treat her supposed horrible complection. She said that the urine helped a little, making her look decent enough so that, with heavy makeup and hours of preparation, she could at least go out in public.

I began to get a feel for what a typical day in Susan's life looked like. Later on, I asked her to keep a record of what was involved in getting up in the morning and getting out the door. With extreme obsessiveness, she produced a one-page record of three mornings' preparations to go out that included the starting and finishing time of each activity. On average it took her three to four hours to wash, dress, put on her makeup, and leave. This level of efficiency was possible because of three to four hours of advance preparation the evening before, including a facial, bath, hair wash, and ironing.

Ironing alone could take several hours for a pair of pants and a blouse, and she was never satisfied that she had gotten all the wrinkles out, and the crease just right. She always thought she looked terrible, and said I must think she just threw on any old rags at the last moment and dashed out of the house. Then she would say that it wasn't worth the effort anyway, because if she took the bus her clothes got wrinkled from sitting down, and if she walked her hair was a mess because of the wind. In fact, she had a perm that wouldn't have deviated a micron in a hurricane.

One Wednesday morning, she started getting ready for a 12:30 appointment with me at 8:15. Her routine was:

8:15–8:30	bathroom, comb hair, make coffee
8:30–8:47	wash face
8:47–9:25	shower
9:25–9:34	brush teeth
9:34–9:41	apply skin freshener and moisturizer
9:41–9:57	apply coverstick
9:57–10:00	make lemon drink
10:00–10:08	apply makeup base
10:08–10:11	blend
10:11–10:16	apply powder
10:16–10:19	blend
10:19–10:24	apply blush
10:24–10:28	blend
10:28–10:58	eyes: brows, liner, shadow, mascara
10:58–11:02	go to bathroom
11:02–11:15	eat
11:15–11:50	fix hair
11:50–12:10	bathroom, teeth, lipstick, dress
12:10	leave home

I was so appalled by this routine that I vowed never to ask

her to record anything else. I didn't want to slow her up by adding the task of recording to her routine, nor did I want to listen to her berate herself for doing such sloppy homework. It was hard to listen to a human being run herself down so unmercifully. If a parent treated a child the way Susan treated herself, the child would be apprehended by a child-protection agency.

All this preparation made it very difficult to work. She had to spend almost a full working day getting ready to go to work! In addition, she had to get in her ten to fifteen miles of walking a day. Some days, she would wake up in a panic state and be driven to leave the house, even when it was 30 degrees below zero, and would walk for miles to burn off energy. All of this made any personal relationships impossible from a sheduling perspective alone.

Complicating this was her eating disorder and her seizures, which in fact were documented by an electroencephalogram and treated with anticonvulsants by a neurologist. She ate irregularly, usually not very much, and often binged, vomited, and took laxatives. She said that, when she didn't eat for a while, she would get hypoglycemic and have a seizure, so she was caught between eating enough calories not to have a convulsion, but not too many to gain weight. She never found a happy medium.

Her chronic pain was treated at a pain clinic. She wore a transcutaneous electrical nerve stimulator (TENS) unit, which helped a little but only if she turned the power up so high that it tended to burn her skin. Without adequate pain relief, she wouldn't sleep properly, would get tired, and would be more prone to seizures. She was always juggling skin breakdown against insufferable pain and poor sleep. Susan said that the pain alone was enough to make her strongly suicidal much of the time.

I was overwhelmed by this insoluble set of problems, and the suffering that went along with them. Realistically, I could not offer much in terms of psychotherapy. I told Susan that she should try chlomipramine, being very careful to explain that this was not a substitute for therapy, but something to be added to it on a trial basis. She had tried another antidepressant a few years previously, but when she gained weight on it, she stopped taking it. Weight gain is a common side-effect of this class of antidepressants. Therefore, Susan would not take chlomipramine.

I did convince her to try trazodone, another more recently developed antidepressant with fewer side-effects than chlomipramine. I increased her dosage gradually to 400 milligrams per day, which is a high dose, but after two weeks at this dosage there was not the slightest change in her depression scores, or life. I tapered the trazodone down, stopped it, and then started chlomipramine, after difficult negotiating with her, and with an assurance that unacceptable side-effects would result in stopping the medication.

I slowly built the chlomipramine dosage up, until she had reached a therapeutic blood level, and all of a sudden it was like someone had thrown a switch. Susan's Beck Depression score dropped to 10. She reduced her walking from fifteen miles a day to three miles. She had not binged once in a week, she no longer felt panicky or driven at any time in the day, and she was thinking positively about returning to work. The only problem was that she was having six to eight petit-mal seizures a week.

When I saw her again a week later, she had had no seizures but the therapeutic effect of the chlomipramine had started to wear off. Within a few weeks, her depression score was back up to 44, and all her other symptoms had returned, despite her blood level not changing. This baffled me. I tapered and stopped the chlomipramine. Trials of two other medications, alprazolam and pimozide, were ineffective over the next year, and she did not want to try a fourth medication called phenelzine. I also considered lithium and electro-convulsive therapy, but we gave up on all physical methods of treatment. Had they been on the market at the time, I would have tried fluoxetine, and, if it was ineffective, would then have tried adding buspirone.

Over the first year I saw her, Susan actually improved a lot. Her hostility became much more muted, she found and kept a part-time job, and her spirits were improved. The eating disorder and obsessive-compulsive disorder were unchanged, but the depression and anxiety were only a fraction of what they had been. Although we talked about many things, I was never sure if anything I did was helpful. I felt that it was the simple act of being with her twice a week that was therapeutic, not anything in particular I said or did. I was someone who would listen and empathize with her point of view.

It was not until two years into therapy that Susan launched into an attack on me for my blindness to her addiction problem. I should have figured out that she was addicted to caffeine, she said. By 'addicted to caffeine' she meant an average consumption of fifty cups of caffeinated coffee a day! Was this humanly possible? Whatever the actual number of cups she drank, I now understood her driven, panicky states better. She was not willing to consider the slightest reduction in her coffee intake, because the caffeine helped control the pain, she said. I could not find a reference to caffeine in my notes, but did find a comment about caffeine abuse in her extensive file from previous therapists and assessments.

Susan joined an Emotions Anonymous group, and found their twelve-step approach and support very helpful. She also attended meetings of a local eating-disorders support group, but she rated the other women as far more attractive and competent than herself, so found the meetings discouraging. Although she was making some progress in therapy, she was really stuck. She still stated repeatedly that the thing she wanted most was to die.

Then one day Susan asked me why I never talked to the Stranger Within. I replied that the main reason was that I had never heard of the Stranger Within. She dropped the topic, and as it was the end of the session, I just left it for later. A couple of weeks later, Susan brought in the following, which she said had been dictated to her by the Stranger Within, and which she had transcribed verbatim.

THE STRANGER WITHIN

As you might surmise, I am the devil in disguise. I am all powerful, all encompassing. I possess completely, and rule absolutely, all of your thoughts and actions. I am the 'Stranger Within.' Your body is merely my mask for survival amidst this gruesome world of humans.

I keep a very negative profile. I give you frustration, hopelessness, helplessness, powerlessness, uncertainty, insecurity, loneliness, and emptiness. I am the voice of fear – fear of rejection, fear of failure, and fear of change.

You refuse to accept that you are not like 'the rest of them' and that you can never be 'one of them.' Sometimes you try to destroy me by going on one of your 'positive attitude' psychology kicks. Then I must bring you failure, disappointment, and pain. I ensure rejection of you by others. I must remind you that I am master of this house. Fail to obey me and I will only cause you more misery. For your agony is my pleasure – my only assurance of mastery and survival. My ever-present, burning, razor-edged spear in your back should be reason enough to submit to me, but still you deny my presence. I have therefore been forced to destroy you completely – body, mind, and soul.

I exist to punish and persecute you for you have failed to live up to human expectations. You do not deserve 'pleasures of the flesh,' but you continue to yearn for them. I teach you your lesson by giving you just a taste of those pleasures followed by overwhelming disappointment, disaster, and failure. I deny you food, for it is a reward only for success, and you are a success at nothing. When you eat I must purge your body, lest you gain strength to overpower me. I urge you to conform to my diet, that I might keep you in a state of drunkenness, under my control. It will damage your skin with blemishes, broken capillaries, and flaming red hands, but that is my assurance of having you rejected by the human race, and fully in the grip of my power.

One big mistake you made caused you to fall prey to me.

Ten years ago you desired a sexual relationship. You failed
to accept that you are born of the devil and therefore
incapable of love. I granted you a taste of such an experi-
ence, climaxing in utter disaster; destroying your career and
your entire being; putting you firmly in my evil grasp. I had
to teach you a lesson: that you do not deserve human pleas-
ures because you are incapable of normal human emotions.

One final thing: I fear change and I strongly sense that
Dr. Ross is causing change in you. In the beginning you said
'this is the man I've been looking for. This is the man that
can help me change my life.' That is why I caused you to
become so aggressive and negative towards him. I fear he
may destroy me.

Remember always, that I am in command. I am master of
your fate, for I am 'the Stranger Within.' Your body is mere-
ly a mask to shield me from the glance that knows. I rule
supremely and in time I will completely destroy you.

Before I had finished reading this, I had decided to talk with
the Stranger Within. After several attempts to contact the
Stranger Within indirectly, with and without hypnosis, I
decided to do a sodium-amytal interview. The most we could
achieve without sodium amytal was to get the Stranger Within
to make a few comments inside Susan's head, which Susan
would relay to me.

Sodium amytal is a barbiturate medication given by vein
which makes a person drowsy and relaxed. Despite popular
perception, it has no truth-serum properties. A person under
the influence of the medication can lie, believe fantasies to be
real memories, remember previously blocked-out events accurately, or simply be confused. It is often difficult to tell which
of these is going on. I use sodium amytal to try to trigger the
recovery of dissociated memories and feelings, and to get in
touch with personality states that are difficult to contact.

Before the first of several sodium-amytal interviews, I asked
Susan what her understanding was of the Stranger Within. She
told me that he is about three feet tall, that he carries a spear,

and that she had known about him for a long time. He jabs her in the back with the spear, which is the cause of her chronic back pain. Caffeine, she said, seems to weaken him, and the chlomipramine, while it was working, took away almost all his powers. Susan told me that the Stranger Within was very scared of chlomipramine.

Susan said she was possessed by the Stranger Within. She thought he could leave her if he chose, and enter someone else, and he was somehow connected with traditional Hawaiian healers, with whom he communicated. She thought that if I went to Hawaii on vacation, the Stranger Within would be able to go there at the same time and pester me. He was bothering her, she thought, because of her ugly, sinful nature.

I told Susan that in my clinical work I have met many entities which claimed to be from other dimensions and times, but that so far all of them impressed me as being psychological in nature, and part of the person I was working with. In Susan's case, I said, the Stranger Within seemed to be a magnified bad conscience. The reason I gave for wanting to talk with the Stranger Within was to get to know him, and to begin negotiating with him for symptom relief, starting with the back pain.

Susan readily became sedated by the sodium amytal. Before I asked to speak to the Stranger Within, I decided to see if there was another personality state I could contact which did not suffer from dysmorphophobia. This proved to be quite easy to do. I asked to talk to 'a part of Susan's mind which does not see herself as ugly and overweight.' Susan said, 'I'm here,' and I began asking questions.

This new part of the mind referred to Susan as 'fat Susan,' and herself as 'thin Susan.' Thin Susan said that she was at most ten pounds overweight, and that she was reasonably attractive. Fat Susan rated herself as sixty pounds overweight, and extremely ugly. Thin Susan's perception was accurate, except that, like many North American men and women, she didn't really need to lose ten pounds, despite saying she did. Thin Susan explained that fat Susan just felt bad about herself. I was never able to activate or contact the thin Susan personality state outside the sodium-amytal interviews.

The Stranger Within was fairly easy to contact. A few repeated requests were required for him to be present and in control of the voice, but nothing excessive. He acknowledged that he was, in fact, the Stranger Within; said that he knew who I was; and said that Susan had accurately transcribed his dictation. He was boastful and arrogant at times, but at other times seemed quite timid and frightened. He said he thought I was against him, and that I wanted to get rid of him, and he acknowledged the negative effect of chlomipramine on his powers.

I asked the Stranger Within if he would be willing to make some deals with Susan which would be mutually beneficial. For instance, I said, if he would jab her in the back less often, she might agree to drink less coffee. The Stranger was so untrusting that all such attempts were futile. He repeatedly stated that I was just trying to trick him, and that everything I did was part of a plot to get rid of him. He didn't believe that I could in any way be interested in his welfare, or that I would ever represent his interests in negotiations with Susan. I couldn't find a 'hook,' no matter how hard I tried.

Attempts to engage the Stranger Within in conversation without sodium amytal continued to be fruitless. I asked Susan to try to talk with him at home, but she always had a reason she couldn't. The main reason was that it had to be quiet, she had to be relaxed, and that it took at lot of concentration to hear his voice. These conditions were almost never met. As a result, there was a period of over a year during which we barely even mentioned the Stranger Within.

A mental health professional I consulted on the case during this period of time said that he thought Susan was literally possessed, and that I should consider an exorcism. When I sought an opinion from a pastoral-care worker, he thought Susan was a typical adult child of an alcoholic, and that she needed group psychotherapy. I got a theological opinion from the therapist, and a therapeutic opinion from the cleric!

We carried on with weekly sessions, most of which were focused on Susan's current life circumstances and problems she was having at work. These stemmed partially from her obsessiveness. Few other employees came anywhere near the standards she demanded of herself, and she considered them to be lazy and morally reprehensible. She always wanted to know why people with no standards and no work ethic got ahead, had good health, and never seemed bothered about their low performance, while she had to suffer so much, and never received praise for her hard work. I had no answer for her.

Although it was true that Susan was excessively perfectionistic, it was also true – if her account was accurate, which it seemed to be – that most other employees were lazy, and even dishonest. There didn't seem to be any real performance appraisal in place, and some co-workers regularly left over half an hour early to go to a second job. Susan was often passed over for better jobs because she lost out on political grounds while someone's friend or in-law got favoured.

Many of my comments were focused on trying to get her to take a more strategic approach to life. Given that she was highly perfectionistic, and given the fact that her co-workers were the kind of the people they were, what was the best survival strategy for Susan in a given situation? Her tendency was to make every conflict into a moral issue, and to take a rigid, absolute stand. My therapeutic approach seemed to be somewhat helpful, in that she was able to be assertive and resolve several problems in a satisfactory way. Previously she would have been fired or quit over them.

Overall, though, there was still only a little progress after several years of therapy. Since we didn't seem to be making any major headway, I decided to try contacting the Stranger Within again, using sodium amytal. I thought that if we could blend in some dissociative techniques, the therapy might become more effective.

Under sodium amytal, the Stranger Within identified himself as Susan's old boyfriend! He said that he was psychic, and that he was monitoring Susan's behaviour through a possession state to keep her under control. The actual boyfriend had been living in another city for almost ten years. The boyfriend said he took on the identity of the Stranger Within as a camouflage. As I asked more questions, a complicated tale unfolded.

According to the Stranger Within/boyfriend, he had to keep his relationship with Susan secret because he came from a different racial background. Members of his own ethnic group would have strongly disapproved of his sleeping with a white woman. He used to go over to Susan's apartment for sex regularly, but didn't go out in public with her. I was clear from the boyfriend's description that he had just used Susan for casual sex, and that there was no real relationship. Susan thought he had loved her.

Then Susan got pregnant. The Stranger Within/boyfriend said he originally thought he was the father, and had learned that it was another man by monitoring Susan's thoughts from within. With the pregnancy, of course, it was necessary to end the relationship with Susan. The reason the boyfriend needed to continue possessing Susan was to remind her of the evil of her ways, to punish her and keep her in a guilty state for the pregnancy, and to make her feel it was a disgrace and all her fault. The purpose behind all this was to ensure that she would never reveal the affair to his ethnic group in Winnipeg.

Understanding now how the logic of the inner drama worked, I asked whether the father of the child was also present inside Susan and, if so, whether I could talk to him. The Stranger Within acknowledged that this was the case, so I asked to speak briefly to the other lover. He came forward. The other lover presented himself as a pleasant and decent man who genuinely cared for Susan, but who was intimidated and pushed out by the Stranger Within. He said that he would have liked to establish a lasting public relationship with Susan, but that she had rejected him.

When I spoke with Susan about all of this, near the end of the interview, she confirmed that she had listened to all of it, and said she was unhappy that her 'secret' had gotten out. She said that she had been pretty sure all along that the Stranger Within was actually her old lover, but she hadn't wanted to admit it to me. She believed that he was literally monitoring her by psychic means, and that he would continue to do so forever. She felt powerless to get out of his grip. Susan felt that this kind of behaviour was typical of his ethnic group. She meant that his chauvinism was typical, and also that it was culturally characteristic to use psychic methods to keep people in control.

Susan also confirmed the other lover's account of the triad and his own character. She had never told me about him before. She lamented her bad decision not to establish a relationship with this man.

I thought this was a very productive interview, and that we had opened up important themes for future sessions. I had always felt that the pregnancy was the single most important event in her adult life, combined with the decision to give the child up for adoption, but I had never been able to make any headway in discussing it with Susan. Whenever I tried to bring it up, she diverted attention to complaints about the medical care she got during her pregnancy. When I pointed out the diversion tactic she was using, she still didn't focus on the real issue.

Susan had created a personified drama inside herself to represent her own self-hatred. I didn't think that she was possessed, and I told her so, but she disagreed. In further sessions, I tried to come back to the pregnancy, the lost opportunity with the father of her child, and her grief about both. I had no success. Trying to work in a dissociative fashion wasn't possible, because I couldn't contact the other personality states without sodium amytal, and Susan wasn't motivated to try to contact them on her own at home. Dealing with the themes in a more orthodox psychotherapeutic fashion also didn't lead anywhere.

I wondered whether an exorcism might make sense. Since psychotherapy was of limited value, perhaps a powerful ceremony aimed at riding her of the Stranger Within might work. For me to take part in such a ceremony, it would not be necessary for me to believe that she was actually possessed, or the victim of a psychic intrusion by her old lover. That was her way of looking at it, but it did not have to be mine. I could view the exorcism as a psychological ritual mobilizing Susan's psychological/spiritual capacity for healing, without any supernatural component being required.

I never got to think more seriously about an exorcism, or to discuss it in detail with Susan. One afternoon, the psychiatry resident on call phoned me to say that Susan had been killed by a car. According to onlookers, she was walking on the sidewalk, had a seizure, and fell in front of an oncoming vehicle in heavy traffic.

Susan's prayers had been answered. I thought of the dozens of times she had asked me to shoot her, or give her a deadly dose of some drug. I thought of the many times she had asked God to stop torturing her, and let her out of this world. And I thought of how little I could do for her. I couldn't understand how one human being could be afflicted with so many different psychological problems in combination. True, she had a history of childhood sexual abuse, but it was relatively mild compared with those of many people I have met, consisting of enforced sexual play with older girls for a few years. True, her parents were very strict and punitive, and did much to undermine her self-confidence. But her problems were far out of proportion to the negative events in her childhood, and other family members seemed to be doing well.

I admired Susan for her perseverance. It took faith to continue living with all that pain. But I didn't understand her. I have met a few people with what I might call a severe atypical anxiety-affective-dissociative disorder. Susan was one of them, the most severely ill. There was something very wrong with her and her life, but diagnostic labels, medications, and psychotherapy didn't have much to offer her. I hope Susan is free of symptoms now.

26

Obsessions and Compulsions

Cindy was the person who taught me that obsessive-compulsive disorder can be a dissociative disorder. When I first met her, she was an extremely anxious twenty-five-year-old housewife with a Hamilton Anxiety Scale score over 30, and an initial diagnosis of generalized anxiety disorder. She had been working as a legal secretary up until a year previously, but had had to quit because of the anxiety. Although I enquired in detail about other anxiety disorders at the time of initial assessment, Cindy gave me a history of pure chronic generalized anxiety, present since her teenage years but worse over the previous year.

She described her marriage as unhappy, not because her husband was unfaithful or unkind, but because he was so obsessive in character that he could never loosen up, relax, and simply enjoy life. Their sex life consisted of intercourse once a week, always on the weekend, with very brief foreplay and never an orgasm on her part.

As I worked with Cindy for a few sessions on strategies for handling her anxiety, she gradually divulged to me a history of panic disorder. She said she wasn't sure why she had not wanted me to know about this at first. She described the precise location and exact date of her first panic attack in a women's washroom at age sixteen, the symptoms and duration of the attack, and the thoughts she had about it. The generalized anxiety began after the panic attack, and in fact consisted of anticipatory anxiety about having another attack.

Once she acknowledged having frequent panic attacks ever since age sixteen, worse in the last year, Cindy was then able to begin admitting to symptoms of agoraphobia and social phobia. She had an additional problem, which was that she would get diarrhoea with most panic attacks. The bowel disturbance consisted of an extreme urgency to defecate, followed by foul, watery stool. She never had diarrhoea except in association with a panic attack. Because she feared having an urgent need to use a toilet when away from home, she became housebound, which was why she couldn't work.

Whenever Cindy went out, she had to plan her route in relation to the availability of washrooms, in case of an emergency. She never wanted to be more than a couple of minutes from a washroom, and actually scouted out the routes to be sure exactly where the washrooms were.

Because I had had other panic-disorder patients with panic-associated diarrhoea, I asked Cindy if she drank caffeinated coffee (the caffeine sometimes stimulates diarrhoea in panic patients). I had seen remarkable results with simply cutting out the caffeine.

It turned out that Cindy did indeed drink coffee before going out, and that this stimulated her bowels. However, she did so deliberately. She reasoned that if she left the house constipated, the risk of having a sudden diarrhoea attack would be increased, and that the larger amount of stool in her bowel would result in a major disaster if she lost control before getting to a washroom. If she drank coffee and had an initial diarrhoea bowel movement before leaving the house, a subsequent panic-driven bowel movement would be smaller in volume, and easier to contain.

The farthest Cindy could go from her house on foot was about five blocks. Every time she went to a local park near her home, she would panic, so she was able to go only to the edge of the park, and stay a short time. I decided to try *in vivo* systematic desensitization for this phobic avoidance of the park, and explained the rationale of the treatment to her. The idea was that, by exposing herself to the park for longer and longer periods of time without leaving, combined with going farther and farther into the park, she would eventually master her anxiety, the phobic fear would be overcome, and the panic attacks would not occur.

This standard behavioural approach just did not work. She had many reasons why it was not possible to work on the desensitization systematically, including poor weather, not enough time, too much anxiety, fear of soiling herself, not believing it would ever work, and fear of fainting. Cindy especially avoided supermarkets, because she feared she would faint during a panic attack in the check-out line. She thought this would be devastatingly humiliating, and that everyone would think she was an idiot.

Cindy had never actually fainted during a panic attack, but no amount of reassurance about the rarity of fainting during a panic attack, no amount of effort to restructure her cognitions, no amount of anything I could think to do, had any effect. She just kept refusing to go to the supermarket without her husband – when he was along, she was all right, as long as the check-out line wasn't too long, and they didn't buy too much at once. They could never go to the supermarket on Thursday night or weekends, because it would be too busy.

Since cognitive-behavioural therapy was having no effect, I decided to try medication. She refused to take more than homeopathic doses of benzodiazepines because she feared getting addicted. When I tried her on a minute dose of chlomipramine, she had an episode of high anxiety and depersonalization for twenty-four hours, and refused ever to take an antidepressant again. She absolutely refused to try a monoamine oxidase inhibitor after I explained the necessity of a tyramine-free diet, because she was sure she would rupture an aneurysm and die.

Because Cindy had worked ever since high school, did not have an obvious history of personality disorder, and did not receive any apparent secondary gain from her disorder, I could not understand what was going on. She was a very pleasant, likeable, and attractive woman, with a good sense of humour and genuine affection for people. She had never overdosed or otherwise acted out, and had never had a clinical depression, or a substance-abuse problem. On reviewing her symptoms during panic attacks, I decided to go back to the first attack, to determine whether it held any clues. I asked about her cognitions before, during, and after the panic attack, as I had before. This time, Cindy made a confession: during the panic attack, she had a sudden powerful urge to take off her clothes and run out in public. She had no idea why she felt this urge, and had never experienced anything like it before. Then she revealed that she was afraid she was going to turn out like her mother, who used to go running naked outside during episodes of uncontrolled mania.

Cindy revealed that this feature of her panic attack had recurred with some but not every attack over the years. She was especially fearful that she would have an attack at work, and disrobe in front of male staff. Recognizing that this was an odd form of compulsion, I began a systematic review of the obsessive-compulsive symptomatology I had done previously.

Slowly, over the next couple of sessions, Cindy disclosed a history of florid obsessive-compulsive disorder. She had both a germ phobia and many checking rituals. Every night, before going to bed, Cindy had to check all the locks in the house three times, and count all her jewellery three times to make sure none was missing. If she did not complete a full set of three checks, or if she felt she had not counted accurately, she would be overwhelmed with anxiety, and have to do another set of three. These checking rituals took forty minutes to an hour to complete.

I realized that the compulsion to disrobe during a panic attack must be related to her other compulsions, and began to consider the preoccupation with diarrhoea as an obsessive symptom. While I was asking her why she felt she had to perform all these compulsive rituals, she replied as the textbooks said she should, saying that it was the only way to reduce the anxiety. However, I saw a hint on her face of not just anxiety but fear, especially when she described checking the locks to make sure they were all secure at bedtime.

I asked her if she was afraid that someone might break in more easily if the doors and windows were not all locked, which she confirmed. To my surprise, though, when I asked who she thought might break in, she replied, 'The Witch.'

Cindy didn't know who the Witch was, but the Witch was more than a purely cognitive phenomenon. Cindy could actually feel the Witch prowling around in the dark outside her house, and had a palpable sense of her presence. I realized that Cindy was making a distinction between an obsessive *thought* and her actual experience of the Witch's presence.

This is perhaps the difference between a delusion of possession and a possession experience. Non-dissociative depressed or psychotic patients will sometimes tell you they feel possessed, but often careful enquiry will disclose that this is an *idea*, not an actual experience of a palpable, internally present entity. By contrast, possessed patients actually feel the entity inside them, may hear its thoughts or voice, and may experience the entity attempting to exert its will over them. The psychotic person has only the *idea* of being possessed; the non-psychotic individual with a dissociative disorder has a full experience of possession, often with behaviour manifestations. DSM-IV contains a provisional disorder, called Dissociative Trance Disorder, which recognizes this distinction and emphasizes it for further clinical study and research.

Cindy was like a possessed person, except that her entity was outside her, rather than inside. I realised that Cindy's obsessive-compulsive disorder was not cognitive or anxious in nature, but, rather, dissociative. I assumed that the Witch was a dissociated aspect of Cindy which she experienced as threatening her from outside. During the day, Cindy said, the Witch was not present; therefore, there was no need to check the locks. I could not clarify how the other checking and counting rituals fit into the experience of the Witch.

Since Cindy had a dissociative disorder, she was likely to have experienced some kind of serious trauma as a child. This I could not uncover fully. Her father had severe obsessive-compulsive disorder, and was extremely rigid, controlling, and punitive. For instance, he used to beat the children if their shoes were not perfectly polished at morning inspection. The inspections were military in nature, with the children standing in line.

I was able to uncover some mild sexual abuse by older girls, occurring when Cindy was about eight years old, but no intra-familial incest. In order to try to understand her symptoms better, I decided to try to make direct contact with the Witch. This proved to be quite simple to do.

Lying back in my reclining chair, Cindy readily went into a trance state, and a straightforward request to talk to the Witch resulted in the Witch asking me what I wanted. I replied, as I usually do at such encounters, that I just wanted to talk, get to know her a bit, and ask some questions.

The Witch was not very forthcoming. She acknowledged that she did indeed prowl around the house at night, trying to get in, and said that, if she ever did, she would hurt Cindy, and perhaps kill her. When I asked the Witch why she would want to do that, she replied that Cindy was bad, and deserved to die. Unfortunately, I could not engage the Witch in sustained conversation, and was never able to explore her reasoning in any depth.

I assumed that the Witch was a personified, dissociated embodiment of the negative self-cognitions Cindy had had ingrained in her by her punitive father. But I was unable to ascertain the relationship between the Witch and the compulsion to disrobe during a panic attack. I suspected that the panic attacks might be attributable to the threatened emergence of a sexualized part-self, and that this symptom might be related to more severe childhood sexual trauma than I had uncovered. It was likely that such a part-self, if it existed, would have a strong identification with the mother.

I then thought back to Cindy's description of her sexual life, and her germ phobia, which were intertwined. She was inhibited and restricted in her sexual feelings and behaviour by a fear of contamination, germs, semen, sweat, saliva, and in fact all body fluids. Fellatio was out of the question, because of the germs on her husband's penis, and she could not stand her husband's body odour. I wondered whether all of this was a convoluted obsessive defence against memories of being made dirty by childhood sexual abuse. I also wondered about the overall rate of childhood sexual abuse in germ phobics as a group.

It was possible that there has been no intrafamilial incest, and that the obsessions had been taught and reinforced mercilessly by her father, along with a general puritanical repression of sexuality. These are the possibilities I would have explored if Cindy had been able to engage in treatment. Unfortunately, she dropped out of therapy before it had really begun, and was lost to follow-up. Why? Had I pushed her obsessive defence a bit too hard? Were there other part-selves or ego states inside that were against therapy, or against the uncovering of sexual-abuse memories? I will never know.

I did learn from Cindy, though. I was amazed and moved by her ability to remain cheerful and humorous in the face of so much symptomatology and suffering. I learned that the old dichotomy between obsessive and hysterical personality styles was an error, since Cindy was actually more a 'hysteric' in her personality style than an 'obsessive,' though she had florid obssesive-compulsive disorder. I noticed this 'hysteria' in other cases of obsessive-compulsive disorder I met later, and realized that, if obsessive-compulsive disorder is often actually a dissociative disorder, it should give an impression of 'hysteria' to anyone who doesn't understand dissociation, just as MPD does.

Cindy was a classical nineteenth-century dissociative patient, as described by Janet. Her obsessive defences were designed, not to repress unacceptable impulses, it seemed, but to ward off dissociated part-selves and their trauma memories. In Cindy's case, the clinical data to support this conclusion were thin, but she taught me the principles of the dissociative model of obsessive-compulsive disorder.

In a psychoanalytical model of Cindy's mind, her anxiety would be signal anxiety about failing attempts to repress sexual and aggressive id impulses. Engaging the 'impulses' in direct conversation is not likely to occur within such a model, because the impulses are supposed to be unconscious, and dominated by primary-process logic. In fact, the Witch could speak as rationally as a bank teller, although she also used extensive trance logic and magical thinking.

The dissociative model of obsessive-compulsive disorder *includes* the psychoanalytical model, but accounts for more phenomena, such as the existence of the Witch. It is evident that the Witch is, in part, an embodiment of id aggression, and that an object-relations analysis in terms of introjects and identifications would be relevant. However, the analytical model misses the fact that the performance of compulsive rituals actually keeps the Witch at bay, and fails to understand that the Witch can take executive control, and can discuss her strategies and motivations with the therapist.

Who would not perform such rituals, if a Witch was prowling outside the house at night, and the rituals actually worked? The primary problem in such cases, it seems to me, is the dissociation, to which the obsessive-compulsive symptoms are secondary. Strictly speaking, the primary problem is whatever is driving the dissociation, but this understanding is implicit in the trauma-dissociation model.

The treatment implications of the dissociative model of Cindy's mind are clear. If the trauma driving the dissociation was uncovered and dealt with, and the dissociated part-selves integrated, the obsessive-compulsive disorder would go into remission. In Cindy's case, the trauma model was of no benefit. She was unable to engage in cognitive-behavioural therapy, psychopharmacology, or dissociative psychotherapy.

Generally speaking, though, obsessive-compulsive disorder is by definition a dissociative disorder, whether it is a primarily biomedical illness or a psychosocially driven, trauma-related disorder. The question is, what percentage of persons with obsessive-compulsive disorder have arrived at their illness by a trauma pathway? I speculate that the percentage is above 25.

I hypothesize that the percentage of trauma pathway patients is higher among behaviour-therapy and medication nonresponders. Given the epidemiology of obsessive-compulsive disorder, and the rate of response to treatment, somewhere between one person in fifty and one in two hundred in the general population may have treatment–non-responsive trauma-pathway obsessive-compulsive disorder. This is the lesson I learned from Cindy, despite the fact that I was unable to help her.